GRIDLOCKED ON THE
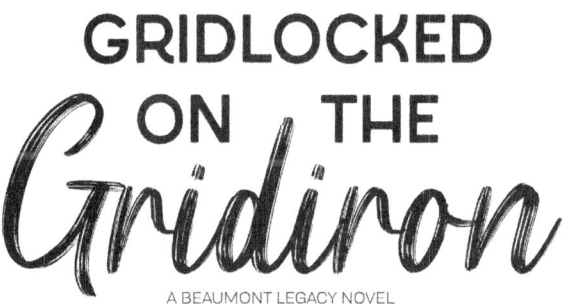

A BEAUMONT LEGACY NOVEL

VAI DENTON

Gridlocked on the Gridiron

Copyright © 2024 Vai Denton

All rights reserved. No part of this book may be used or reproduced in any manner whatsoever without written permission from the author, except as permitted by U.S. copyright law. This book is a work of fiction. Names, characters, businesses, organizations, places, events and incidents are either the product of the author's imagination or are used fictitiously. Any resemblance to actual persons, living or dead, events, or locales is entirely coincidental.

Editing: Rachel Bunner (@rachels.top.edits)

Proofreading: Chelsey Brand (@theimperfictionist) and Laura Hartley

Formatting: Marja Graham

Cover design: Cindy Ras (@cindyras_draws)

ISBN: 979-8-9904429-0-0 (paperback)

ASIN: B0CRGW536H (ebook)

First Edition: May 2024

10 9 8 7 6 5 4 3 2 1

Author's Note

Gridlocked on the Gridiron is the first book in the Beaumont Legacy series. This book can be read as a standalone. There are no cliffhangers.

Your mental health is incredibly important to me, so please take the following content warnings into consideration before continuing: death of a parent (off page, prior to the start of the book), verbally abusive parent, alcohol use, cheating (neither of the MCs), manipulative former partner, explicit sexual content.

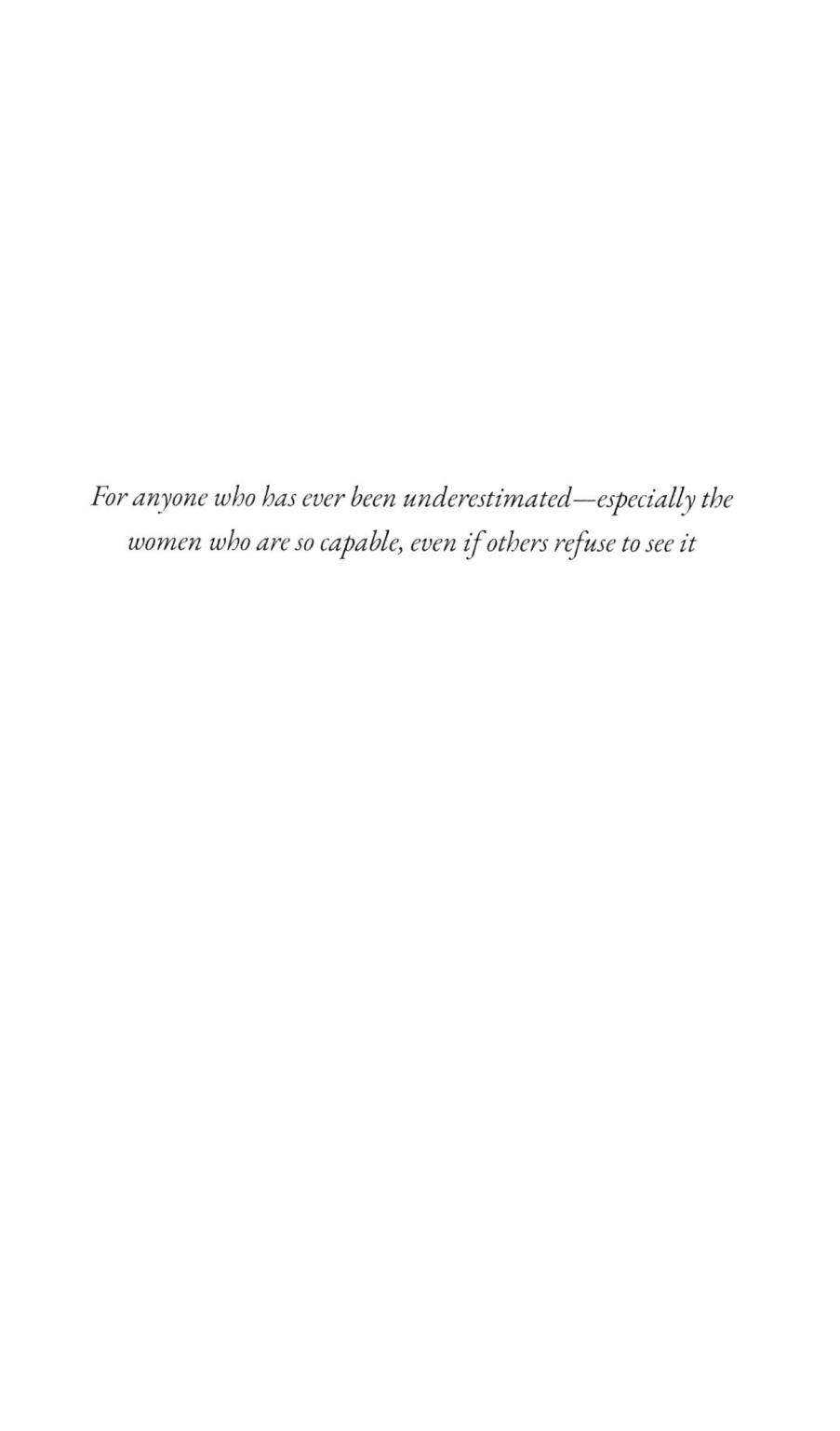

For anyone who has ever been underestimated—especially the women who are so capable, even if others refuse to see it

Chapter One

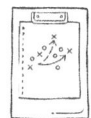

Lucia

Lucia Moretti could attest to the fact that bad news—horrific news—did not, in fact, come in threes. At least not for her, not in all of her twenty-seven years. Not when she'd been eight and her father had told her that her mother had left them and wasn't planning on coming back without even the courtesy of a note. Not when she'd been thirteen and her first and only pet, a sweet yellow lab who'd been like a sister to her, had gotten sick suddenly and died. And certainly not now, at twenty-seven, when the person she'd planned to spend the rest of her life with was caught cheating. By paparazzi. On the eve of their anniversary.

Okay, scratch that. Maybe bad news did come in threes.

Why *The Richmond Herald* chose her for such public humiliation that August afternoon, she couldn't be sure. Maybe it was karma for all the times she'd taken an extra snack from the campus dining halls in college. Or maybe this was the universe's retribution for all the times she'd done a California stop at Virginia stop signs.

Whatever she may have done was unimportant because, there, below a headline that read, "Interception! Vipers QB Caught Passing to the Wrong Woman", was a picture of her intended kissing a woman with blonde hair. And, as if the message wasn't clear enough, beside that was a picture of Lucia with very messy *brown* hair—couldn't they have used a better picture of her, at least?—holding a clipboard, her ring finger and ring on full display.

"They could've *warned* you before they posted this," her best friend hissed over speakerphone, breaking the stunned silence that'd fallen over their collective stupor. Isa's accent sharpened around the angriest word, as if *The Richmond Herald* cared about anything besides sales.

Lucia was still too shocked to speak. Her eyes scanned over every inch of the photo, falling to the clothing he was sporting. *Were those his clothes from last weekend?* That looked like what he'd worn to brunch on Sunday. The brunch he'd told her was with the guys. With the *team*. Was he really so stupid? Had he genuinely thought this wouldn't get back to her? He was a nationally recognized sports player, for Pete's sake.

Her back was still pressed against the concrete of the Virginia Vipers' offices when Isa, voice calmer and tinged with worry, spoke again. "Luc? Are you still at work?" Again, no answer as Lucia's eyes marked where Max's hands were in the photo. "I'm coming to pick you up, hang tight."

Isa's Camry rolled into the parking lot fifteen minutes later, but it felt like only seconds had passed for Lucia. Isa didn't bother to turn down the unintelligible rock music or roll her windows up as she rounded the car and walked toward Lucia.

"Come, *mi cielo*. Let's go to my apartment. Come, come," she said as if coaxing a small child into eating their vegetables. She held the door open as Lucia slid into the passenger seat, cringing at the sounds of Isa's "Rage" playlist, courtesy of her girlfriend.

"Have you eaten anything? Abby just went to Trader Joe's. We have all the cheese and crackers you could ever need." She was kind enough to lower the volume of the music, though Lucia knew it was for her benefit alone and had nothing to do with the glares from the people milling about the facility and offices.

"Luc?" Isa pleaded tentatively when they reached a stoplight.

She'd struggled to string together a coherent sentence, but Isa's presence was like a comforting hug, shaking the words loose.

Finally, "It's so on brand, isn't it?"

Isa just blinked. "What do you mean?"

"I mean, this is par for the course with me. Standard. Expected. *Classic*."

"I'm still not quite sure I follow," Isa said slowly.

Lucia hardly heard her as she began analyzing every interaction she'd had with Max in the previous few months. Nothing had seemed off, but they had both been so busy gearing up for preseason that it would've gone unnoticed either way.

"He's going to find a way to blame me. You know it. He's going to say I was working too much, that I wasn't being attentive enough."

Isa muttered a string of Spanish curses. "He's not getting away with it this time. I'm going to chop his itty-bitty, limp dick right off." She grinned, pleased with herself. She pulled into the alley behind her apartment, diagonally parking in a space that was most definitely meant for straight parking.

Lucia followed her like a zombie up to the third floor and into her apartment, slipping her heels off by the entryway.

"So, how are we ruining his life? Keying his four ridiculously overpriced cars? Setting his hair on fire?" Isa's words were muffled through the half-closed pantry door. Too numb to respond to Isa's attempt to console her, Lucia padded to the table adjacent to the kitchen, pulling her laptop out of her purse and typing in the headline that was branded on her brain.

Did she know the woman? She didn't look familiar, but it was hard to tell with Max's tongue lolling around in the woman's mouth. Her throat constricted as she thought of the house they shared. The house she'd turned into a home over the course of two years.

Lucia didn't notice Abby coming out of the bedroom but felt arms wrap around her shoulders. "Hey, Luc, sweetie." A quick, reassuring squeeze, and then Abby placed a tray down and helped Isa set up the crackers and cheese.

Isa took her extended silence as grief. "I know you're not much of a crier, but you're allowed to mourn, *osita*. Seven years is a long time." More than a quarter of her life, to be exact.

And what a waste.

"I'm fine." At her friends' disbelieving stares, she continued, "Or, I will be. I just—" She sighed, exasperated, closing the laptop. "I thought I'd be on the ground sobbing, you know? Lying down in the shower for an hour, listening to Billie Eilish, crying until dehydration overtook me, and all I could do was stare blankly at the tub. Instead..." She shrugged.

She didn't want to divulge more, didn't want that half-confused, half-sympathetic look as she explained that, instead of grief, she just felt angry. Angry that he'd cheated on her despite everything she'd done for him. Angry that it'd come out publicly, leaving her *humiliated*.

She'd had so many firsts with Max. He'd been there for practically all of her adulthood, or at least the parts that counted. She'd *followed* him from California to Virginia. Yeah, the job she'd been offered was a dream, but she'd said yes because he was the Vipers' quarterback. The monster that was betrayal licked its way up her spine.

They'd done long-distance for the three years before she'd joined him in Virginia, and now she worried what exactly he'd been doing when they'd been apart. There had been times that she didn't hear from him for a few days, and while she'd always chalked it up to him being busy with football, now she couldn't be so sure. Had he been cheating on her the entire time? Could she really be certain that this was an isolated event? Had she been so blind that she'd missed the red flags all these years?

Isa and Abby guided her onto the couch, the long tray of food balanced across their laps. Isa turned on an old episode of *The Bachelor*, knowing Lucia found comfort in the arms of reality television.

During the third commercial break, Isa set the tray down and turned toward her.

"Real talk, what's our plan?" Isa exchanged a look with Abby, silent communication coursing between them, before continuing, "We'll obviously help you pack up your stuff, and you can stay with us until you find a place. But you just say the word, and I'll key his cars, smash his windows and tail lights. Anything. Just tell me what you need."

Lucia slipped her hand into Isa's as Abby excused herself and went into their bedroom. Isa had been Lucia's best friend since their freshman year of college when they'd floundered through an English literature class together. She'd held Lucia together many times as she'd struggled through her advanced computer-science classes. While Lucia had moved around the country working with different teams, Isa got her master's degree and then followed her to Richmond. Her anchor, her rock. Now they worked together for the Vipers, Lucia as an analyst and Isa as an athletic trainer.

"I think…I need to take some more time to process, but I think packing up and moving when he's away would be best. I worry that if I see him, he'll convince me to stay. Or that I'll ask him for all the sordid details." Self-sabotage had always been her favorite form of torture.

"We'll go when he's at lift or practice. Charlotte will completely understand," Isa said, referencing Lucia's boss. "Do you think…" She stumbled a bit. "Do you think you'll stay with the Vipers?"

Lucia hadn't even thought about her job. Over the past two years, the Vipers' offices and training facility had become a second home for her. Richmond, a place she never would've seen herself enjoying, had suddenly become the place where she could picture raising children. And her job? Her absolute dream job? She couldn't imagine leaving it.

She rested her head on Isa's shoulder, too exhausted to respond.

"I'd go to war for you, you know," Isa murmured.

Lucia just squeezed her hand.

Lucia felt eyes following her everywhere she went, from the streets of Richmond, to the training facility, and into her office. It made her skin crawl. Those who were brave enough came up to her and apologized, which only made her feel worse. All it did was remind her of the fact that the affair and inevitable breakup were entirely public knowledge. She'd never minded being in the spotlight, but to be humiliated so publicly felt like more of a violation than usual.

Her phone buzzed for the fifteenth time in five minutes—whether from Max trying to get her to come home and listen to his thousands of excuses, or from journalists hunting her down for an exclusive, she couldn't be sure. If she caught *one* more sympathetic glance, she was going to take a baseball bat to the glass-encased trophies and accolades of the Vipers franchise.

Or not.

But the thought of it was certainly cathartic.

Apparently, spending the night on Isa's couch had imbued her with the same vicious fantasies of retribution as her closest friend. Maybe she'd have to crank up that rock playlist Abby had created.

The intact (for now) glass reflected the now-perpetual crease between her brows. She grimaced at the shortness of the skirt she'd borrowed from Isa, and the woman before her grimaced right back. Charlotte was very forgiving, and Lucia hoped she could look past this transgression just this once. Just while she figured out how best to pack up her entire life during Thursday practice.

All she wanted was to get back to her work. She wanted to disappear for the next fifteen hours, crunching numbers and watching film in her not-so-spacious office. Instead, her brain kept getting sidetracked by the whispers, louder than if her colleagues had been speaking directly into her ear. She'd hoped to find solace in Charlotte's office, but the door had been closed. It was a sure sign John, the general manager, had something important he needed one of the analysts to work on as soon as *in*humanly possible. She hoped the task would be assigned to her so she could finally pay attention to the voice in her head telling her to put her headphones on and stop listening to the unending gossip that threatened to swallow her whole.

She'd been right. When the door opened, John gave her the smallest of nods.

"Lucia." He pronounced her name wrong, the *c* of her name coming out like an *s* rather than a *ch*, but she couldn't complain since she hadn't even expected him to know her name at all. Before she could process that fact, he'd disappeared down the hall, no doubt headed to the beautiful penthouse office he spent most of his time in. Charlotte stopped at the doorway, a momentary panic sweeping across her face. She waved a frowning Lucia in.

"Good morning, Lucia." Charlotte closed the door gently behind her, Lucia's frown becoming more pronounced.

This was new. Charlotte never had closed-door meetings with the analysts, besides for their annual reviews. Bile rose hot and fast in Lucia's throat, her body already beginning to decipher the look on her boss's face.

"Have a seat, please."

"Uh, why are you being so formal? Are you..." Lucia let out a disbelieving laugh. "Are you firing me?"

She'd meant it as a joke, but Charlotte's silence was answer enough. Lucia lurched toward the trash can beside her boss's desk and heaved. The fact that she'd hardly eaten anything that morning was clear as Charlotte ran over to hold her hair and rub her back, making soothing noises.

"It's okay, it's okay." When she noticed Lucia was no longer heaving but also not moving from the trash, she grabbed a water bottle from her mini fridge and forced it into Lucia's hand. "Drink this and sit, please. I promise it's not all bad news."

When Lucia felt more stable, she followed Charlotte's directions and sat, refusing to make eye contact. Charlotte clicked her mouse a few times and then clasped her hands together, laying them on her large, walnut desk.

"As you saw, John was just talking my ear off. He was telling me that he believes your...situation, for lack of a better word, might cause issues with his—"

"Is this about Max?"

"Star quarterback."

"You can't be serious. Max cheats on me, and I get punished?"

It was so like this profession to penalize the woman in this situation. Why should her personal life have had any bearing on her career? Especially when said personal life involved her being a *victim*?

At least the apologetic look Charlotte gave her was sincere. "I'm so sorry, Lucia. You know you're my best analyst by far. Hell, with your qualifications, you should be *my* boss. But unfortunately, my hands are tied. I tried to convince him that you'd be mature about"—she waved her hand—"everything. But he was firm."

Tears were welling in Lucia's eyes, and she wasn't sure she could keep them from falling. How was this fair? She hadn't done anything wrong. She was a hard worker. She'd put in more hours than any of the other analysts, and, as Charlotte had said, she was one of the strongest analysts in the franchise. Maybe even the league.

"This job is—you have to understand, it's all I have right now. I—I don't know what I'd do without it." Her pride was fighting a losing battle against blubbering, and she thought about dropping to her knees and begging.

"He's very insistent that Max Clark remains at peak performance. But I thought this might happen, so I put out some feelers yesterday when I saw the news." She paused, something dawning on her face. "I'm sorry, by the way. I haven't said that yet, but I was so very sorry to see...that."

Charlotte's figure doubled in Lucia's eyes as the tears bubbled over. Charlotte handed her a tissue before turning her monitor to face Lucia.

"Like I said, I put out some feelers. I thought John might pull something like this. Clark is his everything and can do no wrong. But you're very highly sought after, too. And while most teams don't have the bandwidth or budget, they're all well aware that you developed GameFlow Analytics and are falling all over themselves to move money around."

Lucia let out a pathetic sniffle, wiping her eyes angrily. She hated looking weak. One more reason for her to hate Max.

GameFlow Analytics was a software she'd begun developing in her senior year of college, though it hadn't been complete until right before she'd joined the Vipers. She'd patented the software which, at its most basic level, integrated live game data and used machine learning to offer recommendations in real-time. Selling it to the NFL had skyrocketed her stock in the analytics market greatly.

During the three years she and Max had spent apart between college and her move to Richmond, she'd been bouncing from team to team, doing general analytics and starting her career with team quarterbacks. When she'd finally gotten the kinks out of GameFlow Analytics, she'd breathed a sigh of relief, because she knew it meant she'd have a higher chance of getting a job in Virginia with Max. After the sale, she'd had offers from all over the country but had chosen to go to the Vipers. For the *prick*.

"At the moment, only the Sabertooths have been able to find money to take you on, and they're offering quite a raise if you join them. You'd be doing general analytics, just like here, and they'd also like you to continue working on your quarterback software while you assist their quarterback. Apparently, despite their Super Bowl win last year, he's been struggling through preseason."

It only took Lucia a moment to remember the arrogant asshole at the helm of the Charleston Sabertooths. Her whole body went rigid. "Not Colton Beaumont. Tell me it's not Colton fucking Beaumont."

Charlotte turned the monitor back, seeming to realize Lucia was uninterested in looking at the email on the screen. "It's either you take the Sabers up on their offer today before I can formally fire you, and you can say you resigned for a better position"—Charlotte grimaced, apologetic— "or I'm forced to fire you, and the offer potentially comes off the table."

Lucia would have almost rather been fired. *Almost*.

Max may have stripped her of her pride, but he wouldn't take away everything that she'd worked so hard for. She would take the job, even if it meant helping someone she detested.

Chapter Two

Colton

Colton slammed his helmet onto the field, grinding his teeth together to stop himself from cursing wildly. He was a team leader. He needed to show poise and grace in defeat. Out came the journalists and news channels with questions.

"What did you learn from this game?"

"What can you improve?"

"You threw a whopping three interceptions this game. What do you need to do to get that number down?"

"Is this just a rough patch?"

"Where is that great Super Bowl quarterback we saw last season?"

And on and on and on.

It took every fiber of his being not to shove his way through them and into the locker room where he could get a *moment* of peace. At least from the reporters. Once alone, he would spend hours dissecting the game, disappointment in himself growing with every play. They were right. This? After a Super Bowl win? Pathetic.

The only redeeming characteristic of the game was that it was a preseason loss. Not ideal, but at least it didn't tank his team's record. Even if it was their second loss in as many games. A horrible start to a season. A season he'd been positive would come with win after win after win.

When he finally made it to the locker room, his heart stopped at the faces of his teammates. Some had showered already, but most were still sweaty, their jerseys covered in grass stains. He took their disheartened expressions personally. It had, after all, been his fault.

"Guys, this one was on me. When I play well, we all play well, and today was not my best—"

"No, it was not your best, Beaumont. Sit down." Coach Mark Turner stood behind Colton, anger clear from his stance and the ripped papers in his right hand. "Absolutely disgusting. You call that football? You should be ashamed of yourselves. This is not a Super Bowl-winning team, and it's certainly not a Super Bowl-*ready* team—Rudy, what's so fucking funny over there? Offensive line couldn't keep the pocket from collapsing for more than a second or two today. You think that's fucking funny?"

The smile on Rudy's face disappeared the moment Coach said his name, but Coach Turner wasn't done. "Two weeks in a row." He held up two fingers for emphasis, scanning across the room. "Two weeks in a row! I am sick and tired of seeing mistake after mistake out there on that field. It's a goddamn disgrace. You're playing like you've barely started college ball. You want to go back to the NCAA? Be my guest. I don't want to see y'all's faces anymore anyway. Hit the showers, and be ready for the airport in fifteen."

After his five-minute shower, Colton checked the ESPN app, ignoring the burning garbage that was his stats. He searched "Landon Beaumont," noting his brother's game was in the late stages of the fourth quarter. Even so, Landon had put up a whopping ninety-three receiving yards and two touchdowns for the San Jose Sentinels. *Lucky bastard.* His chest swelled with pride for his younger brother, but the competitive man inside of him—who conveniently seemed to have his father's voice—told him he needed to step up.

As if willed into existence, his phone chimed with a text from his father. Below it were ESPN notifications from the games of the day, one of which was titled, "Super (Beau)mont On the Way Out". How original.

He'd heard them all. Over the previous six years and even in college, the media had found a way to crow over everything about him, from his race to his potential love interests, rarely ever focusing on his actual abilities. He couldn't even recall the number of times they'd posted some variation of "Quarterback's Success Spices Up the Game!". It didn't bother him nearly as much as it used to, but he still couldn't fathom why his being Indian warranted so much talk. At least this article discussed his game and not every other aspect of his life.

Before he'd even had time to read his father's text, Colton's screen flashed with his contact, taking up the whole screen with the unsolicited phone call. Colton sighed deeply, sweeping his thumb across the bottom of the screen and bringing it to his ear.

"Dad."

"That performance was abysmal. I'm glad I didn't fly out to watch like I'd planned."

And there it was. His shoulders stiffened at his father's words as they often did. "Hello to you, too."

"What were you thinking with that pass up the middle into double coverage in the second quarter? Of course it was going to get picked off. That was a rookie mistake, and I taught you better than that."

He felt a hand on his shoulder as his father rambled on in his ear. When he turned, Cooper, the Sabertooths' top tight end, cocked his head toward where their teammates were leaving.

"Your dad?" he whispered. When Colton nodded, Coop shot him a sympathetic smile. Cooper Hayes was Colton's closest friend, all too familiar with the pressure his father put on him.

"Are you even listening to me, Colton? How can you expect the Sabers to keep you as their starter if you can't get your yards up and your picks down, huh? And what about everything I taught you about looking across the field as you scramble? I'm ashamed to call you my son today."

The rage that simmered inside Colton any time his father spoke to him like this began bubbling to the surface, but he knew what would happen if he tried to interrupt or explain himself. *How dare you talk to me like that? I'm the reason you're in the NFL. Without me, you never would've made it, even as a free agent.*

And, unfortunately, that was probably true. His father, the famed Troy Beaumont, would've been an NFL great if not for his career-ending hip fracture during the national championship his senior year of college. He'd turned down a college coaching job because Colton was a newborn and their family was already established in Los Angeles. Coached all of his little league and middle school games. Attended every single practice and game through high school. Submitted his highlight tape to college scouts. Sat in the family box during college games, home and away. Without his father's coaching and sacrifices, Colton wasn't sure he ever would've made it to the top quarterback spot at Crestview College, let alone been an early NFL draft pick and a Super Bowl winner. Colton wouldn't have been anything without Troy Beaumont. The debt he owed his father was far too great to ever be repaid.

That didn't change the fact that he hated his father's ceaseless lectures.

Still, he slammed the door in the face of that simmering rage, nodding as he followed his discouraged teammates to the team bus, police escorts already waiting to take them to the airport. He ducked his head as cameras flashed around him, not interested in having this conversation plastered all over the internet. Especially not when he was limping to compensate for rolling his right ankle during the game. He didn't need other teams seeing any weakness from him.

"You're right. I made a lot of mistakes this game. I didn't do a good job of looking down the field, and my pocket performance was less than stellar. My rush game wasn't nearly where it should've been. I need to get more reps in and practice harder before the next game," Colton said like a robot, shoulders slumping in defeat.

"That's right. I'll send you a lift plan to help even out your game a bit more. Just get in the gym earlier than the rest of the team. That's the only way to stay ahead of the other quarterbacks. Reps, reps, reps. Get in there early, leave later, and get more reps in." Colton heard him rummaging through some papers, and he could picture his father sifting through pages of play sketches as he turned on his computer. "Or else you'll get beaten out by that rookie. He had a good season a couple of years ago."

"Well, Elijah's not exactly a rookie anymore, and Coach has no intention of cutting my time."

"*Yet.* If you keep playing the way you have the past two games, that will all change. Especially if the GM and owner get involved."

Colton wasn't going to ask his father how he seemed to know so much about this when he himself had never been in the NFL. He was exhausted. Physically, mentally, emotionally. He was tired of talking to his father—or rather, being berated by his father—and quite frankly, he was getting tired of the sport that used to bring him all the joy in the world.

"You're right." Because that was the only thing his father cared to hear. It was the only thing that would make this call go faster so he could lay his head on the window and try to recover from all the hits he'd taken from giant linemen during the game.

His father hummed his agreement. "I'll be at next week's game." Of course he would. The man had bought a house in Charleston and moved his whole life there when he'd found out his eldest son would be the star quarterback for the Sabers. "I expect a much better performance Friday."

"Of course. I'll be sure to get in the gym before and after practice every day this week."

"Good. And have your brother call me."

As if he couldn't be bothered to pick up the phone and call Landon himself. Colton sighed and checked the time on the call as he climbed the stairs of the bus, noting it felt like it'd been ten times longer than it actually had.

"I'll let Landon know. He played well today, so don't expect a call tonight. I'm sure he'll be celebrating."

"Fine. See you Friday." And just like that, the fever dream that was nearly every conversation with his father was over.

Colton sat in Coach Turner's office, staring out the tall windows that overlooked the training field. They'd gotten back late from the game the night before, and their "rest day" hadn't felt very restful for Colton. He'd gone to the trainer to tape his rolled ankle, taken an ice bath, and then had a meeting with Coach Fillmore, the quarterback coach. He'd thought his day was done, but then he'd been told Coach Turner needed to see him in his office, which was never a good sign. Maybe his father had been right and they were going to cut his playing time.

Mark Turner swept into the office, his clipboard and earpiece clattering onto his desk. He took a seat in a very expensive, plush-looking, white chair and cleared his throat. He waited to speak until Colton met his eyes.

"How're you feeling?"

Like shit. "Fine. A little banged up, but that's nothing new."

Turner nodded. "We're going to have to push o-line a little harder at practice this week. Their performance was subpar at best."

"Coach, it was just as much my fault. I struggled in the pocket and couldn't seem to connect, even when they did a good job." His performance had been laughable at best, and he couldn't put any blame on the men who blocked for him.

Turner was already shaking his head. "You were certainly not at your best, but I won't let you take the brunt of the shitshow in that martyr way of yours. The whole team needs to get it together this week."

Colton nodded, not sure what else his coach wanted to hear.

"Look, I didn't call you in to shit on you or cut your time. I know how good you are, and I know you have it in you. I've seen you at your best. Hell, you helped me turn this team around. I don't know what's been going on, but you're still my best quarterback, and I'm not going to give up on you just yet."

He looked at Colton expectantly.

"I appreciate that, Coach, I really do. I promise I'll work harder this week. I'll do whatever you think I need to do to get my numbers up and get us a win."

He knew how important the next few games were for the Sabers, but especially for him. Colton lived and breathed football. It was the only way he could be valuable to others, and winning was a huge part of that. If he stopped winning, people stopped caring about him, and then who was he? What did he have?

That seemed to be the right answer. "Good. I'm glad to hear it. We've hired an analyst to come in and work with you directly. She's going to do general analytics during games, but you'll also be working with her one-on-one to figure out what your next steps should be. Hopefully, she can help you discern how best to pick up your game."

Colton was already nodding. He trusted all of the analysts he'd ever met. They were wizards, if just a little nerdy for his taste. He'd show up to every meeting with her with a winning attitude, and he'd get his numbers up by the time the season started in September.

"Absolutely. That's a great next step. When does she start?"

"She'll be here Wednesday before practice to meet you. She'll watch practice, and then you'll start working with her right after. She can gauge how often she needs to see you, how many sessions a week, all that."

"I'll be ready."

"Good. Now get the hell out of my office."

Chapter Three

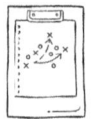

Lucia

Lucia was reluctant to admit that she liked anything about her new situation, but even *she* could agree that Charleston was beautiful. Where Richmond embraced industrial vibes, Charleston exuded coastal relaxation with moss-draped charm. An overzealous intern led her from Sabertooths Walk, a long, tree-lined pathway with twin sabertooth sculptures at the end of it, to Sabertooths Plaza, a large square in front of the entrance to the stadium. He spoke rapidly about the game day atmosphere, the smells of local food vendors who would set up shop in the plaza, and the sounds of the great stadium. It made her miss Vipers game days.

Adjacent to the stadium were the practice fields, surrounded by the training facility and offices, a perk that the Vipers did *not* share. She hated to concede that she liked the idea of her office being so close to the stadium.

She'd been told to come in before Wednesday's practice to meet the staff and Colton, and to watch him in action before coming up with a plan. As if she hadn't already watched his film from the past two games of the season—and, *god*, were they rough. She hadn't mentioned that she'd met him a couple of times in college, and not one interaction had been pretty. She was sure they hadn't mentioned her by name to Colton, and even more positive that, if they had, he would've refused to work with her.

The collar of her blazer dug into her neck, and she readjusted, cursing herself for even wearing one when the August sun was still beating down in South Carolina. Her button-down was likely already showing sweat stains, so she couldn't even take the damned thing off. At least her skirt, though tight, allowed for a breeze to cool her lower half. People were turning to watch as her heels clacked on the concrete, so she stopped adjusting and plastered a smile on her face.

The air that hit her as she entered the first floor of the training facility cooled her in an instant. The man at the desk that faced the tall entrance doors stood as Lucia took in the trophies and display jerseys encased in glass before her. When he saw the intern, he waved them through to the elevators.

"You'll be meeting the team on the seventh floor, Ms. Moretti."

"Thank you both," she murmured, pressing the button and watching the intern and receptionist disappear behind tall, metal elevator doors. The back wall of the elevator was a pane of glass that looked out over the facility, and she took a moment to glance over the meticulously maintained fields.

When the doors opened, she followed the loud voices coming from a large room to the right. Shouting quieted at the sound of her heels, and she wondered if she'd ever get used to walking into a room full of men. She was a woman—albeit a woman uniquely qualified to rectify their quarterback's slump—in a male-dominated industry. An unforgiving industry that only considered a woman successful if she accomplished *more* than men in the same position.

A smile curved her mouth. She didn't have to like Colton Beaumont—and all signs pointed to the fact that she wouldn't, not after the hell he'd made her life in Los Angeles—but she would work with him. Her success in this industry depended upon it. And he needed her as badly as she needed him—or rather, this job.

She took a deep breath and stepped into the now-quiet boardroom, noting that she *was*, unsurprisingly, the only woman. The eyes of the Charleston coaches and analysts rested on her and her alone. She was proud of the achievements that had gotten her to this point, her head held high, confident.

"You have got to be fucking kidding me."

And there was the thorn in her side, standing in the middle of them all. His dark hair was styled better than it had been in college, though that signature scowl hadn't changed. His olive skin was a little lighter without the Los Angeles sun, and his face was clean-shaven. He'd always been handsome, but she'd remembered him as a college boy, and now, he was clearly a *man*. A green Sabers t-shirt clung to a well-muscled chest, and she averted her eyes at the sight of him in glorious gray sweatpants.

Glorious? No. That would not do at all.

"Good morning, gentlemen."

"Tell me this is a fucking joke. Coach? Is this a joke?" His eyes never left her. She stifled a gulp as they traveled down her body and then back up, stopping at the strip of exposed skin above her buttoned blazer before flicking back up to her face.

A middle-aged man stepped forward, eyebrows furrowed as he looked between the two. She knew from the film she'd already reviewed that he was the Sabertooths' head coach, Mark Turner. "Team, this is Lucia Moretti. She is the creator of GameFlow Analytics"—that garnered a mumble or two between the men before they quieted at the coach's look—"and she left the Vipers to work with us. She will be doing general analytics as well as helping Colton. Lucia will be an asset to all of us."

"Hello. Excited to join the team," she lied through the smile on her face.

"Coach, come on. I can't—"

"Do you two know each other?"

"Yes—"

"No," she said coolly. "I went to school in Los Angeles too, so we ran in the same circles, but no," she said again, firmly.

She and Max had gone to Lincoln University, while Colton had played for Crestview College. The two schools had always been crosstown rivals, but she'd felt it firsthand when she'd begun dating Max, who absolutely *despised* Colton.

"Colton, she's currently developing software specifically for quarterbacks. If there's an analyst who'll be able to help you figure out your numbers, it's Lucia."

Lucia stared Colton down, her own confident smirk on her lips, daring him to protest working with her.

Finally, he turned from her, focusing on his coach. "This can't be the only way. I'll work with any other analyst. Anybody but her."

She should've felt humiliated at his rejection in front of this group of men, but instead, she was incensed. He talked like he was above her, and she'd worked her ass off for nine years to be here.

Unclench your teeth, you've had too much dental work for that, she reminded herself.

"You said you'd try anything to keep your spot and prove you want to be on this team. This is anything. You'll start working with Lucia this week, and we'll see how you improve for regular season."

His words left no room for argument. Coaches began filing out of the room, a couple of them nodding at her as they left, though most ignored her. She wasn't surprised.

Colton didn't move, a glare hardening his face. He waited until everyone was gone before speaking quietly.

"How do we even know you and Clark are really over? For all we know, you're here to learn our playbook and take it back to the Vipers."

That, she had not been expecting. The reminder of her ex-fiancé, whose calls she was still dodging a week later, took her by surprise.

"If I wanted to take your playbook, all I'd have to do is study your film for a few games and write some code."

"If you're so good, then why haven't the Vipers won the Super Bowl since you graced them with your presence?"

"What the coaches decide to implement, regardless of my warnings, is not up to me. I do my job, provide my recommendations, and my sway ends there."

"How was Clark after I won? Was he pissed? Fuming?"

Lucia twirled the ring around her right middle finger as the conversation once again found its way to the disaster that was her love life. "Can we not talk about the man who cheated on me publicly and then inadvertently got me fired?"

Colton's eyes narrowed. "Fired? Coach just said you chose to take this job over your job with the Vipers."

She raised her chin, growing tired of his asinine line of questioning. "I chose this job when it was clear to me that I would lose my job with the Vipers."

He stepped closer, pulling his hands from the pockets of his sweatpants. For a moment, his arms flexed, and she watched the veins in his hands, her breath leaving her before she forced her eyes back to his.

"This whole firing business and you not being truthful about your means of getting here makes me think I'm right about you. Maybe it's all a ploy to pull a fast one on the reigning champions."

Lucia scoffed, "You're awfully paranoid for someone who can't even string together a good enough drive to prevent three and out after three and out. Does your punter ever get tired?" The surprise on his face added fuel to her fire. "And what would I even gain from lying about everything and being publicly humiliated like that?"

"I don't know, Moretti. What did you gain from having your best friend sleep with my tight end for a few months just to win a college rivalry game?"

She stepped back like she'd been slapped. What was he talking about? *Who* was he talking about? Isa? She remembered her dating a Crestview player their junior year—before Isa realized she liked girls more—but Lucia didn't know what he was talking about.

His jaw set tightly. "See, you can't even deny it. Clark told me all about it after the game anyway." He shook his head once, angrily, stepping past her on his way out of the room. The arm that brushed hers was strong, and it was quite an effort not to step to the side to stabilize herself.

Almost dejectedly, he called over his shoulder, "See you after practice."

Unsurprisingly, Colton had found an excuse to get out of meeting with her after practice that afternoon, but that was fine. She'd gotten to go home early and wallow in the misery that was her new life.

Home. What a funny word for the two-bedroom house she'd found. Her eyes scanned the unpacked boxes, grimacing at the air mattress pushed into the corner of one of the bedrooms. A fitted sheet was wrapped around it haphazardly, a sure sign the mattress was beginning to deflate.

She ignored the boxes and shuffled to the kitchen, clutching at the denial that surfaced at the thought that she officially lived in South Carolina, a state she'd never even been interested in visiting. And without a single friendly face, Lucia was utterly alone.

She pulled a box of mini ice cream cones from her freezer, sliding down its cool surface until her butt hit the floor. The plastic was loud as she opened it, a reprimand for opening a treat she'd promised to save for later.

In the booming silence of this new place, tears finally came, fast and hot and angry. No amount of mini ice cream cones would fix it. She kept picturing the woman draped over Max, and more than anything, she wished she'd found out about his unfaithfulness from anywhere but the internet.

Her mind then flitted to where it had been for the past week. Had Max and the woman done stuff in their house? In their bed? Her thoughts landed on a year and a half earlier when she'd gone out with Max and his friends, her hair slicked back and her button-down tucked tightly into her pencil skirt. She'd wanted to wear something more comfortable, but Max had insisted her work clothes made the most sense for an outing with him and his teammates.

She'd gone to the bathroom, and when she'd come back, she'd found a beautiful woman leaning over Max, her manicured nails running down his cheek. He'd moved away when he'd noticed Lucia, but her stomach had already begun to turn. When she'd brought it up, Max had looked at her like she was an idiot. He'd always looked at her like that, though.

She'd been so *stupid* then. It'd only taken him ten minutes to explain away the "misunderstanding," and then they'd gone back to normal.

She'd spent her life before him certain that she didn't want to ever be in a relationship, not after witnessing the instability of her father's relationships. And then Max had been there, had pursued her relentlessly, and she'd started to think maybe things would be different. He had been her only relationship, and she'd had no others to compare theirs to, so she hadn't known better. Sometimes, she still wasn't sure she did.

She'd let him get away with missed anniversaries and birthdays, thoughtless presents (that somehow always benefited him, too), and blatant flirting before her very eyes, all because she'd thought he'd loved her. She'd become exactly what she'd promised herself she wouldn't. A sucker. A *victim*.

Lucia felt sick, and she knew she was only doing it to herself, but she couldn't help it. Tears kept coming faster and faster, and she grew angrier and angrier.

Angry at Max for taking seven of the best years of her life from her. For making her believe love was real again. For making her believe that he'd loved her, that he would stay with her for the rest of their lives.

But she was angrier at herself. Angry for letting Max in when she'd always known love didn't last. For thinking an NFL player in the prime of his life would be ready to settle down with his college sweetheart. For not recognizing the signs, especially after being engaged for years with no wedding date in sight.

Her body slid further down until she was lying on her kitchen floor, staring up at the white ceiling, fluorescent lights flickering every once in a while. She swiped at her tears, but more came to replace them.

Even worse than the fact that she'd let herself believe in love, was that she'd become the person she'd always promised she wouldn't be. Her father's monthly heartbreaks had shown her what it was like to believe that love could be true, and she'd spent years in her tiny house in Philadelphia promising herself in the mirror that she would never let herself play the fool.

Yet, here she was. Naive and publicly, horribly, awfully, painfully humiliated because she'd let herself believe that she could be loved. Forced to move to another state, to another job, to work in a place where she knew nobody except *fucking* Colton Beaumont, who'd made it his life mission to make Max, his greatest nemesis, miserable for years.

Colton had done many things to rile up Max, and when Max couldn't take out his frustration on him, it'd ended with her having to calm him down. During her and Max's junior year of college, in the week leading up to their rivalry game with Crestview, the great Colton Beaumont and his teammates had completely trashed the Lincoln locker rooms and field. Lewd drawings and horrible words were spray-painted everywhere. To add insult to injury, someone had taken a shit in Max's locker, and he'd been convinced it had been his nemesis.

Of course, until the game, there had been nothing Max could do. Instead, he'd channeled his frustration and anger into their relationship. She'd walked on eggshells for the rest of the week, not sure which version of Max she'd get—the one who glared at the wall as he thought through how to get back at Colton, or the one who yelled at her until she was shrinking against the wall.

Sure, they'd grown since then. Or rather, she'd grown. Max, in all their time together, still hadn't learned to control his temper, but she'd learned how to handle him, how to not be so afraid when he'd explode and punch the wall near her.

After a few more minutes of quiet sobbing, once the dam had emptied, it occurred to her that maybe she could find the good in this situation. Sure, Isa was miles away, and her father was even further, but she had an opportunity to make even more of a name for herself. And this time, there would be no distractions. No boyfriends, no fiancés, nothing that would divert her from becoming a head analyst for an NFL franchise.

It was a pathetic silver lining to cling to, but she could cling to it nonetheless. When she opened her phone, her thumb wavered over the ten voicemails from Max. She tried not to remember the last time she'd seen him: the night before her entire life was upended, in their bed, that charming smile wide and golden hair shining in the moonlight that filtered through the windows.

They'd had plans earlier in the day, but he'd decided to go out with his friends instead. She'd expressed her frustrations, explained that she was tired of feeling like she was dating someone who was halfway out the door, and to make up for it, he'd bought out her favorite restaurant for the evening. Just like always, she'd let him get away with treating her poorly, reeling her back in just when she'd been ready to let go.

Well, no more. She'd had enough of being treated like shit to last her many lifetimes. The voicemails could wait another day. Better yet, she would force herself to continue to ignore his messages until the sight of his name didn't sting so much. Maybe then she'd be able to have a conversation with him that didn't end with him gaslighting her into taking him back. She would find a way to move on from this, find a way to get what she needed out of her new job.

She typed her best friend's name into her phone, tapping the call icon.

Isa picked up on the second ring. "It took you long enough."

"I left you *last night*, it's been less than twenty-four hours since we last spoke."

"Too many for my liking." She paused, then, "How was it? As horrible as you thought it'd be?"

Lucia disregarded the minor breakdown she'd just had and thought back to the large boardroom. "It's a total testosterone-fest, but that's what we were expecting. Colton is as infuriating and horrible as always. Though..." She trailed off, embarrassed about where her thoughts were leading her. She hadn't expected to be as attracted to him as she had been.

"Though, what?" Isa asked suspiciously.

"Nothing." She said it too fast, so she hurried to the real reason she'd called Isa. "He said something about my best friend sleeping with his tight end so we could win the rivalry game. I know you were seeing that Crestview tight end our junior year. Do you know what he was talking about?"

"Seeing is a very strong word, but yes, I was hooking up with Vinny for a while there. But I don't know what that has to do with the rivalry game." There was shuffling on the line. "All I remember is Max—I mean he-who-shall-not-be-named—being upset with me for it, me telling him off, and then the next time we spoke about it, he was very smug. I just assumed it was because we ended up winning."

Lucia hummed. "Why didn't I know any of that?"

"You had so much going on with your degree and the new project you were working on for the team. And you know how little I paid attention to the wants and cares of he-who-shall-not-be-named. Sorry, *osita*. But I'm sure it's just Colton being Colton. Once he sees how much you improve his game, he'll stop talking about the past."

Lucia hoped so. She'd seen him play the last few years, and she knew he was capable of 5,000-yard seasons. He just needed a little help to get back to his game.

And she planned to be that help, even if it meant wanting to rip her hair out every time she interacted with him. Fixing his season would be her Everest, and then she'd finally get her dream job: running departments of analysts.

Chapter Four

COLTON

Ice baths had always been both the bane of Colton's existence and the thing that kept him sane. Once the stinging wore off and he became numb, all thoughts would disappear. No more thinking about how poorly he'd done so far this season. No more thinking about his father's harsh words. For the next ten to fifteen minutes, he should have been able to relax in complete silence. It had always been meditative.

Except now, that wasn't the case. Lucia Moretti had ripped away that calm, that sanity. The thought of having to work with her for an entire season made him want to scream at the top of his lungs. She was *infuriating*.

The rivalry between him and Max had begun in college and had extended into the NFL, where he was sure it would continue until one of them retired. He'd only seen Lucia a handful of times during his college years, and he hadn't had an issue with her outside of the fact that she was Max's girlfriend. Until he'd learned about what her best friend had done. He remembered seeing the black-haired woman leaving the football apartments but hadn't thought anything of it until Max had taunted him after Crestview lost during Colton's senior year, laughing about how she'd learned their plays just by being around them.

It was bad enough that Lucia, her boyfriend, and her best friend had stolen his senior season with their conniving, but now she was pretending to "help him fix his game"? He didn't buy it. It was too convenient. Even if it had been six years ago, it had lost him the chance at playoffs in his final season, and that wasn't so easy to forgive.

He hadn't cared so much when she was with the Vipers. Max Clark was a slimy weasel, and Colton wasn't sure what she saw in him, but with him in a different state, he'd rarely had to pay the narcissist any heed. But now, with her so close to home, it was all coming back, and he was *bitter*.

How many lectures had he endured from his father after that game? How many extra reps had he forced himself to do to prove to his father that he had, in fact, cared about this sport? How many times had he been told how lucky he was that Max was the year below him, because when draft time came, he wouldn't have to outperform the Lincoln quarterback?

He'd spent weeks perfecting everything about his game before that loss, and all of it had been ripped away from him. She was a reminder of that, and he couldn't stand it.

He couldn't stand her in that little skirt, those ridiculous heels, or that blazer that he was sure she'd been overheating in. He couldn't stand that she knew so much about his game after watching a few hours of film, or that she knew so much about football in general. He couldn't stand that little groove that had popped up between her eyebrows when she got mad at him, the look of disgust on her face clear.

Most of all, he couldn't stand the fact that the moment she'd walked through the doorway of that boardroom, his first thought hadn't really been, *You've got to be fucking kidding me.* It had been, *She's even more breathtaking than she was in college.* And that pissed him off more than any of the other thoughts.

He groaned, pulling himself from the ice as his phone alarm went off. All of that aside, he really didn't want to work with her. It'd been fine when he thought he was just getting some nerdy analyst to come in and give him pointers, but Lucia was, and had always been, the enemy. And he knew she would relish pointing out all of his failures. As if he didn't have enough people in his life doing that.

Coach Turner's words came back to him. *"At the end of the day, it's a numbers game. And she's a numbers girl,"* he'd said, like that was supposed to make him feel better.

It had not, not one bit. And now he had to go upstairs and meet with her one-on-one, and they had to try not to kill each other while getting his numbers up. Because it was a numbers game.

"Coop, I'm heading up." Coop waved his hand, too relaxed in his adjacent ice bath to respond.

Colton had just finished toweling off when Lucia appeared, eyes widening at the towel tied loosely on his hips.

"Oh, I—" She shook her head, cheeks pinking as she looked down at her watch. "You're really dragging your feet. You're fifteen minutes late, and I didn't wanna let you get away with ditching again." She kept her gaze averted.

"Practice ran over. I'll be up in a few. Unless you wanna watch me get dressed." He grinned. If he was going to do this, at least he could enjoy getting under her skin a little.

"I'll be in my office." Her heels clacked against the polished concrete floor, but she'd opted out of wearing a blazer.

When he looked back at his best friend, Coop was smirking back knowingly. "Oh, yeah, you *hate* her."

"Shut up."

Ten minutes later, no less stressed than before the ice bath, but definitely more clothed, Colton strolled into her office. They'd given her a well-furnished room with a view of the practice fields, which was surprising. They usually saved those for the coaches. She must've been *really* good at her job if they were rolling out the red carpet for her.

Lucia had already pulled a chair beside hers, and when he rounded her desk, he noticed one of the monitors had four angles of his last game and the other had a bunch of numbers and symbols. Great.

"So how does this work, exactly?"

"Well, when I click this spacebar here, it'll play whichever of these four videos I click on. And then I can watch you try not to get sacked by the entire d-line as the pocket collapses."

He felt his temper rise at her sarcasm. "I might look like a dumb jock, but I am actually capable of understanding basic computer functions."

She sighed beside him. "Obviously, with the game tomorrow, there isn't much we can do in a couple of hours to get you ready. I'll watch tomorrow and take note of anything I see that could be contributing to whatever's going on with you. From there, I'll plan to watch each practice, and we can work through strengths and weaknesses together afterward."

She waved at the screens before them. "There will be a lot of reviewing film and numbers, and I'll also probably have you run drills alone before or after practice to see how you're doing on your own. Once my equipment comes in, I can get you hooked up to some different monitors to see how you fare during the drills, and even during practice."

He groaned internally. He was tired of reviewing film. It often felt like he watched himself play football more than he actually played it.

"Coach Turner said you'd decide how often we need to meet. After seeing the past couple of practices, what do you think?"

"I think we have a lot of work to do. I was reviewing your stats from last season, and you're averaging well below on everything except turnovers, which are, of course, up."

He felt his hand curl at his side. Did she have to be such a know-it-all?

"Yeah, I'm well aware of that, thanks. ESPN is all too happy to let me know exactly how my stats have been comparing to last season's. What I was asking was how often I need to be here."

She clicked on one of the four windows of film, pulling up a play he knew would end poorly for past-Colton. "Well, that sort of depends on you. Theoretically, we could meet after every practice and go through how you did that day. But, in the interest of us not being at each other's throats five to six days a week, we could cut it to every other day. And obviously not on game days."

"Fine. That's fine." He watched past-Colton step back and read the field before throwing an admittedly beautiful pass, though it wasn't anywhere near his receiver because he'd mixed up his route. A mistake he'd never made before that game.

She moved the video back a few frames and picked up a pen, tapping the screen right before he released the ball. "See that there? That's an early release. You may have read the field wrong, but even if your receiver ran the route you thought he would, that beauty wouldn't have found him."

Dammit, she was right. He'd let go of the ball a split second earlier than he should've.

"I'm not sure if you're just not focused, or if you're getting stressed because your o-line is playing like they're in high school, but that's certainly one of many problems."

His jaw clenched at her words. "There's nothing wrong with my focus," he grumbled. "*You* try reading the field correctly, checking if any of your receivers are going to be open, scrambling to prevent four 300-something-pound linemen from crushing you, all while trying to find an opening in the defense where you can rush for a few yards."

"That's literally your *job*. That's what you get paid millions of dollars to do!" When he turned to glare at her, she met his eyes. "And it's what you've done for years with surprising precision. Everybody knows you're capable of it, you just need to pull your head out of your ass long enough to make the changes I tell you to make."

Colton narrowed his eyes. He didn't like the idea of taking orders from Lucia, but had she just complimented him? "What is this software you're supposedly creating specifically for quarterbacks?"

He was surprised to see her smile. She practically lit up as she turned toward her other monitor. "It'll focus on throwing accuracy and game-time decision-making. So, I'd feed this film, or practice film, through it, and it would pinpoint the things that need to be improved. For example, that early release or your arm angle. Or even your follow-through. There will also be a piece that you can wear, and it'll connect to an app that coaches can use during practice to monitor metrics. Oh! And it'll track progress over time so you can see how you improve!"

She turned back to look at him, and he watched the excitement drain from her face when she caught him watching her.

Even though everything about her pissed him off, he found himself wanting to know more. And maybe a part of him wanted to see the excitement on her face again. A very small part of him he wanted to squash. "How will it figure out if I'm making the right decisions?"

"I'd use all-22 film, and it would determine whether the pass or rush you chose was the best option," she said, referring to when their film crew took video of the entire field, including all twenty-two players.

"Sounds complex."

"And that's why *I* get paid. Though, not millions, unfortunately."

This time when their eyes met, she was *almost* smiling at him, and it *almost* felt like there could be a semblance of a truce between them. Almost.

And then his phone buzzed, and he saw her look down at the screen briefly as his Do Not Disturb turned off and hundreds of DMs came flooding in.

She rolled her eyes, scoffing. "So predictable."

"What the hell is that supposed to mean?"

"It means, of course you leave your notifications on so you can see all your ardent admirers. I bet you like the instant gratification."

Not for the first, not for the second, not even for the third time that hour, he felt his temper rise. Who the hell did she think she was? She didn't know anything about him.

He wasn't about to tell her that he hadn't pursued a woman in years. And he *certainly* wasn't going to tell her the reason he'd even re-downloaded all his socials was to scroll through Max's feed when the news had first come out.

So instead, he said, "There's no need to be jealous."

She scoffed, "Please. If you were to measure my emotions right now, jealousy would be at below-zero levels."

"What's below-zero jealousy?"

It was her turn to narrow her eyes, but whatever she was about to say was cut off by his phone ringing, Maya's name popping up on the screen. She was on the WTA tour, so if she was calling, it either meant something was wrong in the tennis world, or she was making her rounds through the family. She was the one who kept the family together. She had made it her mission to keep everyone in contact after their mom had passed.

"Don't worry, Moretti. There's no need for below-zero jealousy with this one. It's just my sister. I'm gonna take this." Lucia made a noise, but he was already walking out of her office.

"Hey, Mai. You okay?"

"Yep," she chirped. "Just checking in with everyone and wanted to talk to my favorite oldest brother." He knew that meant nothing because he was the only oldest brother, but he loved it anyway. She was his favorite of his siblings, something he did nothing to try to hide.

When their mother had died, Maya had only been twelve. She had been Maya's everything. Probably due to the fact that the minute their father had realized she wasn't a future football player, he'd passed her off to their mother without a second thought.

Their mother had been the most dedicated and loving woman Colton had ever met. She'd sacrificed her career the moment he'd been born, always promising that, regardless of their father, she would be there for her children as they grew up. She'd sacrificed seeing her side of the family more than once or twice a year, had given up teaching her children the culture she'd been born and raised in because she was scared of what might happen to them if she tried to leave.

Maya had taken it the hardest when she'd passed, and the loss had made her cherish her relationships more, even into adulthood. While most of Colton's friends hardly talked to their siblings, Maya always made sure to speak to both of her brothers at least twice a month, no matter how busy she was on her pro circuit.

"How's the tennis?"

"It's great! My coach thinks I have a chance at getting a wild card into a Grand Slam this year, which is exciting."

"That's great, Mai. I'm so proud of you."

"Oh, stop it, you'll make me blush. How's the ol' pigskin? I regret to inform you that I have not been watching football the past couple of weeks."

Probably for the best. "It's good. Landon's been doing really well."

"And you?"

Colton sighed. "I've seen better days, but that's nothing for you to worry about."

"Has our dearest patriarch been up your ass per usual? Who am I kidding, of course he has."

Colton laughed for the first time in a few days, thankful for Maya's sardonic humor. "Yeah, it'll be a cold day in Hell before that stops."

He heard voices on the other end of the phone and knew Maya was probably with her group of tennis friends. Maya was never without them, something else he was thankful for. She deserved better than their shitty, dysfunctional family. "Go ahead, Mai. I know you're busy. We'll talk again soon. Love you to the moon."

"Love you to the moon, Colt. Good luck on your next couple of games, and I'll text you if I ever go to the house in Charleston."

He put his phone on Do Not Disturb again—indefinitely—slipped it into his pocket, and walked back into Lucia's office. He couldn't decipher the look on her face, but at least it didn't seem like she wanted to knife him. She didn't make any more comments about his "ardent admirers," and they managed to get through an hour without killing each other.

Chapter Five

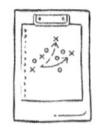

LUCIA

Lucia watched Colton lead the Sabers across the field as the crowd, a sea of green, cheered. The intern had been right. Game day in Charleston *was* intoxicating. Even the hot South Carolina sun, which had been hidden by clouds the past week, came out to say hello—and was doing its best to burn every fan to a crisp.

Luckily, her position had many perks, one of which was an air-conditioned box where she could work during games. Unluckily, that meant she had to sit with the rest of the analysts, all of whom were men, and none of whom would give her the time of day.

She couldn't say she was surprised. It had taken over a year of dedicated effort to make friends with her coworkers in Richmond, excluding Charlotte. She was sure it would take many months, maybe years, before her new colleagues saw her as an equal. If they ever did.

Her two laptops sat in front of her, one running diagnostics on the software she was trying to finish by the end of the season—though that appeared to be a lofty goal—and the other displaying game stats. The large screen hanging on the left side of the room showed the game in crisp high definition, which was good because she could hardly see who was who from all the way up here.

She clicked through the different views on her second laptop, making sure her all-22 view and replay options were both working before kickoff. Now was when the adrenaline usually hit, though she was still technically in training, learning her new team's processes. She'd been told to shadow the other analysts to get a feel for how different her old procedures were from what they did, and to focus her attention on Colton's performance.

In the first quarter, Lucia watched the team as a whole, taking in the sloppy offensive line and an asleep-at-the-wheel defense. As she already knew, Colton was not the only reason this team was trudging painfully through preseason.

After she'd made some shorthand notes for herself to review when looking at film, she focused on a very *un*focused Colton. He seemed oddly out of sync compared to where he'd been in February of that year. To the untrained eye, he still seemed to have a semblance of rhythm, but she could see that the lack of offensive line protection wasn't the only issue. Sure, the collapses were messing up his timing and confidence, but his reads were predictable. He was making it easy for their opponents to pick off the ball.

Despite that, Lucia had to admit that his mechanics were nearly flawless. Every once in a while, he'd release the ball too early and miss his mark, but for the most part, his motion looked solid. She wondered how he would do without pressure. If he were just to throw a long pass without giant linemen descending upon him. She made a note to herself to have him do some drills alone the day after next.

After a particularly bad drive, he stomped off the field, tossing his helmet to the side. Lucia couldn't be sure what he was saying, but his hands were waving wildly. What she wouldn't have given for a *Mic'd Up* episode right then.

Halftime was busy as the analysts ran data and numbers to the coaches and broadcasters. Through the hustle and bustle, she offered to proof the numbers. Instead, they had her take the physical copies over to the coaching box. She smiled (read: bared her teeth) as she took the sheets of paper from them, cursing whatever high being decided to make her love this sport so much.

The second half was slightly better. Cooper Hayes, Colton's favored receiver and Charleston's beloved tight end, had finally been cleared to play again after a pretty bad concussion in the first quarter of the first preseason game. It appeared to give Colton the confidence he needed to send up two beautiful passes for seventy yards, setting up a first and goal at the three-yard line. After two failed rushes by the running back, Colton ran the ball into the end zone himself.

The crowd roared, finally seeing their star quarterback tapping into his potential and giving the Sabertooths their first lead of the game. A few minutes later, near the end of the fourth quarter, Colton connected with Cooper for another touchdown, putting a nail in the Lions' coffin.

It had been a hard-fought win. Everyone, from the players, to the fans, to the coaches and analysts, knew the Sabers should've obliterated the Lions. Even so, fans filing out of the stadium yelled and cheered and stomped to show their support for a team that had brought their city so much success in previous years.

It was an ugly win, but it gave them hope that the season might not be over.

Colton was late. Again. Forty-five minutes late, to be exact. Lucia wasn't surprised, but she *was* annoyed. It was a Saturday, and while she normally worked weekends, having a Friday game meant Saturday was optional for staff. She could've worked from home, at the very least. She'd gone out of her way to be there today to help Colton, and he didn't even have the courtesy to let her know he was going to be late. Or not come at all.

She checked her phone again before walking out of her office and down the hall. She stopped, quieting her steps when she heard a voice.

"I told you I'm busy right now. I have to—" Silence.

Colton must've been on the phone. Lucia wondered if she should back away, sit down in her office, and wait for him to finish his conversation. She'd overheard his call with his sister two days earlier—though, to be fair, that was his fault for barely stepping outside of her office. *This* eavesdropping was on her. Maybe she was nosy, or maybe she was tired of him snubbing her and strolling into their sessions late (or never), but she didn't move away.

"Yes, Dad, I understand. I played poorly and am lucky we won...Yes, I know you moved to Charleston to come to my games..." A sigh. "Yes, I'm sorry I've been playing in a way that disappoints you."

Lucia's eyebrows pinched together. His father sounded like a grade-A douche.

The apple doesn't fall far from the tree, she mused.

"Yes, I'll be in the gym twice a day this week. I'm well aware that, starting now, the games count, Dad. I've lived and breathed football my entire life. I think I know the difference between preseason and regular season." There was that hint of temper in his voice, and Lucia wondered how he kept a hold of it so well with his father but seemed unable to with her.

Lucia was so focused on her own thoughts that she didn't hear his approach. Around the corner he came, phone still to his ear, and his eyes fell to her. Oh, and he was *pissed*. There was the wrinkle between his brows that always accompanied their encounters, and his frown was more pronounced than usual. Her eyes fell to his jaw, which had clenched quite a bit since he'd found her listening to his conversation.

She wagged her fingers in a pitiful wave, a faux-innocent smile curving her lips. She tried to look apologetic but had no idea if it came across that way.

"I'm gonna have to call you later, Dad. Something's happened at the facility, and I need to go." His eyes searched her face as he listened to his father.

Colton stepped closer, and she stepped back, her body pressed to the wall. She couldn't put her finger on what he smelled like, but whatever it was, it was *good*.

"Yeah, I'll come by sometime this week." Suddenly, the phone was in his pocket, and his full attention was on her. "Why am I not surprised that you don't know how to mind your business? Snooping to see if I'd give up something valuable for you and the Vipers to use against me?"

Lucia swallowed, and his eyes tracked the movement. "I was coming to drag you up here since you're late. *Again.* It's not my fault you have private conversations out in the open."

She shouldn't have been listening in, but she was fed up with all the men in her life treating her like she didn't deserve a seat at the table. She didn't know what else she could do to prove she'd earned her place in Charleston and in the NFL, but she wasn't going to keep taking it lying down. Especially not from Colton.

Colton's eyes narrowed. "How much did you hear?"

She shrugged nonchalantly. "Not much, I really was just coming to see where you were." She crossed her arms, trying to appear confident. "I'm tired of you acting like showing up to our meetings is optional. I have been waiting here since our agreed-upon time. I could've been at home."

"Yeah? You have plans you're missing out on?"

"My life outside of work is none of your business."

"Got a hot date?"

"Colton."

"Lucia." Something dangerous flickered in his eyes before he stepped back, giving her a little more room to breathe. "I'm surprised you don't have the schedule. We have clinics with local kids with cancer once a month. I was out in the stadium with them, and we try not to put time restrictions on it when possible."

Her knees almost gave out at the confession, but she braced herself against the wall. Now *she* was the asshole. Colton didn't even look smug. He just turned on his heel and walked to her office.

Lucia took a second to collect herself, brushing out her skirt before following him. He was already sitting in the chair she'd pulled beside hers, gazing out over the practice fields.

"I'm sorry. Look, neither of us wants to do this, but both of our jobs rely on us being here. We should try to communicate better."

"I'll be better about letting you know if I'm going to be late. But just so we're clear, that doesn't mean I don't still think you're working with the Vipers."

She sat in her chair, moving it away from Colton so she could think better. "You're welcome to your paranoia. I don't care what you think."

Thirty minutes later, after getting through less than half of the film from the game, Colton slammed his fist onto the desk. "You know I watch film all the time? I don't need you going through every minuscule aspect of my game in film. My dad already does that every day, and then I have to endure it with the whole team throughout the week."

"Colton, what do you think I'm here to do? Did you think I was gonna tell you how well you're playing? Coddle you into getting your shit together? Tell you 'Good luck on the season' and be on my merry way?" When he didn't respond, she continued, "No! That's not why they brought me in. They hired me to help you because you're a world-famous quarterback having a bad preseason, and we need to figure out how to get you back."

"Actually, they brought you in because your boss asked them if they needed an analyst."

Lucia sighed. "If you don't want my help, just leave. I'm not dealing with your shit today."

He didn't try to hide the surprise on his face, just stood and walked out. She knew he was angry—whether from a shitty game, talking to his father, having to work with her, or all three—and nothing she said right now was going to get through to him anyway. They had two weeks until the regular season started. She would find a way to show him she was there to help.

With Colton gone, she pulled up film from the previous season, scooting her chair forward and searching for anything she was missing. Hours rolled by with nothing. The sun began to set, and she placed her head in her hands, angry. His questions echoed in her head.

"You have plans you're missing out on? Got a hot date?"

So smug. Like he couldn't imagine her having anything better to do than meet with him. She *despised* him.

Still, she couldn't help but feel a little bad for him. The call with his dad seemed to have made him even less amenable than usual, and she wondered how many times he'd had that same conversation. She'd noticed in film that he'd seemed brighter in past years, smiling more on the sidelines when it was the defense's turn on the field. She wasn't sure whether those smiles were correlated with winning or if there was more to it.

Maybe he needed to find a way to enjoy the game again.

Chapter Six

COLTON

Colton's muscles ached as he lay on the turf of the practice field. Most of the team was heading to the showers, but Colton had a session with Lucia before the season opener. He actually felt that they were making progress. Not that he'd ever tell her that.

Colton was not proud of the way he'd acted with Lucia after the last preseason game. He'd made an effort to be on time for their meetings over the next week, and to her credit, she'd begun to implement productive ways to help him that weren't just picking apart film. Namely, practice drills.

When Colton turned his head to the left, he was met with the tallest, most ridiculous pair of heels he'd ever seen. Lucia peered down at him, and with the glow of the floodlights behind her like a halo, she looked like an angel. His eyes traveled over her legs briefly, marveling at how long they were.

When he met her eyes, she raised an eyebrow.

"What do you want, Moretti?" He let out a groan as he turned his head to look back up at the night sky.

"Why are you so sore?"

"I've been going to the gym before and after practice this week to get ready for the game."

"Who told you to do that? You need to rest. Causing extra strain on your muscles isn't a good idea so close to the season. You're on a plan for a reason."

"And yet here you are, about to ask me to do extra drills."

Lucia sighed. After a moment, something thudded next to his head. "Put that on. We'll keep it light today, but I need to get some metrics to keep your tracking consistent."

When he picked it up, he realized it was the vest she'd had him wear during their field sessions. "I don't want to wear the sports bra today."

Another thud. The bands he wore on his wrists to track his arm movement. "It's not a sports bra. Stop whining and get up. I have shit to do."

"Like what?"

"What did we say about asking questions about our lives outside of these sessions?"

"Ask them?" She didn't look amused. "Well, how else am I supposed to know whether or not you're working for the Vipers?"

"I'll be sure to show you the part of my paystub that says 'Sabertooths Football.' Now. Get. Up."

Colton stood, groaning. When he started to remove his shirt, she made a noise that sounded like a squeak.

"What are you doing?"

"Putting the sports bra on."

"Put it on over your t-shirt."

Colton grinned, having learned that making Lucia uncomfortable was one of his favorite pastimes. Especially to get back at her for all the rude comments she'd inevitably make about his sloppy form. "What? Can't think when my shirt's off?"

"Another comment like that, and I'll have to have a conversation with HR. Put the vest on. I already put cones and ladders out, I just need to track your acceleration for some agility drills, and then we can focus on your throwing." Under her breath, but not quiet at all, she continued, "God knows you need agility training. You can't scramble for shit right now."

"I heard that."

"Good. Get up and prove me wrong."

Despite the strain, Colton completed five rounds of the agility drills she'd laid out for him, his legs screaming from the effort. After each round, Lucia checked her tablet, her bottom lip tucked between her teeth. Finally, she seemed content with the numbers.

"Okay, put the wristbands on now. We'll do the same throwing drills as last time." When he listened, her eyebrows came together. "You're being more amenable than usual, have you finally decided that I'm not a Vipers minion here to spy on you?"

Colton slapped the ball once before letting it roll off his fingertips, up, up, up. She glanced down at her tablet again, tapping on it a couple of times.

"I'm too tired to think of anything mean right now. You're still Clark's little helper, as far as I'm concerned." It was lazy, but Colton liked to win, and any comments about her being Clark's minion seemed to get under her skin.

She looked up at him angrily. "Colton, on the field, you're supposed to scramble your feet, not your brain."

He picked up another football from the ground near his feet, his whole body aching with the effort. He took a step back and repeated the motion, this ball coming up a little shorter than the last.

"Early release. Focus on the field. You have no d-line descending on you, absolutely no pressure. Give me eight clean throws, and you can be done."

"Since when did you become a quarterback coach? I didn't even know analysts did field work."

"Since you showed Coach Turner—your biggest supporter, by the way—that he can't trust you to lead his team anymore."

Ouch. He'd walked right into that one. "I'm plenty capable. We just beat the Lions, didn't we?"

Lucia scoffed, "You and I both know that was an ugly win. If they had been even slightly better, we probably would've lost…again. And honestly, Cooper coming back helped you immensely."

He didn't respond. She was right anyway. He played better when Cooper was out on the field. And if the Lions had been on their A game, he would've struggled a lot more to get that win.

"What do you love about the game?" she asked, tossing him a ball that'd rested beside her foot.

"What?"

"Why do you play? What makes you want to keep playing?"

"Winning." He said it without thinking. Winning was, and had always been, his driving force. His father had instilled it in him from a very young age. If he wanted people to see him, he needed to win.

Lucia gave him a look that seemed equal parts pity and contempt. "But there has to be something that makes you *enjoy* football. The fans? The feeling of a great throw? Being able to do what you love with a team that you love? What about the game gets you giddy?"

"Giddy? What am I, a teenager?" He let another ball fly, knowing how perfect it was before Lucia even said anything.

She let out an exasperated sigh. "Never mind. Seven more."

He listened, letting a few more go until she was satisfied. He jogged over to the balls he'd thrown and dropped them into a nearby bin. She was already heading back toward the offices when he caught up to her.

He pulled the wristbands and vest off, handing them to her. Her hand stilled when his fingers brushed hers, like he'd startled her. The tired look on her face made him ask, "What about the game gets *you* giddy?"

She searched his face as if looking for any signs he was mocking her. "Everything." She shrugged and kept walking.

"That's a half-assed answer."

"Better than yours!" she called over her shoulder, disappearing into the tall, glass building. Colton smiled at that.

He jogged toward the locker room, excited at the prospect of a warm shower to soothe his aching muscles. When he turned on the hot water and stepped in, he realized he was still smiling.

The hooting and hollering that accompanied their win didn't end on the bus to the airport and continued well into the flight back to Charleston. The coaches, including Coach Turner, were still talking excitedly together. Everybody was admittedly surprised that the season would be starting one and zero.

Even Lucia was smiling when Colton walked past her on the plane to use the bathroom, though he quickly realized it was because of something Cooper—who, for some reason, was in the seat beside hers—had said.

When Coop saw him, he waved him down with an evil grin. "Colt, why didn't you tell me how lovely Ms. Moretti here is?

Were you gonna keep all this intelligence to yourself? I could use some help too, you know."

Cooper only grinned wider when Colton scowled. "There's nothing lovely about Lucia," he grumbled as he walked away.

A few minutes later, when he came back from the bathroom, Cooper was nowhere in sight, and Lucia was typing rapidly on her tablet. When she noticed him watching her, she glared. "Oh, hello, asswipe. Come to tell me about how ugly I am again?"

There were stifled snickers across the aisle from Lucia, though the staff members quieted and looked away at Colton's glare.

He turned back to look at Lucia.

"I *never* called you ugly." The fervor with which he spoke seemed to stun them both. He rolled his neck, saved from having to say anything further when the pilot let them know they were descending. He pointed toward his seat, which seemed to be enough of a goodbye for Lucia.

While Colton sat back down and fastened his seat belt, Cooper turned to him with that same grin on his face. "Not your smoothest moment, my friend."

"What were you doing talking to her?"

"What would you say if I told you I was asking her out?"

Colton's head whipped to look at his best friend, who was quickly becoming his least favorite person. "You didn't."

Cooper's laugh was answer enough, though he still responded. "No, I didn't. I was asking about GameFlow Analytics. I took a couple of coding classes in college and really liked them, so I wanted to learn a bit more about her process and her favorite programming language. Pissing you off was just a bonus." That didn't warrant a response from Colton, and Cooper chuckled again. "What do you care, anyway? I thought you didn't like her."

"I don't," he ground out.

"But I can't ask her out?"

"Correct. Plus, she's probably still with Clark. You know my theory."

"Yes, Einstein, I'm well aware of your outlandish theory. You talk about it so much, I bet even your pillow knows about it."

"What?"

"When you talk about it in your sleep."

"I don't think it's outlandish. Her best friend in college literally—"

"Yes, yes, she slept with Vinny, who divulged all of your team secrets. Does that even seem like something that would've happened? Or did you just let Clark get in your head?"

Colton mulled it over, hating to concede it was entirely possible Max had said that after the win just to piss him off. It was definitely a signature Max Clark dick move. Still, that didn't change the fact that she was the fiancée—or ex-fiancée—of his sworn enemy.

"She's still potentially going to marry the person I hate most in the world."

Cooper shook his head. "I think you know you're being ridiculous. Nobody allows themselves to be publicly humiliated like that, and then moves their entire life to another state, where they don't know anyone but the guy they're being forced to work with, for their fiancé's personal vendetta."

"What, did you take psychology classes in college too?"

"As a matter of fact, I did. They went hand in hand with my anti-bullshit classes."

Colton rested his head on the seat, closing his eyes for a moment as the plane's wheels touched down.

Colton shut the door to the locker room, letting it click quietly behind him. After his father's call, which had only been marginally better than the ones he'd received after losing, he'd spent an hour in the weight room doing some light resistance training, stretching, and rolling out. He didn't usually do more than a quick stretch after a game, but he was feeling antsy after his conversation with Cooper.

The building was quiet, just the way Colton preferred it. He often stayed behind after everyone left, enjoying having the vastness of the facility all to himself. The elevator dinged, letting him out on the third floor where they had fridges stocked with healthy food and protein shakes. His stomach growled, the few slices of pizza he'd had after the game long digested.

Just as he started to grab a stack of food, the door opened, startling him. When he turned around, he expected to see a janitor. Instead, standing there in her matching, dark-green, game-day pantsuit was Lucia.

She squeaked when she saw him. "I—I thought I was the last one here."

He was at a loss for words. Her hair, normally in a clip or tight bun, was down, falling well past her shoulders. When he finally regained the ability to speak, he said, "Nobody's allowed in here but coaches and players."

"No, I know. I just—I got hungry, and I haven't had much time to get groceries, and everywhere's closed, but...you're right. I should go." She turned to leave.

"What are you doing here so late?"

"One win does not a Super Bowl-winning team make, Colton. There's a lot to do." Her hand still rested on the door, her back to him.

He took a step forward, then another. "But it's late. Way past midnight."

Lucia turned around, eyes widening as she took in how close he'd moved to her. "Well, my job depends on making sure *you* keep winning. Not the team. You, specifically. And just because we won doesn't mean you're back to yourself. So, I came back to watch film."

She worked harder than the coaches. Even they had gone home already, content to watch film the next morning.

He took another step forward until his shoes were practically touching hers. He waited to see if she'd move away, push herself against the door, but she didn't. She just stared up into his eyes defiantly.

"I won't tell if you won't," he whispered.

He watched her throat as she swallowed, then her mouth as she bit her lip. Her eyes were as hazy as his head felt.

"H—huh?"

He tilted his head back toward the fridges. "I won't tell anybody if you grab some food."

"O—oh, right." But she didn't move. Her eyes didn't leave his.

"What's the matter? No witty quip for me? My, my, Moretti. That's very unlike you."

"I—I—"

He loved making her stutter, and apparently, his proximity did the trick.

"Please don't stay here this late after everyone leaves. It's dangerous."

"You're...you're not my boss. And...and you're here, too. Who should I be afraid of? You?"

He inched closer, their noses almost touching. Her eyes fluttered closed, and he wondered if she wanted him to kiss her as badly as he wanted to. It was an unsettling thought, so instead, he whispered, "Go grab something from the fridge, and I'll walk you out."

Chapter Seven

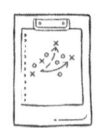

LUCIA

Isa had been silent for long enough that Lucia was beginning to get worried. "Isa? Did you hear what I said?"

A garbled noise came from the other side of her phone. "What! He *what*? That piece of shit almost *kissed you*?"

Lucia didn't know how to explain that she wasn't sure she was upset about it. She also wasn't certain he had *actually* almost kissed her. It seemed more like he'd been toying with her.

"Well, it was more like he leaned forward to close-speak with me, you know? I'm not positive that he wanted to kiss me. I mean, the guy hates me and thinks I'm working with his greatest nemesis."

"Close-speak?" Isa asked incredulously. "Why don't you seem as upset about this as I am? And why aren't you emphasizing how much *you* hate *him*?"

Lucia blew out a sigh. "I don't know, I've been working with him a lot recently. He's definitely rough around the edges, but..."

"Oh, don't tell me. Don't you dare tell me you wanted him to kiss you. Lucia Moretti, don't you tell me that."

Isa took her silence as an answer.

"*Puta*! I can't believe you. What's changed?"

"Nothing's changed! It's not like I *like* him, but you have to admit he's hot as hell. He was in my space, and I couldn't think, and yeah...I guess I would've been okay with it."

Isa groaned, but then seemed to think for a second. "Well, maybe you'll get a better lay outta him than you did Max."

Lucia set her glass of wine down on the counter, shocked. "I'm not gonna sleep with him, Isa. It was just a momentary lapse in judgment. Again, I *must* remind you that he hates me."

"So, the only reason you won't get laid is because he hates you?"

"No!"

"Mm-hmm. Well, just saying, it doesn't sound like he hates you."

Lucia finished her glass, needing the burn.

"Lu, have you talked to your dad since you moved?"

Lucia regretted finishing her wine. She should've waited.

"No."

She loved her father. She really did. But she wasn't ready to hear his optimistic take on her failed engagement. And he would absolutely have one.

The man had been cheated on and abandoned, left to care for an eight-year-old daughter on his own. Her mother had left them because she couldn't handle being a mother, because having a child hadn't fit her lifestyle. She'd thrown years of marriage into the trash to go do who knows what. Despite that, her father had managed to continue giving his heart away, getting back up and dusting himself off after every heartbreak. Her whole life, she'd watched him get hurt over women who didn't deserve him.

She'd promised herself she wouldn't be like him, and then she'd met Max and had thought that maybe she'd been wrong. But Max Clark had proven her right, right, right, and now she was an absolute fool, following in her father's footsteps. So, no, she hadn't spoken to her father.

"Lu, the longer you wait, the worse it might be. And you never know what he'll say." When Lucia didn't respond, Isa continued. "He's the only family you have––besides me, obviously. Don't push him away."

Lucia sighed, knowing Isa was right. "I'll call him this week. I promise."

"Okay, Abby's giving me that 'get off the phone' look, so I've gotta go. But you owe me details about sexy Colton Beaumont."

"Now he's sexy?"

"I'll say anything to get you laid. Goodnight, *osita*. Kisses."

Lucia huffed a laugh before responding, "Kisses."

She ignored the glass on the counter and grabbed the bottle of wine instead, tucking herself under a blanket on her couch and turning on *The Bachelor*. Maybe scripted, pretend love would make her feel better.

The hair on the back of Lucia's neck rose, and she remembered Colton's warning from a week earlier. Despite finally pulling her car door open, throwing herself inside, and locking the doors, the panic didn't subside. It took her a couple of minutes, but she finally realized why.

Her car wouldn't start. She was alone—she hoped—in the Sabers' parking garage, and her car wouldn't start. She weighed her options, wondering if it would be better for her to sleep in her car for the night than to call a rideshare. Just as she'd decided that was her best option, a knock on her window startled her. She let out a shriek, jumping out of her seat before searching for her pepper spray.

"Moretti, open the damn door."

Lucia breathed a sigh of relief, thankful it was only Colton. She cracked the door a little.

"Yes?"

"Get out."

She stuck her chin out defiantly. "Stop. Telling. Me. What. To. Do." Just for good measure, she added, "Asshole."

"What did I tell you about staying here so late? Why don't you listen to *anything*?" He looked like he was ready to throw her over his shoulder and walk over to the car she'd been too scared to even notice. She *really* hadn't done a good job of casing her surroundings.

"There's only so much work I can do from my house without my equipment."

"Get out."

"Can't you just give me a jump?"

His jaw ticked, but he didn't respond. She opened the door and folded herself out of the car slowly, deliberately making him wait. If he was going to boss her around, she would do everything in her power to make it harder for him.

She followed behind him, astounded when he opened the passenger-side door of his Ferrari.

"Why the hell do you care anyway?"

"I'd rather my personal sports analyst not get murdered during the season." His jaw was clenched. He seemed oddly stressed.

"Wow, you're so kind. I'll be sure to only dangle myself in front of the Charleston murderers once the season is over."

He apparently didn't find that funny, his face stoic as he pulled out of the parking lot.

"Guide me to your house." He nodded toward his phone, which was held up by a magnet connected to the air vents.

She picked it up, pointing it at him so he could enter his password.

"It's one-one-zero-seven."

Lucia nearly dropped the phone. Max hadn't ever given her his password. She was so shocked that she just listened to him, typing in the password and then her address before placing the phone back.

They sat in tense silence until Lucia couldn't take it anymore. "How much did you see?"

"Of you jumping into your car like you were being chased by a man wielding a chainsaw? Pretty much all of it. I had just gotten into my car when you came out of the elevator."

She closed her eyes, dreading her next words. "Well, thank you. I'm not gonna apologize, because I didn't do anything wrong. But thank you for saving me from sleeping in my car."

He didn't respond, didn't even nod, just flicked on his blinker as he turned onto a residential street.

Just when she thought they would stay silent for the rest of the ride, he said, "I worry about my little sister every day. I don't know if she'd ever tell me if something happened, or if, god fucking forbid, something has already happened, but I worry about her being outside at night every single day."

Lucia tried not to melt at his confession. Once again, he'd surprised her. She twirled her ring around her middle finger, not sure how to respond. She looked out at the beautiful mansions with manicured lawns, cursing herself for investing all of her money instead of spending it on the finer things in life. Like an NFL player's old house.

A few minutes later, when they'd moved away from the player mansions, Colton pulled in front of her new house. She wondered for a moment what he thought of it, brushing some invisible dust off her skirt awkwardly. He stopped the car, got out, and walked over to her side.

Why was he being so…chivalrous? What happened to the annoying, hard-headed Colton she couldn't stand?

She locked eyes with him as she stepped out of the car, nearly teetering on her heels as his eyes slid to the bottom of her skirt and then down her legs. He started to reach out like he was going to offer her his hand, but she was nearly standing already, and he seemed to think better of it, stuffing his hand into the pocket of those damn gray sweatpants she hated that she loved.

The moment was broken when a flash went off. Lucia spun around, eyes narrowing as she tried to decipher the shape in the shadows before them. Another flash.

"Ignore it," Colton whispered gruffly. Her stomach flipped. At what? She wasn't sure. "We passed my house on the way here. They must've been waiting and followed us. I'll have some of my people work on keeping those off the internet."

The media made her jumpy, and she didn't like the idea of them taking pictures of her, but she could hardly focus on that with Colton beside her. Colton shut the car door behind her, a hand on her lower back, ushering her toward her front door as she located her keys in her purse.

"Oh, you don't have to walk me. It's just right there."

"Shut up, Moretti. We're already halfway there."

He was right. It only took them a few strides to reach the three steps that led to her little stoop. She pulled her keys out and pushed them into the doorknob as another flash went off behind them. She really hoped the pictures were just of Colton, but the sinking in her stomach made her think otherwise.

Before twisting the doorknob, she turned to look at him again, flushing when she realized his eyes were already on her. "Thank you again."

His eyes searched her face for a second before he responded, "Goodnight, Moretti."

She turned the knob, went inside, and shut the door. She rested her forehead on it as she locked it, closing her eyes and cursing her damn car.

Chapter Eight

COLTON

Colton's chest had been aching ever since he'd left Lucia at her house the night before. Something about the way she'd looked at him on her porch had made his whole body react, his heartbeat increasing. It pissed him off.

They still hadn't talked about that night on the third floor, though he supposed there wasn't anything to say. He really needed to keep his head in the game and stop focusing on Lucia's every little movement. How had he gone from convinced she was the enemy to being stupidly attracted to her in the course of a couple of weeks?

He thought a little bickering might do him good, a comment about her messy office already on his tongue; until he caught sight of her through the slightly open door. She was devastating.

Her face was puffy and red, tears streaming down her cheeks no matter how much she patted them away with tissues. When her eyes flicked to him, she swiveled her chair around so he couldn't see her.

What'd happened? She'd seemed fine when he'd dropped her off the night before. Had he said something? No, he found it hard to believe he was the cause of this. She was much too strong to care about any of his useless jabs.

She must've still been upset about her breakup with Clark, then. He supposed that sealed it for him that she'd been honest the entire time. He could finally admit to himself that, in all likelihood, she was probably not a spy for Max Clark. Just a heartbroken ex-fiancée.

He knew he should leave and give her the privacy she obviously wanted, but his feet started moving toward her before he could even think. He kneeled before her, pushing away the urge to reach for her face.

"What's wrong?"

The words came out gruffer than he'd intended, and she flinched. *Fuck it*.

He reached out, lifting her chin so he could meet her eyes. "What's wrong, Lucia?"

She opened her phone and handed it to him, closing her eyes as if scared of his reaction. He looked at the screen, noting the somewhat grainy photo. He pinched the screen, seeing the headline at the same time he recognized the people in the picture.

It was him and Lucia gazing into each other's eyes. Taken in front of her house the night before.

"Fuck."

She shook, sobbing quietly as he read the headline. The words "Sports Analyst Makes Quarterback-Hopping an Olympic Sport: Vipers QB ex-fiancée shares a moment with Sabers star" glared up at him.

Whoever wrote that was a piece of shit. And to make matters worse, a moment later, a text message from Max fucking Clark came in as a banner at the top of her screen.

"You're pathetic," it read. He clenched her phone so tightly that the power-off screen greeted him after a few seconds.

How *dare* Clark talk to her like that. As if he hadn't done enough. Had he been sending her messages like this the entire time, or was this a new development because of the news?

He didn't have time to think through it all, placing the phone onto her desk and taking both of her hands in one of his. He placed his other hand on her cheek, wiping away the moisture that rested there.

"Shh, I know. I know. I'm so sorry, Lucia. This is all wrong." He glided his thumb over her soft cheek again. "They're assholes, all of them." He held her like that for a minute, tentatively brushing away new tears that sprung up.

When she'd calmed down a bit, he squeezed her hands softly. "They'll say anything to sell whatever they can. Believe me. They've dragged me through so many variations of 'Shouldn't he be a doctor or engineer?' and 'Does this look like a *Colton Beaumont* to you?' that I've lost count."

He still remembered the first time he'd seen a news site talk about his race, as if being half-Indian made him so different from the rest of the NFL that it warranted putting him in the headlines. As if the color of his skin changed his abilities on the field. Big deal. Most people didn't think twice about his race, but leave it to the media to sensationalize something that had no bearing on the sport.

This information seemed to stun her. She blinked at him slowly, then sniffled. "They said that about you?"

He nodded once, not wanting to dwell on it. "I'm telling you, the press will say anything. I'm sorry you got sucked into it because of me."

She scoffed, "It's not exactly the first time this has happened to me. Not even this season."

"No, they haven't been too nice to you, have they?"

She sniffled, shaking her head.

He realized how close they were, how both his hands were on her. She seemed to come to the same realization because she released his hand. He removed his other hand from her cheek and moved a few feet away.

"What do I even do? This is going to affect my job again, I can just see it." Another sniffle and then a groan as she planted her face in her hands. "I'm so screwed."

He didn't know what possessed him to say what he did next, but he knew he would regret it. Dearly. "What if we went along with it?"

Her eyes were as wide as saucers when she looked back up at him. "*What?*"

He thought about trying to find a way out of it but remembered Cooper's words. She was alone in a new place. She had nobody she could rely on in Charleston, and this was the last thing she should be dealing with on her own. Plus, it was nice knowing it would get under Clark's skin.

So, he shrugged nonchalantly. "We could pretend. You know, until everything blows over. Everyone will already think something's going on either way. This way, you can take control of the narrative. Plus, it'll get that fucking *dick* off your back." He had to rein in the anger that threatened to take hold when he thought about that message.

She waved her hand between the two of them. "Aren't you forgetting the part where we can't stand to be in the same room as each other? Or the part where we've hated each other since college?" She smoothed her skirt. "This conversation notwithstanding, because I'm vulnerable, and you're going to pretend you never saw any of this later." She looked at him pointedly and he nodded.

"We've been doing a fine job of it for a month. And I think we can put our college rivalry behind us."

She gave him an incredulous look, wiping at her face. At the very least, this conversation had taken her mind off of the news for long enough that she'd stopped crying. Colton was thankful for that.

"What about my job? There's no way they'd let us work together if we're in a relationship, right?"

"I can handle Coach. Don't worry about that."

Her eyebrows came together as she thought.

He continued, "I'm going to go and get to pretending that this never happened—if that's what you really want. But think it over, you don't need to decide right now."

Practice was hell the next day, and his teammates giving him a hard time didn't help. Cooper eyed him suspiciously the whole three hours, but Colton had to keep his mouth closed until Lucia decided for them.

He still wasn't positive about what had made him volunteer for a fake relationship. What had he been thinking? He hadn't been in a relationship in years. He barely had enough time to sleep, let alone have a girlfriend. No matter how fake it might be. It had been so dumb, but the rationale he'd given her seemed to have made even her pause. As if she had truly been thinking about it. And he had to admit that controlling the narrative was likely their best option in this situation.

At the end of practice, Coach Turner asked Colton to follow him, ominous as ever. Colton was bummed to miss out on an ice bath, but obeyed, wondering what he could've done to get Coach so twisted up.

He realized what it was the moment he walked into the HR Coordinator's office, a wide-eyed Lucia looking back at him. *Shit*. This was happening a lot faster than he had expected. He'd thought she would have had at least a couple of days to think through his offer.

Coach Turner pointed at the seat beside Lucia's, walking around the desk so that he stood behind the coordinator whose name Colton couldn't remember. A few steps away was a woman about his and Lucia's age with black hair tied back in a ponytail, dressed in a black pantsuit, and glaring down at her phone. When Colton sat beside Lucia, the woman looked up, a glare still fixed on her face.

"I'm sure you're both aware of our policy on disclosure of relationships." The HR coordinator paused, waiting for their responses. Colton looked to Lucia, wanting to take her lead since he'd given her the reins. She refused to meet his eyes.

The man continued when neither of them spoke. "Is the headline true or not? We need to be aware if you're together, as it will affect your working relationship going forward."

Colton was still watching Lucia. She closed her eyes, sighed deeply, and then nodded once, resignation in her tone. "Yes, it's true. We wanted to disclose our relationship when we realized that we wanted to be together, but the press beat us to it."

And there was her decision. He didn't realize his heart had been pounding until he heard it in his ears, a rush of blood at her words. Coach's narrowed eyes never left his face, and Colton was sure he was trying to figure out whether this would be a good or bad thing for his game.

"In that case, we do have to put some protocols in place to ensure that your working relationship remains what it's meant to be. Lucia will be given a superior. She will have to write a report after each session to make sure she's remaining objective and that all your work together is being logged."

He wasn't sure if that was better or worse than he had been expecting. At least he wouldn't have to fight for her to keep her job. He absolutely would have fought, though, just like he'd promised her. He did feel bad about the extra work she'd have to take on. He would try to be better during their sessions.

This was good. This was good for both of them. She would get Clark off her back while giving the press what they seemed to want. They would control the narrative the media was trying to spin. And he could focus on his game. His girlfriend would be the one to help him win the Super Bowl again.

The woman near Coach Turner stepped forward. "Hello, I'm Tessa. I'm a publicist for the Sabers, and I was asked to help curate media associated with this relationship. The team wasn't prepared for a scandal of this magnitude between a player and a staff member, so we'll have to do some damage control. I can handle most of that, but I have a few requests."

Lucia was turning the ring around her middle finger, a semi-distressed expression on her face. Colton nodded at Tessa for the both of them.

"Great. As I said, I can handle most of the press, but I will ask that the relationship be kept above board from now on. That means you'll need to post each other on social media, and I'll send an email to you outlining what content is acceptable and what isn't. You'll also need to be seen outside of work together—whether that be eating out, at each other's houses, or what have you. And finally, Lucia, you will need to be in the end zone with the rest of the spouses and partners during home games for the pre-game kiss. We want to make it clear to the press and the public that we are aware of this relationship, and that it has been okayed by management. The last thing we want is for it to seem like something against protocol is going on under our noses. Make sense?"

Colton's eyebrows raised at the requests. He'd had plenty of experience with PR teams and had even asked his agent to work with the Sabertooths' publicists to ensure those pictures didn't go public, which had clearly been a waste, but he'd never known how controlling they could be. He didn't have an issue with the requests, but this was certainly a lot to ask of Lucia and him, especially during the season. Though, he supposed, not to people who believed they were seriously together.

Lucia cleared her throat before answering softly, "Yes, of course. We will be sure to do all of that."

Tessa nodded, tapping a few times on her phone as the HR coordinator slid a sheet of paper across his desk toward them. "Sign this disclosure agreement, and Tessa will be in touch if she needs you two to do anything specific. And Lucia, look out for another email regarding your new supervisor, Tim."

Colton looked over at her, but her face was devoid of emotion as she signed the sheet in front of her. He followed suit, and then they were dismissed. They didn't speak until they got to her office and she closed the door behind him.

"We need guidelines." She cleared her throat, sitting in her chair and folding her hands together.

Colton was still in shock that this was really happening. "Guidelines?"

"Well, we need an end date, at the very least."

"An end date."

"What are you, a parrot?"

"No, I'm just—what sort of guidelines do you mean?"

"Well, when do you see this mutually beneficial agreement ending? When will it stop being mutually beneficial? We'll both have to put effort into this outside of work hours, so it's important that we establish that."

She was so analytical, even when she was taken by surprise. He didn't know how she could be so logical all the time.

Regardless, he thought through the season, and his answer to her question landed squarely in January. "Before playoffs start. We have an amicable split before playoffs and focus on winning." He wouldn't even ponder the possibility of them not making it to playoffs. "That makes sense, right?"

"That's over three months."

"Okay, I'm open to suggestions," he drawled.

She rolled her eyes. "Fine. Before playoffs it is."

Chapter Nine

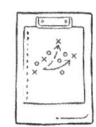

Lucia

Max's incessant texts hadn't let up for the first two days after the news had come out. They'd slowed after that when he'd realized she was still ignoring him. Isa, on the other hand, had been texting her about it every hour, even after the phone call when Lucia had given her all the details, including the fact that it was all *fake*.

Despite knowing she'd likely regret her impulsive decision to agree to Colton's plan, Lucia knew it was better to be able to call the shots than take them as the media threw them. And she was also big enough to acknowledge that, no matter how immature it might be, there was some satisfaction in knowing what dating Max's nemesis must be doing to him. All she had to do was look at the hundreds of texts he'd sent to know an extra report a day was absolutely worth it.

Lucia knew no matter what Colton said, his game was getting better. They'd won all three of their regular season games to that point, and Colton was leading the charge for all of those wins. She liked to believe it was, at least in part, because of her. He'd even lightened up during their sessions, as if their relationship was some kind of truce.

The more she was able to improve Colton's game, the higher the chance that other teams would want to bring her on to do something similar for their quarterbacks. She wasn't sure if the Sabers would extend her contract after her first season, but at least if she did this right, she would have her pick of the other teams.

She was startled from her distracted film perusal when the man in question opened her door, a grim expression on his face.

"Okay, don't be mad."

Her eye twitched. "What did you do?"

"Well, it's not what I did so much as what I didn't do."

She was not amused, and she hoped her face made that clear. To really hit home, she crossed her arms over her chest, ignoring the split second where his eyes traveled down to the newly exposed skin of her chest.

"I forgot to tell you that I have outreach today, so I actually can't meet right now."

She sighed. "We really need to work on your timing on *and* off the field. You're supposed to let me know if you can't make a session *before* the session, not five minutes into it."

"I know, I know. Like I said, I forgot. I'll make up for it tomorrow, promise." He started to walk out but turned back around. "Actually, why don't you come?"

"Oh, I don't know. I don't think they really let analysts go to those things."

"How about girlfriends?"

"I don't think that's any better."

"Oh, come on. I know you're not busy right now because your boyfriend skipped out on his session. So let's go. It'll be fun, I promise. And if not, I owe you any food of your choosing. Even if it's just player food from the third floor." He grinned. "Plus, the publicity will be good for us, and Tessa will be jumping for joy."

"Fine, but know that I'm only going for your wallet and all the food it'll buy me when I don't have fun."

He nodded once, the grin never leaving his face. It'd thrown Lucia off, how disarmingly charming he could be when they weren't trying to kill each other. She kind of liked seeing him like this. Not that she'd ever say it to his face.

They took the elevator to the first floor before walking over to the stadium through one of the private side entrances.

"What're you guys doing for outreach today?" She shivered when he placed a hand on her lower back, willing the butterflies that formed to fly away. Or better yet, die.

"A bunch of kids from local elementary schools are coming to play with us. We're gonna run some drills with them and then do some seven-on-sevens."

"You know, a week ago, I thought you ate kids for breakfast."

"What changed your mind?" he asked with humor in his voice as he led her to a nearby bench, far enough from the fray that she felt safe from any stray footballs.

"I realized you *are* one."

He placed both hands on her shoulders, pushing her gently onto the bench before stepping back. "That's funny, I thought the same about you."

She crossed her legs as he backed away from her slowly. "Real original, Beaumont."

After Colton joined his teammates, he squatted down to talk to the elementary school kids. Lucia noted their ages varied, though most of them were so small, they had to clutch the football with both hands.

She watched Colton stand behind a group of seven- or eight-year-olds, helping them with their stances as they learned how to throw the ball. Luckily, someone had brought junior footballs, so they were able to throw them without much of a struggle.

Her eyes rarely left him. He was like another person with them, a bright smile on his face as he corrected their forms or let them tackle him to the ground.

"Ref! Did you see how hard he hit me? Ref, come on!" It took her a moment to realize he was talking to her. Colton beckoned her to them, and she walked over hesitantly.

"Hm, I didn't see anything. Looked like a clean hit to me." She winked at the little boy who'd taken Colton to the ground, fist-bumping him before he grabbed the little ball and ran.

"Something tells me this ref is dirty. Who paid you off?"

"Colton Beaumont, a sore loser?"

"I might be sore, but I'm no loser." He chased after the little boy, picking him up and raising him high in the air before he could reach the end zone.

Lucia felt someone sidle up to her. She hadn't registered there were any girls there until she saw this child's little ponytail and ruddy cheeks.

"Do you play football too?" the girl asked.

Lucia smiled down at her. "No, I'm not nearly as cool as you. I bet you run laps around all these stinky boys, huh?"

The little girl beamed. "I try. I'm a lot faster than most of them." Her smile fell. "But Mama says I have to stop playing when they stop doing flag football."

Lucia tried to hide her frown. "Why's that?"

The little girl shrugged, placing her small hands onto the vee of her football pads. The motion was adorable, and Lucia wanted to hug her. "She keeps telling Daddy that she doesn't want me playing with the boys because I'll get hurt. Daddy thinks I'd be a good wide receiver, though."

"I bet you will be." Lucia's eyes found Colton, who was letting another little boy wrestle him to the ground. "What's your name?"

"I'm Sadie."

"Okay, Sadie. You see that big, stinky boy over there?" Lucia pointed at Colton, who was standing back up. When Sadie nodded, she continued, "You go tackle him, and tell your Mama you took out an NFL quarterback."

Sadie took off. Colton's eyes widened as she approached at full speed, slamming into him. He made eye contact with Lucia as he went down, and she bent over with laughter at his expression. She knew it was to show the little girl she was just as strong as the boys, but that made her smile wider.

He was a big softie. He never should have invited her to watch, because she wasn't going to let him live it down. All his douchebaggery had been a front. Or maybe he'd saved it just for her.

He raised his hands in faux frustration. "Ref, come on! I saw you tell her to do that, I didn't even have the ball."

She jogged over to them as best she could in her heels, already yelling, "Play on!"

Their fourth regular season game coincided with the start of Lucia's favorite month: October. The air was crisp, the sweaters and sweatshirts were out—even if Charleston didn't always provide the coolest of weather—and the football was getting good.

Lucia felt oddly excited to stand in the end zone for Colton. The Vipers never had a tradition like this one, and even if they had, who knows if Max would've wanted her on the field. Excitement swirled in her chest.

Colton led the team out onto the field, and the screams of the crowd were deafening. Lucia shared a smile with one of the wives who stood beside her as they covered their ears. Blade, the Sabertooths' mascot, jumped up and down on the field, engaging the crowd in a Sabers roar as partnered players ran over to their spouses and significant others.

Colton approached Lucia, taking his helmet off as he jogged over. The crowd was so loud that she didn't hear the words he whispered to her. He set the helmet down at her feet and gently placed his hands on either side of her face. His forehead met hers.

"Next time, you should wear my jersey. Like them." He inclined his head toward the women beside her, but she couldn't move her head to look, so focused on him. Before that evening on the third floor, she'd thought his eyes were brown, but up close, she'd learned they were lighter. And was that a hint of green? She hadn't noticed that in the darkness of the meal room.

"You forget that I'm working. I can't very well sit in the analyst box in your jersey."

Colton grumbled. The crowd was still cheering around them, but Lucia saw the other players start to head back toward the field.

"Are you going to kiss me? Or keep staring aggressively into my eyes?"

He sighed. "Dammit, Moretti. I was trying to bring some semblance of romance to our first kiss." His eyes fell to her mouth. Then he leaned forward, pressing his lips to hers firmly.

It was a little more than a peck, and he was gone in an instant, but she was light-headed. *Just the crowd, and the lights, and the cameras,* she assured herself. She'd felt this rush before when thousands of eyes had rested upon her and Max during his proposal, except that had felt disingenuous, like Max had been doing it for the attention. This felt right somehow, and she didn't know what to think about that new, excited fluttering in her chest.

It was just the attention making her feel that way. It wasn't the kiss, and it definitely wasn't the look in his eyes before he'd kissed her. Or that decidedly arrogant smirk she thought she'd hated until recently.

She followed the rest of the partners back through the tunnel, then found her way to her box. For the first time, the rest of the analysts acknowledged her, some of them smiling, others waving. During the first half, they listened to her both times she spoke up. They even let her proof the numbers during halftime before one of the interns ran the data to the coaches and broadcasters.

She was thankful to finally get the respect she knew she deserved, but hated that it was only because of who they believed she was dating. It was infuriating, especially when she knew she probably worked as hard as, if not harder than, all the men in that room with her. She stewed during halftime but forgot all about it in the third quarter.

Colton was taking sack after sack. His o-line was completely disrupted, giving him no time to find a receiver. Even when he handed the ball off to his running backs, they were getting stuffed at the line.

She could see how tense he was getting, could see the frustration in each of his throws. She didn't know when she'd keyed into his movements so distinctly, but it was as obvious to her as the sun rising over the horizon on a clear day. He was pissed, and it was affecting his motion. He looked like he had during preseason.

The fourth quarter wasn't better. Colton threw a pick, took two more sacks, and ended the game with far less yardage than their past three games. The team was deflated, and Colton was there at the center of it, yelling at the sky as fans filed out of the stadium dejectedly. The energy in the box was just as dim, and she excused herself.

Only as she walked toward the press conference room did she see the texts from Max.

> Max
>
> This little game of yours is getting pathetic, Lucia. Stop messing around.
>
> This is ridiculous. If that kiss was for my benefit, you're acting like a child.

She was so sick of the tone in these texts. As if he wasn't the reason their relationship had ended. She finally broke the radio silence she'd been giving him.

> Lucia
>
> Fuck you, Max.

She knew it was immature, but she was still angry, and maybe it was time for her to stoop to his level.

> Lucia
>
> Hope you're enjoying the blonde.

She put her phone on Do Not Disturb, tucked it into the pocket of her green pantsuit, and continued her walk.

Colton had asked her to be at his press conference after the game, though he'd been in far higher spirits when he'd made the request. When he finally entered the room and the cameras began rolling, his eyes met hers, and she could see the disappointment in them. She was sure all he wanted to do was jump into an ice bath and sleep off the aching in his muscles and tightness in his chest he'd once told her accompanied a loss.

The moment he sat down, the questions began.

"Tough loss today, Colton. Can you walk us through what happened on that crucial interception in the fourth quarter, and what you might have done differently looking back?"

He paused to think. "Yeah, I mean, I saw the coverage and thought I had a window to make the throw. I should've recognized the pressure from the defense and scanned the field for another option."

"It seemed like the offensive line had some struggles today, allowing multiple sacks. How did that impact your ability to execute the game plan, and do you think protection is an area that needs improvement?"

"I think we were struggling as a unit, but the blame is on me. I need to do better at scrambling when the time is right."

She had to stop herself from scoffing. He needed to stop taking responsibility for things that weren't his fault. His offensive line had been shit all game, and he'd been scrambling well until the last quarter.

As if he sensed her thoughts, he met her eyes again. "We talk about protection every week. It's always an area that can use improvement."

Her chest constricted as she watched his shoulders droop a bit. She realized he'd completely internalized the loss as his fault, just like the preseason losses, as if he were a one-man team. When the Sabers lost, it was his fault. When they won, it was a team effort. No wonder he was the team captain.

"You've had some great moments this season, but today was a setback. What's the team's mindset moving forward, and how do you plan to bounce back from this disappointing loss?"

"Absolutely, today was a setback, but our mindset remains positive and determined. We've had great moments this season, and we're fully aware of our potential. We'll go back to the drawing board, study our mistakes, and use this loss as motivation. We're not defined by one game, and our goal is to bounce back stronger and more focused for the next challenge."

"Thanks, Colton." The journalist turned to Coach Turner. "Coach, tough loss. What will you be focusing on this week during practice?"

Lucia tuned him out as she watched Colton stand and walk out of the room quietly. She left from the other door, meaning to catch him before he went home for the night. At first, he didn't notice her in the shadows as he stalked toward the exit that led to the facility. His jaw was tight, his lips pressed firmly together.

He finally saw her, pausing in front of her. His eyes were dark, swirling with all kinds of emotions she couldn't place, but she knew he was mad. She knew it from the set of his shoulders and the dip between his brows.

Lucia didn't know how to make him feel better. All she was good for was numbers, and that was the last thing he needed. She stepped forward into the light, and his eyes tracked her movements warily, fixating on the hand that raised slightly at her side.

Before she knew what she was doing, heart pounding, she'd placed her hand on his stubbled cheek, the way he had when she'd seen that dreaded headline a week and a half earlier. He leaned into it, just barely, just for a moment.

Then the moment was over, and his large hand was clasping hers, gently pulling it away from his face. He squeezed it once and disappeared out the door, leaving a very confused and *very* warm Lucia.

Chapter Ten

COLTON

Colton knew he was wearing on Lucia's nerves, but watching her temper rise distracted him from that familiar tightness in his chest. It'd been less than two days since the loss, and his father's words still echoed around in his head.

"Your season is up. It might be time for you to hang up your helmet and look for some coaching jobs. You'll be lucky if you can get a spot as a quarterback coach with a D3 team." And more like that. His dad was such an ass, but once again, he couldn't disagree. He hadn't played well, and he could very well be on his way out of the league.

"Colton, are you even listening? God, it's literally like working with a ten-year-old," Lucia sighed exasperatedly.

"You'll be pleased to know that I am, in fact, smarter than a fifth grader. I got a very prestigious degree from Crestview."

"I wasn't insulting your intelligence that time, just your attention span."

"What's that? You want to know my wingspan? My, my, Moretti. I love it when you talk dirty to me."

She smacked his arm, pushing away from her desk and walking to the tall windows. "I can't stand you. It's a wonder anybody believes we're together."

"About that. I need a picture of you for my locker. You know, for believability's sake. The sexier, the better. Anything involving lingerie is a plus, but I won't dock points if you go full nude." He winked as she whirled around to face him.

She threw the only thing she could find at him: her pen. It bounced off the desk, half a foot away from him.

"I'm going to have to tell the coaches that the analyst who's supposed to be helping the quarterback can't even hit a large, stationary target. They generally frown upon things like that."

"You should be glad I don't know where you live, 'cause the moment I find out, you'll have to sleep with your eyes open." She pointed at him, eyes narrowing. "Wide open."

She continued to glare at him until he put his hands up in defeat. "Come back, Moretti. I'll be on my best behavior, Scout's honor. Tell me what your fancy quarterback software says I need to fix."

She let out a deep sigh but complied, walking back to her desk. "It doesn't take my fancy quarterback software to see what's wrong, Colton."

He didn't like that tone. She sounded like she was pitying him, and that was the last thing he wanted. He wanted more of their bickering. He needed it.

"What do you mean?"

"I mean, maybe it isn't all a numbers game. Maybe it's not just the pressure from the opposing team coming down on you. Maybe there's more to it."

He was very uncomfortable with where this discussion was heading, but he tried to play it off. "Don't tell me you think I need a sports psychologist. I'll really lose favor with the coaches and management if they need to hire another consultant just for me."

She was quiet, and he hated that most of all. She couldn't be serious. Yes, he was struggling, and yes, even his wins weren't his best work, but they were still up three and one for the season. He'd fucked up on Sunday, but he would make it up to the team.

"Colton," she said gently. "Do you even enjoy the game anymore? When you go out there, do you focus on having fun, or is winning truly all you care about?"

He didn't even have to think about his answer. Like a robot, he responded, "Winning is all I care about." Because that's how it'd always been, and how it needed to be. If he wanted the adoration of the fans and the love of his coaches, teammates, and family, he had to keep putting in the effort and getting the wins.

"I see you, you know. I can see how you're feeling at any given point. I saw your frustration manifest in those plays on Sunday. You're not having fun, and that might be a part of the problem. Maybe you need a break?"

He ignored her question, going over each of her previous words carefully, savoring them slowly. She'd been paying attention to him during the game? She knew him well enough that she could tell just by looking at him how he was feeling? What did that mean, exactly? What exactly had she meant when she'd said, *"I see you"*?

"I don't think I need a break." His words were sharper than he'd intended, but they left no room for discussion, just as he wanted. A break was not an option. If he took a break, then somebody else would come to take his place, and then he'd never be able to prove himself. What he needed was to get his shit together so he could keep winning.

"I understand that, but I want you to know that I can't guarantee everything is going to fix itself just because I'm here, or just because you're getting more reps in. I won't overstate my abilities, especially if I don't believe the problem is entirely outside your head."

"Go back to telling me you see me. Say more things like that."

"Colton…"

She paused as he leaned closer to her, like he'd wanted to do from the moment he'd walked into her office and seen her in that stupidly tight blouse that made it hard for him to think.

Or, if he was being honest, from the moment she'd walked into the boardroom at the end of August.

"Colton, what are you doing?" She was whispering.

He followed suit. "Exercising my duty as your boyfriend."

"But there's nobody around."

He paused for a moment, watching her for any sign of discomfort. Her eyes were hazy, like that night on the third floor. Her lips were parted slightly, beckoning him.

"Tell me you want me to stop."

He waited five seconds, then ten. Her eyes fluttered closed, and he leaned a little closer. He brushed his lips against hers gently, reveling in the softness of them. *God*, what a bad idea. This moment was going to drive him out of his mind, especially since he knew he wouldn't, couldn't, let this move any further. They were both there to do a job.

He pulled away, just far enough that their lips no longer touched, but close enough that they brushed together when he said certain words. "Look at us. We haven't even tried to rip each other apart today."

Her eyes fluttered open, and she blinked at him. "I guess you're growing on me."

Her stomach grumbled, and he chuckled, pulling back. "Let's go get dinner."

"What, together?"

"Yes, together. That's what couples do. Plus, think of the nice message we'll get from Tessa for being seen together publicly."

"I have to write a report for this session."

"So write it in the morning. Nobody's going to look at it before then anyway. And that's assuming they look at it at all."

She clicked her tongue at him. "But you've been entirely uncooperative. We've barely done anything worth discussing in the report."

He shrugged. "So write that. It's not like Colton Beaumont being uncooperative is news to anybody. They'd believe that shit in a heartbeat. Might be the most believable thing you write."

She rolled her eyes, placing the errant pen she'd thrown at him into her neat little pen holder and closing her laptop. "I swear to god, you're going to cost me this job someday."

"Maybe." He grinned. "But today's not that day. Come on, you're clearly starving."

Lucia's phone kept lighting up with messages, the vibration shaking their table. Finally, she tucked it under her leg, shaking her head at Colton apologetically.

"Who's that?"

"Oh, no. I don't ask you about all those women on your phone. That's not a part of the agreement."

He clenched his jaw. Sure, their agreement was purely for show, but it wouldn't exactly be a good look if either of them were linked to someone else. As they both were aware, the media would find a way to expose that.

Plus, he wanted to be the only person she was talking to.

"I only downloaded my social media apps to see the fallout after the situation with Clark. All those notifications were from DMs, which I never respond to, and I've deleted all the apps since."

She sipped from her water. "Why were you looking at the fallout of our engagement on social media?"

Colton shrugged, embarrassed. He hadn't planned on ever telling her that. "Wanted to see if he'd post about it, I guess. I don't know what I was looking for."

She grimaced. "Max rarely posted about me when we were together. He wasn't going to say anything after we broke up."

"Would you like for me to post about you?"

He knew Tessa had told them they needed to post about each other, but he wanted to know what *Lucia* wanted.

She waved her hand as she shook her head. "No, no. That's not what I meant. He just posted about so many other things, it would've been nice to be on his profile somewhere. I wouldn't expect someone who doesn't use those apps to post." She reached for her water again. "Plus, we're getting a little old for social media."

He heard her phone vibrate, eyes flicking down her body at the noise. He reminded himself, not for the first time, that this was all a ruse. She didn't owe him anything, not even fake loyalty.

"It's Max, by the way. I'm not, like, talking to other people while we're publicly together. He just hasn't left me alone since the news came out."

He mentally counted the number of downsides of their deal, at least for her. She had to report to a supervising analyst. In addition to all of her regular work and the work she did with him, she now had to create a report after every session. And, apparently, Max was so pissed off, he was blowing up her phone. The piece of shit had probably treated her like garbage during their whole relationship and had just expected her to be there for him after he cheated.

"What's he saying?"

She swirled her water with her straw, ice clinking against the glass. "Keeps saying it's pathetic that I left him for you. That you *would* be the type of person to take his sloppy seconds."

Colton's right hand clenched his glass tightly. The next time he saw Max Clark, he was going to deck him. Pummel him. Eviscerate him.

Lucia must've noticed him tense, because she continued, "Sorry, don't take that personally. It doesn't mean anything."

Colton cleared his throat, his voice low but dangerous. "I'm not mad he said that about me. I'm pissed he said that about *you*."

Her eyes met his, and the corner of her mouth quirked up. "I haven't taken him seriously in a while. He went from a shitty boyfriend, to a shittier fiancé, to the shittiest ex."

"Why don't you block him?"

She swirled her straw again, and Colton had to stop himself from reaching out to halt her fidgeting. "I know it might seem stupid, but a part of me thinks he might, maybe, apologize? Finally see that he was wrong for cheating on me, and say sorry?"

"Would you take him back?"

She scoffed, "God, no. But I spent seven years of my life loving him. Or at least thinking I did. I'd like to see some kind of redemption arc for him." Colton watched her fiddle with the ring on her middle finger.

He really didn't want to say the next words. He'd been enjoying their fake relationship and truce, and he wanted it to continue, but he couldn't ignore all of the hardships she was having to endure because of it. So, quietly, he asked, "Do you think it'd be easier if we broke up?"

Her hand stilled. "Oh, uh, why?"

"Well, just, if it's making your life more difficult, both by adding extra work and an even shittier Clark, maybe you want an out?"

She watched him, her mouth opening and then closing.

"Lucia, I'm not saying *I* don't want to continue, just so we're clear. But the point of the arrangement was for us to both benefit, and if you aren't benefiting, then I don't want you to feel like we have to continue." He smiled at her warmly. "I'd like to think we're the kind of people who can play nice and maybe one day be friends if we were to break up."

She shook her head. "No, I don't think it makes sense. You were right about this allowing us to control the narrative the press spins, and that's what I need right now. The added report and a few more texts from Max a day aren't a big deal. I think it'd be worse if we broke up now." She placed a hand on his, startling him. "But I appreciate the offer. And what you're giving up by fake dating me."

Giving up? What was he giving up by dating her? Having fewer laughs a day and very empty—albeit rare—free time?

Before he had an opportunity to voice that, she asked, "So, if we're going to keep doing this, I need to know more about you."

"Anything specific? Or should I just dump anything meaningful from my life onto you?"

"Why don't you tell me about your family?"

His family. That was a bigger question than she knew. "Well, I have a younger brother and sister. Landon plays tight end for the Sentinels, but I'm sure you knew that. My sister plays pro tennis, and she's on the women's tour right now."

"Jesus. Athletic family. I know Landon went to Crestview, too. Did Maya?"

"Yeah. We grew up near LA, so it just made sense to stay nearby. Especially after our mom passed."

Lucia's eyes widened, and the waiter chose that moment to bring their food.

The young man, little older than a boy, placed Lucia's pasta and Colton's personal pizza in front of each of them. He stopped when Colton looked up at him.

Excitedly, he said, "Oh my gosh, Donovan said it was you, but I didn't believe him. I—I'm so sorry to do this, but would you sign my shirt for me? My family will lose their mind."

Colton always felt awkward when people asked him for pictures or autographs, but he smiled. "Of course. Do you have a pen, or...?"

"Yes!" He rummaged around in his apron pockets, pulling out a black pen and lowering his shoulder so Colton could sign where he pointed.

When Colton capped the pen, he motioned toward Lucia and asked, "Don't you want her signature? That's Lucia fricking Moretti, the greatest NFL analyst and football software creator the league has ever seen."

Lucia's eyes widened again, for a different reason this time. The poor waiter began stuttering. "Oh, oh, oh, I'm so sorry. I—I'm so sorry. Would you...?" He sank down, pointing out a place on the opposite side of his shirt.

"I don't think—"

"Moretti, do the man this one small favor."

She sighed, smiling politely at the waiter before signing on his shoulder. When he walked away excitedly, she glared at Colton. "Why would you do that? He seemed so stressed out, like he thought he should've known who I was."

"I always feel uncomfortable when that happens on a date. At least this time, I'm dating someone important enough to warrant an autograph."

Lucia twisted her fork in her pasta, pulling out a steaming bite. "Right. Like I'm going to believe you've never dated a celebrity." Colton couldn't stop watching her lips as she placed the bite delicately in her mouth. When her eyes met his again, she covered her mouth with a hand. "Stop watching me eat!"

He averted his gaze, grabbing a slice of pizza. "No, I've never dated a celebrity. I spend so much time prepping for the season that I don't have much time for dating at all."

"But so many of your teammates have partners. Why do they have time but you don't?"

"Because they rely on me to win, so I spend most of my time outside of practice in the weight room or on the field." He was the leader, which meant there were higher expectations resting on his shoulders.

Lucia set her fork down. "This is what I mean. We have *got* to work through this. Football is a team sport. You are a *part of* the team, you are not *the* team."

Colton pondered that as they ate in silence. Remembering their earlier conversation, he asked, "What about your family?"

"It's just me and my dad, actually." He didn't want to pry, so he finished off his pizza and waited to see if she'd add anything else. "My mom didn't want kids in the first place, so there was no chance of siblings. Then, you know, I guess she couldn't handle it all, and she left us."

Fuck. He didn't know what to say. How do you help someone feel better when they've been through something as traumatic as that?

Lucia laughed. "Yeah, that's about how most people respond to that."

"Fuck, Lucia, I'm so sorry. I know it's not the same, but I lost my mom eleven years ago." He'd hoped it would assuage some of that sadness and anger he'd seen in her eyes, but he was worried it sounded like he was trying to take hold of the conversation and focus on himself. He cursed his brief dating history, wishing he'd spent more time learning about the women he'd taken to bed so he could be better at dinner conversation.

"I'm sorry about your mom."

"I'm sorry about yours."

They smiled at each other as they enjoyed their dinner, a comfortable silence settling over them.

Chapter Eleven

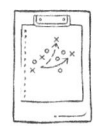

Lucia

The team's private plane was divided into sections, with regular traveling staff—Lucia included—in the back, players in the middle, and coaches in the front. There were curtains to partition and separate each group from the other, allowing each of them to do their different types of work.

Lucia sat near the back of the plane, tablet resting in her lap as she scrolled through analytics from the past few games. She was figuring out if there was anything in particular she wanted Colton to focus on before their next game. She didn't even notice that someone had sat beside her until they jostled her with their elbow.

She turned to give a reprimanding look to the culprit but found Colton grinning at her instead. "Hi, beautiful."

Her heart tripped for a second, and her stomach knotted up until she saw his head subtly tilt in the direction of the others in her section. Most of them had their eyes fixed on them, whispering amongst themselves.

"Hi…"

"You can call me handsome if it helps," he whispered against her ear.

"Pass."

"You're not being a very good girlfriend. How will anybody know that we're truly together if you won't give me the verbal praise I yearn for? Tell me how hot I am." He was still keeping his voice low, but there was a teasing to the words.

She laughed. "You're an idiot. Shouldn't you be going over plays or being a team leader? Or doing something even a little productive?"

He nodded. "Sure. What should I do to get my numbers up this game, O Learned One?"

"Honestly, I want to see you having fun on the field. This is something you're passionate about." She paused looking at him for confirmation. He nodded again. "So let that show."

"Are ya gonna watch me have fun?"

She began typing notes to herself on the tablet, highlighting Colton's relevant numbers and copying them into a separate document. "Well, it is my job."

"I don't wanna have fun all by myself."

She turned to him again, and there was that wicked grin on his face. He was so handsome, even when he was trying to annoy her.

"Good thing you have a whole team, who, by the way, you should go bother instead of me."

"Don't you wanna know what kind of fun I have by myself? And why it would be *so* much better with, say, a girlfriend?"

Lucia held back a giggle at the insinuation. Colton was an idiot, but he certainly knew how to make her laugh.

"I'm going to start recording our conversations and showing your teammates. Just so you've been made aware."

He groaned. "Lu-chi-uh, I'm so bored. Talk to me."

She wondered why he'd chosen her to talk to when he was bored when all of his best friends were on the plane with them. She felt almost honored that he'd chosen her to annoy.

In keeping with her faux-irritation, she said, "Colton, you get on my very last nerve."

"Good."

He placed his head on her shoulder as she continued to work. Minutes later, he was asleep, and she was too busy trying to make sure he didn't hurt his neck to finish what she'd planned to get done on the plane.

Lucia's phone vibrating was no longer new, but she *was* surprised to see two texts from Colton, especially since she knew he was supposed to be in his hotel room for the night.

> **Colton**
>
> Please come bother me.
>
> Luc pls, Coach locked me in my room and it's so early and I'm so bored.

Lucia rolled her eyes as she clicked open her phone. She had never met a man who could switch up like Colton. One minute, he was this manly, angry, hard-headed jock, and the next, he was a five-year-old.

> **Lucia**
>
> You text like a teenager.

She tried to focus back on her laptop where her checklist hadn't even begun to dwindle. Most of her prep work for the game was done, but she also needed to prepare her and Colton's sessions for the next week. Of course, those would change if something crazy happened during the game in a couple of days. If they won, she'd have to adjust a little, but if they lost, they'd have a lot more work to do. Some of which she was not equipped to handle without a sports psychology degree.

> **Colton**
> That's fine. Bring some snacks, I am a man starved.

> **Lucia**
> I saw you scarf down an entire pizza during meetings. How does your body function with the amount of pizza you consume?

Lucia weighed whether staring at her computer for another two hours was a better or worse way to spend her time than taking snacks to her juvenile-esque, fake boyfriend. She opted for the second, knowing she wouldn't be able to concentrate when he inevitably continued texting her.

> **Colton**
> Wouldn't you like to know?

> **Lucia**
> Aren't you guys supposed to be on a diet during the season?

> **Colton**
> Are you body-shaming me? I'm HURT. Here I was thinking you liked my physique.

Lucia pocketed her phone, put her laptop and tablet onto the desk, and made a snap decision to remain in the pajamas she'd changed into earlier—sweatpants and a Virginia Vipers t-shirt. She smirked at herself in the mirror, already picturing the glare on Colton's face when he opened his door. To be fair, she'd only packed for a couple of evenings, and it was the only sleep shirt she'd brought.

The vending machines were mostly a bust, but she managed to scrounge up two bags of M&Ms, a bag of Chex Mix, and a bag of regular Lays. It would have to do, especially on short notice.

He'd texted her his room number—conveniently on the top floor—and she could see by the tape on his door that it was his. She laughed at the three layers of scotch tape on the top, middle, and bottom of the door. He must've been known for taking late-night trips out of his room.

It was an antiquated tradition and made the coaches seem like toxic partners who needed to know where their players were at all times, especially at night when they were meant to be resting and relaxing. Yet something about Coach Turner trapping the fully grown, six-three, 200-and-something-pound, twenty-eight-year-old man made her giggle. She knocked lightly, holding up the measly snacks she'd acquired for his peep-hole approval.

"Pull the tape up," he instructed through the door. She pulled the tape from the door, leaving it stuck only to the frame.

The door opened slowly. He rested a shoulder against the frame, his long, muscled arm opening the door wide enough for her to walk underneath. She ignored his narrowed eyes as they found her shirt.

His room was, obviously, a suite, even though he only used it at night. She walked into the living area with a full dining table, couch, coffee table, TV stand, and TV. Past that was a sink, microwave, fridge, and coffee stand.

"This is so much nicer than my room. That's not fair."

The sounds of college football filtered in from the bedroom, cheering clear behind the sound of an announcer. Lucia set the snacks next to the sink. The bedroom, which connected via a hallway to the living room, had a separate door, desk, and king-sized bed. She wasn't sure what exactly the plan had been after she brought him the food, so she turned around.

He was eyeing her incredulously, and she wasn't sure if his eyes were fixated on the goosebumps that cropped up on her arms, or the shirt.

"Cold?" he asked. She supposed that answered the question.

She crossed her arms. "Oh, no, I'll be fine."

He was already fishing a dark green sweatshirt out of his duffle bag, tossing it to her. "Put that on. And keep it, I don't wanna see that shit again." Under his breath, he mumbled, "Imagine wearing a Vipers shirt in front of me. The gall."

"Oh, you don't like my shirt?" She batted her eyelashes at him innocently but pulled the sweatshirt over her torso. It smelled so much of him, rich and earthy and surprisingly...*nice*.

"I'd like it a lot more if it were in the trash. Or better yet, burned." He grabbed the snacks and threw them onto his bed. He hooked his thumb behind him toward the other side of the bed as he sat, grabbing the remote.

"Oh, are we...Am I staying? I thought I was just bringing snacks."

"Moretti, sit your ass on the bed. I'm not treating you like an intern. Or a food delivery service."

He clicked to the TV guide, perusing. She took a moment to take in the tight, white t-shirt and dark green sweatpants that were no doubt a part of a Sabers sweatsuit. She was starting to get annoyed with the way her body responded to him, hating the familiar, tight coil of desire behind her belly button that she noticed any time he walked around in sweatpants. And that damn t-shirt. She chalked it up to being celibate for months, but damn did his body look good.

"Not that I don't enjoy you ogling me, because trust me, I do, but I need your help choosing a movie. Otherwise, I'm going to pick something you'll probably hate."

She could feel herself flushing, warmth creeping over her cheeks. She cleared her throat. "Sometimes I forget how highly you think of yourself."

"I think the only person who was thinking about me just now was you."

She didn't have a response to that, because he was right. She sat beside him, leaving enough room between them that she didn't feel like her breath was stuck in her chest. Another interesting body quirk she'd experienced in his presence recently.

"If Coach Turner asks, you forced me to come see you on the threat of a breakup."

He slid down on the bed a bit. "I sound like a terrible boyfriend."

She shrugged. "Well, if the shoe fits and all of that."

She was startled when he turned and looked at her meaningfully. "If you don't want to be here, I understand. I appreciate the snacks, but you don't have to stay if you don't want to." He sounded surprisingly serious.

"Well, it all comes down to what movie you choose. You already scrolled past *How To Lose A Guy in Ten Days*, so I'm not sure I can trust your decision-making."

He stopped scrolling, moving back up toward the movie she'd indicated. "Sounds dumb. What's it about?"

Lucia mock gasped, a hand on her heart. "How *dare* you! That is prime romcom."

He clicked on it and, just as it was starting, said, "Okay, but what's it about?"

"I could write an essay on this movie, but it's about a journalist who wants to write about politics but is assigned the How To section at a gossip magazine. That's all you get, you just have to watch."

"You shouldn't work in movie marketing."

Despite what he would probably say at the end of the movie, Colton seemed engaged in the story. Lucia spent more time watching his reactions from the corner of her eye than watching the movie itself.

She couldn't believe she was sitting on a bed with Colton Beaumont. Watching a movie. Sharing snacks. Not wanting to murder him. Sometimes even laughing with him.

A few months earlier, if someone had told her she would find herself in this situation with him, she would've thought they were on all kinds of drugs. Lucia Moretti and Colton Beaumont did not mix. And if they did, it was for an MMA fight to the death.

This new, fragile alliance was confusing. He was being nice to her. Gone was the douchebag with a stick up his ass. He'd been replaced with someone kind enough to kneel in front of her as she sobbed, wiping away her tears and offering to make a serious change to his life to save her the embarrassment of the press shitting on her. Someone who, despite harboring a very serious vendetta against her ex, had spent his free time being her only acquaintance in a city that hadn't been the kindest to her. Maybe even a friend.

She actually *liked* this Colton. He was goofy and made her laugh, at least internally (she couldn't show all her cards, after all). He showed her how good a boyfriend he *could* be to someone—someone who would one day enjoy his love and attention.

That was a weird thought. Once they broke up in January, he might find someone who he could love. He might show the new woman Charleston the way he had Lucia. He might stow her away on the plane and have her join him in his hotel room, watching a romcom with her two days before a big game. Lucia wasn't sure why that bothered her, but it did a little. At least the part of her that could acknowledge how attracted to him she was and how much she enjoyed his company.

She turned to look at his profile, taking in the strong nose, chin, and hardly-there stubble. The angled cheekbones and dark hair. The full lips that were twitching into a smile.

"What?" he asked, his eyes still on the movie.

"Huh?"

"Are you ogling me again?"

"No." *Yes.* "It's just…"

"It's just what?"

"Look at us. Being friendly." She paused, remembering something that'd flitted through her mind during their first dinner date. "Do you finally believe that I'm not trying to screw you out of your season?"

He finally turned to her, eyes holding hers. "I stopped believing that the day you and Coop talked on the plane on the way back from our first regular season game."

"Really? What changed your mind?"

"Coop just talked some sense into me. And, really, I should apologize for the way I acted when you first came to Charleston. I know the move must've been hard on you after everything, and I'm sure I didn't make it any easier."

"Mm. You know, saying that you should apologize isn't the same as apologizing."

"You want me to get on my knees and beg you to forgive me?" Her breath hitched, and he must've noticed it, his eyes falling to her parted lips. "Because I will. Just give me the word."

She rolled her eyes to ease the tension between them, turning back to the movie. "No, that's not necessary. But I will take a 'sorry I made your life miserable and your job difficult during the worst weeks of your life.'"

"Lucia Moretti, I'm sorry I made your life miserable and your job difficult during the worst weeks of your life."

She nodded once, a small smile on her face. "Better."

She didn't realize until the movie was over that he hadn't touched the snacks she'd brought him. "If I didn't know any better, I'd think you asking me to bring you snacks was a ruse to trick me into coming to see you."

He grinned as he stood. "Good thing you know better." When she started to take the sweatshirt off, he pulled it back down, holding firmly onto the fabric. "I said you could keep it, and I meant it. I have a thousand of these. And I never wanna see you in a Vipers shirt again."

"Noted."

He grabbed a keycard from the coffee table as they walked to his door. She raised an eyebrow.

"Wasn't the whole point of me bringing you food so that I could leave and fix the tape for you? Coach'll be pissed."

"I don't give a damn. I care far more about making sure you get to your room safely."

Were those...were those butterflies in her stomach? Fucking butterflies. She was going to have to have a serious talk with herself. And maybe Isa. Isa would talk sense into her. This was getting out of hand.

They stood on opposite sides of the elevator, Lucia looking everywhere but at him, though she could feel his eyes on her. When they finally reached her floor, she walked to her door quickly.

She felt him move behind her as she dug around in her little purse for her key card. His chest was nearly pressed to her back, his arm beside her head, resting against the door, caging her in. Gentle fingers found her waist, and Lucia dropped her purse, every muscle in her body coming to a standstill. She could feel his breath tickling her neck, and her eyes closed involuntarily.

There was something intimate about the closeness, his front nearly touching her back, his fingers just a whisper in the dip above her left hip. She wasn't sure how long they stood there, but she couldn't find it in herself to push away, or even to bend down to grab the purse and keycard.

"Colton..."

As if he hadn't even realized what he'd been doing, he jolted away from her, reaching around to grab her purse from the ground. She put all of her focus into curling her hand around the bag, separating the two cards, and swiping one into the slot. When the light flashed green, he reached past her again to push the door open.

"Goodnight, Lucia. Double lock your door, please."

"G—goodnight." She stepped forward, and the door closed behind her. Her hands shook as she locked the door.

She felt jittery, like she'd just had two shots of espresso, and even when she had turned off all the lights and sunk into bed, she couldn't stop tossing and turning.

Chapter Twelve

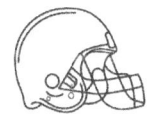

COLTON

Bye week could not have come any sooner for Colton. He loved football, truly. But no one could deny how physically taxing the game was for the body, and no amount of ice baths and massages could heal him the way rest would. Luckily, winning the prior two games and getting their record to a solid five and one meant bye week was slow. Practices were shorter, less demanding. They mostly consisted of walking through play calls, and rarely did he even have to throw a ball.

The week leading up to bye week had been hectic, though. He'd gone from early morning lifting to meetings to film to practice, and while that was pretty standard, somehow, his days had felt longer than usual, bleeding from one to the next. He'd only had thirty-minute windows here and there to meet with Lucia, where he'd normally been able to make two hours available for her.

She'd seemed fine with it. He was sure she'd had plenty of work to do, but he also wondered if she'd been avoiding him since the hotel room incident. He wasn't proud of his lapse in judgment, but he also wasn't sorry.

He realized that his feelings for Lucia were changing. Before, she was just the infuriating analyst helping him with his game who needed a hand with the media. But now, he wasn't so sure.

Whatever his feelings, he knew he needed to set them aside. He needed to make sure he kept his performance up for the rest of the season so the Sabers could have another shot at the Super Bowl. There was a reason they'd set the end of their relationship for January.

If his father saw him now, could read his thoughts, he'd be alarmed. Worse than alarmed—*furious*. He'd probably say something about how he hadn't given up his coaching job all those years ago, spent Colton's entire life training him, perfecting his form, and convincing scouts to come to see him play, for it all to go down the drain on *some girl*. The few times the press had linked him with a woman in the past, his father had been none too pleased. Hell, the man had called Colton when the article about him and Lucia had come out to ensure she wasn't affecting his focus, and he had been fuming when he learned that Lucia was an analyst *working* on his game.

He tried to quiet his thoughts as she walked into her office, seemingly startled to see him already there. That white button-down hugged everywhere *he* wanted to hug, and she'd chosen black pants instead of her usual skirt. Her ever-present heels clicked as she resumed walking to her desk.

"You're early! I never thought I'd see the day."

"I figured if Coach can be nice to us during bye week, I can try to be nice to you, too."

"How chivalrous of you." She unclipped her hair, and he watched, mesmerized, as she twirled the light brown strands around her hand and back up into the clip.

"What are we working on today?"

"That depends on you. If you don't feel like doing fieldwork, we can go through film."

An idea popped into his head. "You know what? That's a great idea. There's actually some film I've been meaning to watch. Mind if I take over for a second?" He pointed at her laptop.

She narrowed her eyes at him but scooted it in his direction. "If you pull up porn on my work computer, I will hire an attorney and bring you up on sexual harassment charges."

"Oh, please, you think so little of me. I don't need porn." Nope, all he needed to get off were thoughts of her backside. Or her in a button-down. Or worse, her in his Sabers sweatshirt.

He shook his head and pulled up his network television provider. After logging in, he clicked around a few times until he reached the livestream he wanted to watch.

When he turned the laptop back to her, she blinked. "What did I do to you? Why would you choose this?"

Before them was Thursday Night Football. And who was playing on that beautiful Thursday night? The Vipers.

"No, I promise I'm doing this for you." When she glared at him, he tried to contain his grin. "Okay, and maybe a little for me too. I want you to analyze him. Tell me everything he's doing wrong and how he could improve. It'll make you feel better, *and* it'll serve as a teaching moment for me."

Lucia mumbled something under her breath. Then, "I don't know how you manage to get away with shit like this, but I can't even provide a valid reason for why it's a bad idea."

His grin grew. "Exactly. I might look like a dumb jock, but sometimes, just sometimes, I figure out how to use this thing up here." He poked his temple.

She pulled the video onto her monitor so they could watch on a bigger screen. For the hour and a half that remained of the game, she pointed out quarterback mistakes on both sides of the ball, though there was a barely muted joy in her eyes when she pointed out Clark's mistakes.

Despite the Vipers winning, she was smiling. "Okay, pop quiz. What'd you learn?"

"That Clark is nothing without his o-line. Dude's a worse scrambler than me."

Lucia snorted, throwing her pen onto the desk and leaning back. "This is now the second time I'll have to write a report that's pure bullshit."

"I'm surprised they're not all pure bullshit. The idea that you have to write reports because we're together doesn't even make sense."

"Well, no, I understand why I have to. What if we were actually together and I was getting paid for these sessions but we were"—she waved her hand around—"hooking up?"

"I didn't take you for a hooker, Moretti."

"That's not...God, you're infuriating. Has anybody ever told you that? Are you aware of how annoying you are?"

He tapped his chin. "Hm, let's see. You've told me more than a dozen times. Coop's told me a few times. I guarantee both of my siblings have, especially Landon."

"So, nobody outside of your inner circle? That tells me everyone else you interact with is lying to you."

"Did you just describe yourself as a part of my inner circle?"

Silence. "Well, at least to the media. And if I'm not a part of your inner circle, then I'm the only outside person in your life being honest with you."

"Am I a part of *your* inner circle?"

She sighed. "Colton, I have, like, three friends, only one of whom I currently speak to, and she doesn't live in the same city as me. Plus my father. So, anybody who I spend as much time with as I do you, no matter how miserable that time is, they're bound to be a part of my inner circle."

This was a perfect bridge for what he'd been waiting to ask her for over a week. "Well, come to our bye-week party on Saturday, then. Devin's hosting again, and all the wives and girlfriends will be there. You'll get to meet people and make some friends in the city."

"I don't know…"

"It'll be fun, I promise."

"That's what you said about outreach."

He scoffed, "Don't pretend you didn't have fun at outreach, I was watching you." When she didn't respond, he said, "You can hold my hand the whole time."

She smacked his shoulder. "I will *not* be doing that."

"Well, you probably should since you'll be coming as my girlfriend."

She groaned. "God, don't remind me."

"We're going to need an attitude makeover before the party. This whole 'pretending to hate me' thing isn't gonna look good in front of our friends."

"Bold of you to think I'm pretending."

"So that's a yes to the party?"

"Fine, Colton. I'll go. But only because I'm starved for friendship and having you as my only acquaintance here is beginning to cause me real problems."

"You're so good to me."

That dress was going to be his absolute undoing. He'd kept it together for two months of button-downs and tight skirts and heels. He'd even managed to get through the night when she'd worn his sweatshirt in his hotel room. But that dress? Shimmery green, flaring around mid-thigh, a bunching of fabric right above her breasts. He was struggling to keep his eyes off of her, even as his teammates tried to engage him in conversation.

"Colt."

"Huh?" He turned to Cooper, whose eyes traveled from him to Lucia.

"Did you hear me?" His friend adjusted the cowboy hat he often wore when he wasn't on the field.

"No, sorry, what'd you say?"

"I was asking what you think the over-under will be next week, but now I want to know what the hell happened between six weeks ago—when you were still spewing your nonsense theory to anyone who'd listen—to now. One minute, you're pretending you can't stand her, and the next, you're dating her."

Colton clapped Cooper on the back. "I've got you to thank for that, actually. After you called me out for being an idiot, I tried to right the ship a bit between me and Lucia." He hated lying to his best friend, but he'd agreed to keep the secret a secret, even from his closest friend.

"So, now what? You're not exactly a dating kind of guy."

Colton shrugged. He'd have taken offense if he didn't agree. He'd just been so busy with football that dating hadn't been a priority. "I don't know, man. Let's call it a crush and see where it goes."

Cooper's words were lost as a gaggle of women sat beside them. A couple of them moved closer to Colton, trying to trap him in a conversation about—were they talking about vegetables? Colton wasn't paying enough attention to them to say for certain.

He watched Lucia throw her head back and laugh at something Rudy's wife said. They'd found each other quickly in the maze of bodies that took up the first and second floor of Devin's house and back patio, and he was glad she was making friends. It warmed his heart to see her getting along with people who meant so much to him, especially so quickly.

Her eyes met his, though they slid away quickly, landing on the two women beside him. Just as one of them placed their hand on his bicep, Lucia tracking her every move, Colton stood. He mumbled an "excuse me," knowing Cooper would be perfectly content without him.

Lucia had already turned back to Jenna and another woman when Colton approached. In keeping up with appearances, he slid an arm around Lucia's waist. She tensed for half a second before leaning against him.

He bent his head down to rest his lips against the shell of her ear. "Moretti," he whispered. Her whole body shivered, and he grinned wide.

When he was satisfied with the teasing, he turned to Jenna. "Hey, Jen. How are you? And the kids?"

"Colton damn Beaumont. Come here." She gave him a bear hug, and because his arm never left Lucia, she became a part of it. "The kids are good. Rudy's mom's got them tonight. I'm so glad she lives nearby. Can't miss a party at Devin's."

Devin. Star wide receiver and notorious partier. He'd bought his house between two other teammates to ensure he wouldn't get noise complaints. Not Coach Turner's favorite man, but he certainly did his job well.

Lucia turned in his arm slightly, her nose scrunched. "What's so great about a Devin party?"

Jenna answered before Colton could, gesturing above them. "Besides all the condoms hanging from the trees out here?"

Lucia's eyes widened, and she turned her head to take in her surroundings. "Oh my god, I didn't even realize."

Jenna laughed. "That's tame. Once Devin gets nice and drunk and convinces some of the rookies to drink too much, you're really in for a treat."

Lucia whispered to Colton, "I'm scared."

Squeezing her waist, he whispered back, "It'll be so much fun, just you wait."

She raised an inquisitive brow. "Do you party with him a lot?"

"Nah, not really my scene. I'll come to bye week and New Year's. Maybe a couple others during offseason, but I'm usually—"

"Yeah, yeah, focused on winning. I know, Superstar."

"Mm, trying new nicknames? I like that one, you should call me that more." Her cheeks pinked, and Jenna and her friend seemed to take the hint to turn further toward each other and talk.

"I'll keep that in mind."

They continued mingling. He introduced her to as many of the partygoers whose names he knew, and some he didn't, his arm never leaving her waist. She was nursing her third drink by the time Devin's antics started.

The minute all the rookies came out of the house naked (but for a tiny, incorrectly-sized loincloth) and shivering, Colton knew it was about time to go. They each had one green and one yellow pompom, shaking them awkwardly.

"Alright, now for the pyramid. Sanders, you're on top. Don't look at me like that, you lost at straws."

Lucia's hand came up to cover her mouth as she giggled. Colton joined the rest of the people at the party as they cheered and whooped for the oversized men pretending to be cheerleaders.

Only a moment after they got into formation, the pyramid began to sway, and nine NFL players fell into the Olympic-sized swimming pool, splashing everyone within thirty feet. Devin clapped gleefully and jumped in after them.

"Alright, this is about the time I typically leave. Let me check on Coop..." Cooper somehow had three women wrapped around him—one of whom had stolen his cowboy hat—and the biggest smile on his face. "Yeah, I think we're probably good to go."

Lucia looked in Cooper's direction, her laugh melodic.

"Okay, let me say bye to Jenna and Leigh."

He reluctantly let her go, making his rounds quickly before meeting her at the door. She swayed as she stepped onto the front porch, and Colton reached out a hand to steady her.

"Alright, Moretti. That's it, we're gonna walk this way. Remind me to tell you tomorrow morning that you plus alcohol plus your highest heels are not a good combination."

"Hey! I'm great in heels. And, I wore them for you."

That lump in his throat hadn't been there a few seconds before. He tried clearing it, to no avail. "What do you mean?"

"You know, in case you annoyed me. They double as a very solid weapon in dire situations."

He guided her toward his car, shielding her from the flashes of cameras around them. "You won't find yourself in any dire situations when I'm around."

"I don't know about that," she said breathily, falling into his passenger seat the moment he opened the door. He stopped at the insinuation, taking a step back in shock. Had he been giving off strange vibes? Was it clear how attracted to her he'd been all night? He'd tried to be on his best behavior, his hand never going lower than the small of her back.

"I would—I'd never do anything to you that you didn't want, Lucia. Tell me you know that."

Her head swiveled to his, her eyes wide. "I didn't mean it like that, Superstar."

"How did you mean it?"

She blew out a breath, crossing her arms across her chest. "You make me feel jittery. And warm. And I don't like it. It's very disconcerting, especially because I'm just here to do a job. My dream job."

That wasn't so bad. He would take jittery and warm. "I'm your dream job?"

She rolled her eyes, tucking her legs into the car. He closed the door and walked around the car, sliding inside and starting the engine.

"There's that big head of yours again."

"Yeah, TBI brain. Gets the head all swollen."

He waited for a witty comeback, but when he turned to look at her, she was watching him.

"You okay?" She seemed mostly coherent, using words like *disconcerting*, but that didn't mean she wasn't feeling sick.

"Have you had a lot of concussions?"

He hadn't been expecting that. "Oh. Two, maybe three." He felt her eyes remain on him as he drove. He'd already memorized the route to her house, though he'd only been there a couple of times.

She was startled when he pulled to the curb out front, as if she hadn't realized how close they were. He helped her out of the car and up to her front door, once again trying to shield her from the person who had seemingly followed them from

Devin's house, camera flashing. He thought she'd search for her keys, but she turned to him instead.

They stared silently at each other for a moment, neither sure what the next move was. Logically, he knew she should go inside, and he should walk back to his car and go home. But she was glowing from the small porch light she'd left on, and she was breathtaking, and he couldn't stop staring.

He watched her hand warily as it came to rest on his chest. She moved forward slowly, leaning in just enough to place a soft brush of her lips on his cheek. She didn't pull back, and he wrapped his arms around her, tight, breathing in the smell of her shampoo. He liked it when she wore her hair down.

She rested her head on his chest, their breathing synchronizing. "Mm. This is good. Very good for the cameras. Tessa will love this," she whispered.

"Oh, don't pretend you don't like it too."

She fisted his button-down with the hand that was on his chest. "That's not your business." The right side of his mouth lifted slightly, involuntarily.

After a few minutes, when he thought she might be falling asleep right there on her porch, he pulled away gently. "Where are your keys?"

"Purse."

He kept one arm around her as he pulled her keys out. "Are you going to be able to change and get ready for bed okay?"

"If you're insinuating that I should let you in to help me undress, think again, my friend. We may be fake dating, but none of that nonsense."

He slid the key into the doorknob and opened the door slowly. "You're right, you're very coherent despite all the stumbling." She walked into her house, pulled the keys from the doorknob, and stared back at him smugly from inside.

"Goodnight."

"Lock the door, please."

"Aye, aye, Captain."

He waited until he heard the lock click into place before he walked back to his car.

Chapter Thirteen

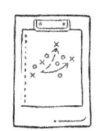

Lucia

Utterly, totally, completely embarrassed. That was the best way to describe how she'd felt the next morning. She couldn't believe the things she'd admitted to Colton, even if they were true. And the kiss? The hug? What the hell was she doing? She was still working through the end of her last relationship, the last thing she needed was another...complication. She'd come here to do her damn job so that other teams would see her value and clamor to have her join them. From there, she would go on to be a head analyst. She had no guaranteed contract with the Sabertooths after this season, so she had to work extra hard to make sure she had a place to go for the next one.

And yet she couldn't deny that she'd wanted to invite him in, wanted him to push her against the wall of her little house and make her moan like Max rarely had. For the next week leading up to their home game, Lucia had gone out of her way to stay away from Colton. Sure, they'd still met for their sessions like normal, but she'd given excuses for why she couldn't go to dinner after, or she'd left early so they wouldn't run into each other in the parking garage.

It was too embarrassing, and being near him brought up feelings she wasn't willing or ready to address. She'd always been professional with Max at work, never so much as having the urge to kiss at the Vipers' facility. It was strange for her to feel this way with Colton.

At least she could usually get away with not seeing him after game day. Especially not on game days at home after a hard-fought win. They'd put up such a fight, each and every one of them beat up and bruised, but with winning smiles and bright eyes. She was sure he was already out celebrating with the team, enjoying the whooping and hollering of his teammates as they congratulated him on being back.

And he kind of was. Whether or not she'd helped him, he'd played a hell of a game and deserved to go out and enjoy it. She was proud of him and the fight he'd put up to prevent the mistakes of prior games. He'd also nearly doubled his yardage, which was truly a feat.

Knowing he was long gone, she felt comfortable removing her hair from its clip and downloading the film from the game. She could go through it before she left for the night so she'd be ready for their sessions that week. Which also meant she could continue to leave early on days they didn't meet because she'd be ahead. It was a great plan. Maybe she'd even take Jenna up on getting a drink on King Street.

Charleston was growing on her. She'd despised it when she'd moved, so set on ending up in Virginia for the rest of her days. But Charleston's energy, its Southern charm, both on game days and in general, was intoxicating. She'd yet to explore much of the city, but what she had enjoyed had made her think twice about applying to other teams for next season. Maybe there was somebody she could beg at the Sabers to let her keep this job, especially with how Colton's performance had improved so far.

She spent twenty minutes watching and clipping the first half of the game to put through her software. Her program was glitching a little bit, so her head was buried close to her laptop as she tried to debug the code. Someone knocked on her door, and she jumped a little, her knee hitting the underside of her desk. She winced.

When she looked up, there was Colton, freshly showered and—unfortunately—rather mouthwatering. She shot up, unsure why she felt so embarrassed. Her knee screamed in pain from the beating it'd just taken.

"H—hi. What are you doing here? I thought you'd be out celebrating."

He looked serious, far more serious than he normally did in her presence. At least recently. He'd been goofy and silly almost every time she'd seen him since they'd come to their tentative truce. The taut set of his facial muscles was jarring, and she grew even more confused when he closed the door halfway.

"I thought I would be too."

"Oh." She said it like she understood what he meant, but she really, *really* didn't. What was he doing in her office?

"Everyone invited me out, but as I was showering, I realized I didn't want to go."

"Oh?" She needed to find something else to say because this was getting out of hand. And what was with that breathless thing going on with her voice?

He took a step forward, then another. "I realized there was something I wanted to do first. Something I *needed* to do."

Dear god, his voice was husky. So deep, she had to clench her thighs together to stop the feeling that started to unfurl there. *Embarrassing*. She needed to get laid so *badly*. This was not like her at all.

His eyes flicked down to her thighs, like he'd seen that subtle movement, and when they came back to her face, his pupils were dilated, his eyes darker. He still hadn't thrown her that grin he'd been sporting so much recently, and his chest was moving fast, like he was struggling to breathe.

He moved even closer to her, and she felt it too, that feeling in her chest that constricted her lungs, just a bit. She remembered his last words, vaguely.

"Wha—what was it that you needed to do?"

She blinked, and he was right in front of her. Despite her heels, she was still looking up at him. She struggled to swallow with him so close, and he tracked that with his eyes too, seemingly so in tune with the subtle movements of her body. Their chests rose in unison, breaths mingling as he looked at her lips through lowered lashes. Her abdomen warmed, liquid and needy. A small, reedy gasp left her as his right hand found her waist. *Had* that been her? That hadn't *sounded* like her.

"Can I..." He trailed off, and Lucia hoped he was asking if he could kiss her because the answer was yes. Absolutely yes. One thousand percent yes.

She nodded her head.

His lips were on hers in an instant, his left hand on her cheek and both of hers fisted in his shirt. It was different from their pregame kisses. Hotter, harder, faster. Open-mouthed and wet and half bites of each other's lips as they fought for control of the kiss. He won, and she gave up easily, letting him push her against the window of her office, pushing closer and closer and closer until there was no space between them.

She slid her arms around to his back, pulling him tightly to her, nails digging through the material of his shirt. He grunted into her mouth as she hit a spot below his neck, which only urged her on, sliding her nails into his hair.

He pressed wet, open-mouthed kisses against the column of her throat, and her head fell back against the glass as she moaned. She wanted him so badly. *Needed* him. Now she understood his words.

When he lightly bit below her ear, she slid her hand down toward the top of his pants, wanting so badly to touch him.

She rubbed him through his sweatpants with the heel of her hand, enjoying as he moved against her, groaning deeply. She felt her own slickness, warm against the fabric of her panties, quickly growing uncomfortable. She wanted to feel him inside of her, his tongue, his fingers. *Him*.

He seemed to sense her urgency, his hands on her ass as he picked her up, allowing her legs to wrap around him. And then she was grinding on that spot that—*fuck*. She was wild, crazed. She needed more, she needed him.

She felt like she was going to explode. He was so hard, his abs, his cock. *God*, it was huge, and the feel of it against her center made her whole body quake.

"*Fuck*, Moretti. You make me fucking crazy." He held her up with one hand on her ass, her back still against the glass. His other hand buried into her hair, and he pulled gently, grinding himself into her as she cried out. "Yeah? You like that? Gonna come all over that sexy little pantsuit just for me?" His words were quiet but gruff, and she already felt herself getting close to that edge she'd rarely crossed with anybody else.

The hand in her hair slid to hold her chin so her eyes met his, his thumb slipping into her mouth. She sucked on it, and his eyes darkened even further. He grinded against her again and her eyes started to drift closed at the pleasure.

"Nuh-uh. Eyes on me, Moretti."

Just as he started the motion again, the door to her office swung open.

The curse that left Colton was angry. He set her down softly and turned around, shielding her from the view of whoever had just ruined the moment. Her brain wasn't working, neurons firing in all the wrong ways as she tried to comprehend what was happening. She adjusted her blazer and pants, running a hand through her mussed hair.

When she peeked over Colton's shoulder, there were Coach Turner and her semi-newly appointed superior, Tim, both with varying degrees of horrified expressions on their faces. Her heart was still racing, whether from what had just happened or what might still happen—her imminent firing and departure from the Sabers—she couldn't be sure.

"Hello." She cursed her breathless voice, moving to stand in front of Colton, worried about what might be on full display in his sweatpants. Clearing her throat, she tried again. "Hello. Can I help you with something?"

Coach Turner glared at Colton behind her. "We were coming to check if you needed more time with Colton or more equipment since he seems to be improving with your work. Though now, I'm not sure that's necessary."

"Coach, this was my fault. Lucia was trying to work, and I'm just amped up from the win."

Tim's face still held that appalled expression as he spoke. "I must remind you of the disclosure agreement you both signed. You are not permitted to have relations on team property. Do we need to get you a chaperone for each time you meet? If this is how your sessions have be—"

"It's not." Colton cut him off. "Our sessions are very professional, as you'll see from each of the reports Lucia puts together afterward. She's the reason I played as well as I did today. Her sessions have been invaluable to me."

Lucia's heart flip-flopped at his praise. Then she remembered his lips on hers and then on her throat, and she had to clench her legs together again. She felt movement near her waist, like Colton might reach out to steady her, but he must've thought better of it. Probably for the best, considering their predicament.

"I'm very sorry, Tim, Coach Turner. It won't happen again." At least her voice was starting to even out.

Coach Turner gave a curt nod as Tim walked out of her office. "If you need anything extra…" His voice sounded pained, but he followed Tim.

With both of them gone, Lucia turned back to face Colton. He smiled down at her, the ghost of a dimple in his cheek.

"You're gonna be the death of me, Moretti." He pushed his hands into her hair, massaging her scalp as he pressed a feather-light kiss to her forehead. "I'll see you tomorrow."

Her stomach dropped as she watched him go. She knew what they'd done was wrong, but that didn't change the fact that it'd felt so, *so* right. She knew, just by looking at his face, that he felt the same way.

She hadn't had time to call Isa in the previous weeks, so busy with the season that she'd barely even had time to sleep. Luckily, they were both free for a few minutes before her next meeting with Colton.

It was their first time talking since *The Night,* and she just let the words tumble out of her, making sure to shut and lock her office door before she divulged anything too juicy to her colleagues.

Isa was, once again, shocked into silence.

"Isa, please. Colton will be here soon, and I really need your thoughts."

Silence.

"Isa..." She drew out the last syllable for a few seconds.

"Oh, I'm sorry. I thought my best friend just told me that she dry-humped the man she was pretending to date, whom she also claimed to hate the last time I saw her. But that can't be right. I must've misheard. So say what you just said again, but a little clearer, please." Lucia heard the edge of Isa's accent, a tell-tale sign of her distress.

"Yes, totally agree, I hated him, and now I don't and all that. Can we focus on the fact that I spent a seven-year relationship thinking I couldn't come unless my hand was involved, only to learn from *one* encounter that Colton can do it without his hands or tongue or dick? And because of that, I've been avoiding him for a week because I'm scared if I don't, I'll jump his bones?"

"God, you need dick more than I realized. He *never* made you come?"

Lucia groaned. She hadn't mentioned this to Isa before because she was, quite frankly, embarrassed. Isa was always talking about how good things were with her partners in the bedroom, and Lucia just nodded along, believing something was wrong with *her*. The further removed she became from her relationship with Max, the more she realized how bad it'd been and how much better it *could* be.

"Isa, please, not the point."

"What am I supposed to say? Do you want me to tell you that this is a good idea? Because I'm not sure I think it is. I'm sorry, *osita*. I want to be happy for you, and I do think you need to get laid, and maybe he's the best person for that for the time being. But I also think that'll get messy, especially if feelings get involved."

Not exactly what Lucia wanted to hear, but that was why she'd called Isa. She needed honest advice.

Isa continued, "He offered to do this to get back at Max. And at the end of the day, you guys will have to stop whatever this is in January, and then where will you end up? I don't want you to get hurt."

"But what if it's just sex? What if I get the perks of this weird, friends-slash-fake-relationship-with-benefits situation and don't let feelings get involved?"

Isa made a *whoosh* noise, like she let out a big puff of air. "That's pretty advanced for somebody who's only ever been in one serious relationship, *mi cielo*. I'm not sure you know how to not let feelings get involved."

A knock sounded on her door. "Shit, I have to go. Can I call you tomorrow? We need to talk about something other than my sex life."

"Of course. I'm planning a trip to see you soon, so we can figure out when would be best for that. Kisses."

"Kisses." That put a smile on Lucia's face. She was so thankful to live in an age where her best friend was just a quick call away, but she needed to see her friend in the flesh. She needed a hug.

Lucia unlocked the door and opened it slowly, breath catching as she took in a dejected-looking Colton. They'd lost the day before, and it showed all over his face and in the set of his shoulders.

"I can't today, Luc. I'm too tired, and I don't wanna watch film, and I don't wanna go out on the field. I just wanna..." He stopped talking, eyes pleading with her.

"Okay, okay, no worries." She thought for a moment, trying to find a way to distract him, while also apologizing for being somewhat MIA since *The Night*. "Will you show me Charleston, instead? Apparently, Coach Turner likes me too much to fire me just yet, so I need local spots to enjoy."

She grinned, hoping Colton might smile with her. It was innocent enough, right? Isa might not agree, but Lucia believed in her ability to keep her feelings removed from the situation.

What could go wrong? It was just dinner. Plus, she'd hopefully be gaining a new restaurant to enjoy in the area.

The surprise on his face only lasted a second before he smiled. It wasn't the goofy one she'd been hoping for, but it was better than the frown he'd been sporting before.

"Of course I will."

Chapter Fourteen

COLTON

Colton had many hats when it came to Lucia, and the moment she'd asked him to show her Charleston, he'd donned his tour guide cap. He'd noticed all week the way she'd run out of their sessions as soon as they were over, likely as confused as he was about where they stood. It was nice that she'd chosen him to take her out into the city. Now that she'd met Jenna and Leigh, he knew she could've asked them, but she'd chosen *him*. There was something in that gesture that made him feel special and wanted. Something in it that eased the tense feeling in his chest that was normally reserved for losses. And he was thrilled to show her the city he loved to call home.

He knew it had been wrong, knew he never should have gone up to her floor to see her after that win. He had been high off of it, and he'd known the only reason he was getting back to his game was because of her. She was probably the smartest person he'd ever met, and he was slowly beginning to regard their sessions as sacred. Required, if he wanted another championship win. He wondered if she might actually know more about football than him, and the thought made him grin. Really, he'd gone up to convince her to celebrate with the team.

But the moment he'd seen her with her hair down, her eyebrows knitted together as she glared at her laptop screen, all of that had left him. Reason itself had gone out the window, taking a swan dive from those tall, glass walls of her office. And sure, it had been wrong, but it'd been the best fucking kiss of his life. He'd almost come undone at just her touch, something he hadn't even known was possible.

Colton decided to take her to his favorite restaurant in all of Charleston—Saltwater Cowboys. Rudy had brought him there his first year with the Sabertooths, and it'd quickly become his favorite spot to be at sunset on a free day, rare as they were.

He placed his hand on the small of her back and led her to a spot outside, pulling his baseball cap lower. Luckily, it was so busy that nobody seemed to notice them, and if they did, it was because of Lucia, not him. The woman knew how to drive a man right out of his mind.

"Colton," she breathed out, her eyes wide as she surveyed everything around them. "This is beautiful." She sat in the chair he pulled out for her, her smile reward enough.

"Rudy brought me here years ago, and since then, I come every chance I get."

Her eyes scanned the horizon, watching the sky sink from blues to pinks and oranges.

"This might be the best sunset I've ever seen."

"Wow, that's saying something since you lived in LA for years."

She scoffed, "Yeah, right. If you got far enough away from the smog to see the sky, even at the beaches, they didn't look like this."

He didn't know if he agreed with that, but he was a little biased. He'd lived most of his life near LA and had grown up enjoying most of the California sunsets from football fields.

"Have you had time to go to the beaches here?"

She shook her head, a small frown on her face. "No, not with the season."

He vowed to take her to the beach at least once before they broke up in January. He wanted her to love Charleston as much as he'd come to over the previous years. Sure, he was an LA boy at heart, but if Charleston let him, he'd be happy to grow old here.

He could tell she had more to say, so he waited.

"Maybe once we get into offseason. If I'm still with the team by then." She mumbled the last sentence.

"What do you mean?"

She shrugged but didn't respond immediately. He watched the sun's slow descent. When their waiter arrived, they ordered, and Colton looked back at her.

"I don't know. They signed me for the season, you know? There are no guarantees past that."

"But look at us! Look at my numbers compared to preseason. How could they not want you to stay?" He caught the blush that crept over her cheeks.

"Oh, well, I don't know. I can't take all the credit there."

Colton called bullshit. He didn't think there was a single thing that factored into his performance more than her help. Not even the extra days his dad wanted him at the gym had made the impact on his game that she had.

"I know we lost again, and I know that was on me." There was that feeling in his chest again as he remembered going down three, four, five times. Remembered his head hitting the turf, the ball that he normally tucked so well during a sack coming out of his hands and giving their opponents the ball at the ten-yard line in the last seconds of a tied game. It'd haunted him in his dreams the night before.

She seemed to sense where his head was, her hand coming to rest on his across the table. "Colton, we've talked about this. This is a team game, nothing is ever completely your fault. That fumble was rough, but it was a tied game because defense struggled. And your o-line still needs work."

He tried to smile but wasn't really feeling it. "Maybe you should be working with them too."

"Eh, I specialize in quarterbacks." And wasn't he thankful for that.

"Where did you grow up?" he asked, shifting the conversation from him and his failures.

"Philly, actually. Very different from here or LA."

"Would you go back?"

She looked past him, and he knew she was looking at the little fishing boats that bobbed in the water behind him. "I barely visit, and that's mainly to see my dad. I don't really see myself ever living there again."

He didn't want to pry, noting the expression on her face and remembering what she'd told him about her mom leaving when she was younger. "You an Eagles fan, then?" He narrowed his eyes, trying to hide the playful smile that threatened the corners of his mouth.

She grinned wickedly. "All this time you've been worried about me taking your secrets back to the Vipers, you didn't even think about the field day I'll have with the Eagles, my *true* team."

"I *knew* you were the villain in my story, Moretti."

She laughed. "That's okay, I always knew you were mine."

"Really?"

Her eyes flicked back to his, the light in them dimming a bit. "No." She twirled her ring around her middle finger like he'd noticed she always did when she got anxious. "That spot is reserved for Max Clark."

Colton grimaced, hating to even hear her say his name. Even if he'd never had an issue with Clark before meeting Lucia, Max would be on Colton's shit list just for what he had—and continued to—put her through.

"Is he still bothering you?"

She lifted one of her shoulders half-heartedly. "Here and there. He gets especially mad on game days if he watches, 'cause it seems the camera likes to focus on our kiss. Which, if you think about it, is crazy because that's usually game day for him too. And if the media or anybody posts about us online, he'll say something. It's a lot of the same shit, I kind of just ignore it. Seems like he only cares about me when he's reminded that I'm with someone else."

Colton went rigid at that. He'd hoped Clark would've just left her alone after a few weeks, but the fact that he'd publicly ruined her life and then continued to terrorize her made Colton see many shades of red. If they both made it to the divisional championship during playoffs, he was going to rip Clark's head off.

"Still waiting on his redemption arc?"

She glared at him. "There's no need to be a dick." He held up his hands defensively. "But yes, I'm still holding out a little stupid hope that he'll apologize." She paused, eyes finding her hands. "Because if he never does then it makes me wonder why I was ever with him. Was he this terrible the whole time? Can I even trust my judgment in men? Of people in general?"

That admission, that vulnerability, had wiped away any anger he'd been feeling. She looked so sad, he wanted to reach across the table and hold her to him, but he reined in the urge. He needed to stop giving in to the feelings he got when he was around her, especially ones that made him want to kiss her silly. Kiss her until she moaned like she had in her office, until she moved against him like a woman who needed to be sated.

Right. Those were the inappropriate thoughts he was *not* supposed to be having. He was, thankfully, pulled from the mental image of her against him by her question.

"So, who's your favorite sibling?" She leaned forward conspiratorially, and he knew she was trying to move past the admission she'd made.

He laughed. "You have to promise not to tell, but definitely Maya. No doubt about it."

"Aw, poor Landon. He probably spent his whole life overshadowed by you, and now he can't even be your favorite?"

He rolled his eyes. "Landon is one of the best tight ends in the league right now, nobody's overshadowing him."

"Colton, if I know anything about you, it's that you were probably always the best at everything growing up. You just seem like that kind of asshole." She laughed at his expression. "It's true. Come on, tell me I'm right."

"I will do no such thing. I was a very nice child, I'll have you know."

"I find that hard to believe based on who you've become."

"You, Moretti, are a scourge on my very being."

She laughed melodically but didn't respond.

He took the moment of silence to bring up what he'd been wanting to talk to her about for the past week: the upcoming dinner his siblings and father had every year in honor of their mother.

"Are you free this Saturday?"

"Oh, uh, I'm not sure. I assume I'll just be going through film from Thursday's game."

He bit the bullet. "Well, my family and I have a get-together once a year, usually in November, to honor my mom. We try for her birthday, which is November seventh, but we're all so busy that we just do the closest day that works for all of us. Which is this Saturday."

He'd been holding off asking her for a couple of weeks so as not to scare her. He hadn't even been sure he was going to ask her initially, but when he thought of having to face his father alone, even with his siblings, it made his skin itch, and he knew Lucia's presence would help.

She blinked at him, wide-eyed. He continued, "Um, so, well, yeah. It'll be at my dad's house here in Charleston, and you can meet my family. Maya is especially excited to meet you. But only if you're comfortable, I don't want you to feel pressured to come." He took her silence to mean she wasn't interested. "I completely understand if you don't want to, Lucia. It's a huge thing, even if we were dating for real."

For the second time, she reached across the table to place a hand on his, quieting him. "Of course I'll be there,

Colton. What are fake girlfriends for, if not for fending off their boyfriends' fire-breathing-dragon fathers and supporting them through a tough time?"

He had no idea that the title held such all-encompassing duties, but he let out a relieved breath, a small weight lifting off his shoulders. He was never technically alone, since his siblings always came, but it would be the first time someone came to support *him*.

Colton's heart was thudding in his chest. He didn't know why his father had this effect on him. Every cell in his body was on high alert as he looked at the two-story, white, antebellum house. His father had spent an unnecessary amount of money on this place just so he could be close by for Colton's games, despite having a massive house in Los Angeles that was rarely used.

He made a move toward the curved staircase that led to the front door, but a gentle hand stopped him. He'd been so caught up in dread that he'd almost forgotten Lucia was about to meet his family and was probably more nervous than he was.

He turned to her, trying to put a brave face on. "You ready?"

She nodded, worried eyes on him. "Are you okay?"

He tried to shrug, but it came out robotic and strange. Her eyebrows drew together more.

After a moment of staring at each other, Lucia reached up and placed her hands on his shoulders. "Hey. I'm only going to say this once because it feels weird to be nice to you, so listen closely." She took a deep breath, like the next words would pain her. "You are more than football. You are more than a winning season, you are more than a Super Bowl-winning machine, okay? You would be important to plenty of people regardless of whether you win a million games, regardless of whether you leave the NFL right now. Your dad can shove his 'constructive criticism' up his ass." She pulled her hands away to air quote with her fingers, then placed them back at her side.

He smiled gratefully at her, even as his heart rate picked up for an entirely new reason. He hadn't realized how badly he'd needed to hear those words.

And a part of him wondered if *she* was one of those people who believed he was important regardless of whether he was in the NFL. But he didn't have time to think about it too much as they turned and approached the belly of the beast.

Chapter Fifteen

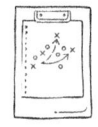

Lucia

Colton's father's house was huge. Admittedly, it was not nearly as big as Colton's massive, seven-bedroom, $7.5 million home—yes, Lucia *had* found his mansion online—but it was still looming and beautiful.

Lucia was quite nervous. Sure, the stakes were lower since she wasn't *actually* dating Colton, but she still had to *pretend* to be dating Colton, and she honestly didn't know what that entailed. It was hard enough not to drool over him in that long-sleeve button-down that put his muscles on full display. She was also struggling to work through the whole *they almost had sex in her office* thing, but that was the last thought she needed to be focused on as she walked up the stairs of the white house, clutching tightly to the gift bag that held a bottle of whiskey.

The door opened before they even knocked, revealing a tall woman of about twenty-two or twenty-three with tan skin and dark-brown hair. She was stunning, and she smiled wide as she launched herself at Colton, who realized just in time that his sister was hurtling toward him.

"Hey, Mai. Missed you." The woman, Maya, gave Colton one more squeeze before turning to Lucia, smiling wider, if that was even possible.

Lucia held out her free hand. "Hi, I'm—"

"Lucia!" Maya's arms were around her, and Lucia hugged her back tentatively, smiling at Colton from over his sister's shoulder. Even in her kitten heels, Lucia was a couple of inches shorter than her.

"You have no idea how thankful I am that you're here. Family functions are so boring with me as the only girl." Maya slung an arm around Lucia's shoulders and led her inside the house, leaving Colton to walk in behind them.

"It's really nice to meet you. Colton speaks very highly of you."

"As he should! I'm his favorite sister, after all."

The foyer was open and spacious. Maya pointed out where Lucia could leave her shoes.

"My brothers and father hate it, but especially when we're honoring our mom, I insist we take off our shoes. It's how we grew up, and it's what Mom would've wanted."

Lucia smiled kindly as she stepped out of her heels. A man a couple of years younger than Colton but a few inches taller walked into the foyer, making eye contact with Maya as he hooked a thumb over his shoulder. "Mai, Liliana needs your help in the kitchen."

Maya scoffed, "Oh, what? You're too tall to help her out yourself? Sexist pig." She turned to Lucia. "I won't subject you to their sexism by asking you to come with me to help Dad's chef. You hang out with Colton and Landon, and I'll be back."

Landon smirked at his sister before stepping forward and focusing that smirk squarely on Lucia. "Well, hello there. You're even prettier in person." He extended a tattooed hand. "Landon Beaumont, Colton's younger and sexier brother."

The cocky smirk grew wider as Colton came up behind her and placed a hand on her back. She put her much smaller hand in Landon's outstretched palm.

"Ah, yes, the famous tight end. I'm Lucia, Colton's very serious girlfriend."

As if to reward her, Colton's pointer finger dragged little patterns on her back through the fabric of her floral dress. She squashed the urge to lean into him, pulling her hand back from the handshake.

Something strange passed between the brothers, and Lucia wasn't sure how to read it. She didn't have siblings and had never known the competitive feeling that accompanied playing the same sport and trying to one-up one another. She didn't know much about their relationship, but even she could see that it was a little strained. Still, they leaned in for a hug and clapped one another on the back.

"Your stats are looking much better."

"Thanks, you've had a great season too."

From an outsider's perspective, the interaction might've seemed odd. But just as she'd imagined, Landon's body language told her he wasn't Colton's biggest fan. It was clear there was a lot of family trauma the boys needed to work through together, and she hoped one day that they would.

She walked beside the brothers into the living room and connected kitchen, Colton's hand still resting on her, though now around her waist. Maya and an older blonde woman, who Lucia assumed was the chef Maya had spoken of before, were facing away from them, chopping something. The smell of food cooking made Lucia's stomach grumble, and she saw the quirk of Colton's lips at the sound.

The sound of footsteps had all of them turning. Lucia felt like the entire room was holding its breath. The spell was broken as the shortest Beaumont man with green eyes and graying hair walked in. His eyes landed immediately on Colton before they slid to Lucia, narrowing almost accusatorially on her.

"Hi, Mr. Beaumont. I'm Lucia. This is for you." She held out the pretty gift bag, almost embarrassed as he took it from her like it was a bomb. He peered inside, and seemingly satisfied that she wasn't trying to blow up his family, he set it on the counter.

When she'd asked Colton what his father might like, the only thing he'd been able to think of was whiskey. She had spent longer than she should've researching the best one to buy him, hoping to make a good first impression, but she could tell he'd made his mind up about her before she'd stepped through the door of his house.

"Nice to meet you," he said in a way that made it seem like it was *not*, in fact, nice to meet her. He turned to Colton. "Let's go talk about the game before dinner."

She saw Colton's shoulders sag as he grimaced. He shot her an apologetic look but followed his father out of the room. Lucia couldn't figure out why he'd deflated, since the Sabers had won the game by three scores and Colton had played quite well.

"Landon, make yourself useful and go set the table, please. We'll start setting out food in a minute." Maya wasn't even facing them as she said it, though she turned around and winked at Lucia as Landon grumbled.

"Lucia, join me."

Lucia followed Landon into an adjacent room. The dining room was massive, with a huge, wooden table and matching chairs. Intricate placemats of red, gold, and blue sat at each setting, though they looked old and worn. A blue table runner lay down the middle of the long table, tying into the decor well. Besides the table, there was little else decorating the room. There were no family photos, pictures of pets, or even paintings. It felt very cold, just like the rest of the house.

"So, you're the minx who dated Colton's sworn enemy, right? I can't tell you how much I've heard about Max Clark over the past nine years. I was surprised when I heard you and

Colton got together." She tried to detect any note of suspicion in his tone as she grabbed the plates from the head of the table, setting them out as he laid out silverware and thinking through how best to respond.

"I was working as a Vipers analyst, and it didn't work out for me there, so I transferred to the Sabertooths to help Colton after the first two preseason games. We didn't see eye to eye in the beginning, as you can imagine."

That got a chuckle out of him as he continued around the table.

"We started spending more time together, and we realized that we had a lot of common interests. After that, everything kind of just fell into place, I guess."

It felt odd lying to Landon, but the last thing she wanted was for him not to believe that they were together. Colton already had to deal with his helicopter parent of a father, he didn't need his brother teasing him for lying about a girlfriend too. If it meant protecting him from that, she had no qualms about fibbing.

Landon chuckled again. "Well, I'm certainly surprised. Colton's probably the best of us at holding a grudge. Granted, he's had to deal with the most shit from our dad, but still, he can be a real dick sometimes. I don't know how he managed to get his shit together enough to convince you to go out with him."

Lucia grinned. "He's very stubborn."

"That, I knew. But glad to hear he put that particular personality trait to use at something that matters. One thing we have in common is that we are both no good at relationships. I haven't seen him date someone seriously in years."

"Do you think he just didn't have the time before?" She was being nosy, but she really wanted to know why he'd spent so many of his best years alone.

"I'd joke that he has no game with women, but I think we can probably agree that's not true."

She shook her head. The perpetual warmth that swept through her when he was near was a good indication that it wasn't even a little true. Not to mention how she'd nearly come apart in her office.

"Right. Anyway, I think Colt was dealt a tough hand with our dad. He's got it so deeply ingrained in him that his football stats have to be perfect all the time that he probably never even thought about it. You must've really taken him by surprise."

She laughed as she leaned against one of the chairs. "I think what surprised him was that I didn't take any of his shit."

He gave her a genuine smile, not one of his cocky smirks, as he said, "Good. He needs it."

She thought back to what he'd said about their dad. "Your dad's pretty hard on all of you, huh?"

"Hard's an understatement, but like I said, Colton gets the worst of it. He was the first-born son who could do no wrong." There was that tinge of bitterness. "Unless, of course, he is on the field. No matter how hard Colton works, no matter how he perfects his game at the expense of his life, his relationships, his everything, it has never been enough for dear ol' Dad."

The thought made Lucia's heart hurt for a young Colton. "Why has he pushed you and Colton so hard in football? I mean, I know he played in college and was a first-round favorite for the draft, but it feels like a lot of pressure to put on someone else."

Her dad had a lot of faults, but even with the small family hardware store he ran, he'd never expected Lucia to follow in his footsteps. The moment he'd learned she was good at math and had an interest in computers, he'd made sure to hire someone to help with her college applications, even when they hadn't had much money to spare.

Not only had she found Colton's house online, but she'd also looked into his family. Troy Beaumont's college career had been incredibly promising. He had been predicted to be the first pick in the NFL draft after his senior year of college, but the injury during the national championship had changed everything. She had been surprised to see that he'd quit the football world and moved on to something else. Still, it made no sense for that to be his only reason to push his sons so hard.

Landon leaned against the doorway. "Right after Dad got injured, he met our mom through some friends. She swam at Crestview, and I guess with them both playing NCAA sports, they understood each other. A few months later, she was pregnant with Colton, and my dad had to find a job quickly. I'm not sure either of them were thrilled about it, but they got married right out of college."

Landon rubbed his jaw, an odd look on his face. "A few months after Colt was born, my dad was offered a coaching job at a college across the country. The offer was only on the table for a week or so, but with a newborn and a recently purchased house, there was no feasible way for them to uproot their life. Plus, Dad would've been gone all the time, and Mom didn't want to have to rely on her parents too much, so they ultimately decided it wasn't the right path."

Realization dawned on Lucia as Landon continued. "So Dad put all of his free time into coaching Colton. He wanted to make sure Colt was the next best NFL great, no matter the consequences. Then I was born, and he'd been out of the football world for so long that he couldn't find professional coaching jobs anywhere. Instead, he threw himself into coaching all our Little League and middle school games. Taught Colt and me everything he knows. Made sure Crestview scouts came out to watch him play in high school and then went to all of his college games."

Lucia whispered, "And Colton's believed his whole life that it was his fault? That his father missed out on a career in coaching because of him?"

Landon nodded slowly, lips pressed into a thin line. "Dad made sure he knew that story. Any misstep, and he would remind Colt what he'd given up for him. Mom tried her best to stop it, but there was nothing she could do, short of leaving him. And there was no way he wasn't going to fight with everything in him to keep Colt, if only to live out his dreams."

"And what about you?"

"I spent years trying to live up to my dad's standards, but with Colton as good as he was, it didn't make sense for me to be a quarterback. Plus, I'm taller, so tight end was the best choice for me." He grinned. "Let's just say I'm glad to be across the country. It's nice being out of Colt's shadow, but it's even nicer being away from Dad."

As horrible as Lucia felt for all of the Beaumont children, her heart ached for Colton. He'd had the weight of his father's goals and dreams placed on his little shoulders from the moment he was born, his life already planned out for him. No wonder all he cared about was winning. It was all he'd known. He felt he could only get his father's love if he won, and she was sure that translated to everyone else as well.

"Sorry, I thought you would've known this stuff. It's textbook parental projection. Unfortunately, Colton's too indebted to him. He's so consumed with the idea that he must get Dad's approval that he won't even say no when Dad berates him for a win during Mom's memorial dinner."

Absent-mindedly, Lucia responded, "No, I had no idea. Colton likes to keep his private life private, even from me."

Maya walked in with a casserole dish, a pained expression on her face. She'd clearly heard what they'd been talking about, her eyes flicking between the two of them.

"Casserole's ready," she said quietly.

"I'll help with the rest of the dishes. You've done enough. Let me bring the stuff in, you'll burn yourself." Landon followed his sister out of the room as he spoke, leaving a shocked Lucia to stare at the pristine table, her body leaning against a chair to steady herself.

She knew Colton had invited her, had wanted her there for moral support, but she couldn't help but feel as though she'd overstepped the bounds of their relationship by having that conversation with Landon. She'd learned things so intimate about Colton that it genuinely made her question all the interactions she'd had with him, all the mean comments she'd made about his game since they'd first seen each other in the Sabertooths' boardroom.

She didn't know how to act. On one hand, this didn't change their relationship at all, but on the other, she felt for Colton. She really did. Someone who was supposed to have nurtured him, taught him how to ride a bike, taught him how to play a *relaxed* game of football, taught him all the ways of the world, had cursed him with high expectations and a life mapped out for him.

Moments later, Landon and Maya had set up all of the dishes on the table, no thanks to the still-shocked Lucia. Maya led Lucia to a chair.

"Here. Colton usually sits in this chair anyway." She pointed to the one beside Lucia.

Sure enough, a few moments later, Colton walked in and sat beside her, his jaw tense. When he saw the expression on her face, his eyebrows knitted together.

"You okay?" he whispered as everyone sat down at the table around them, their father included.

She nodded. "You?"

"I'll be fine."

Lucia spent most of the dinner observing the dynamic between Colton and his father, though her silence also allowed her to notice how Troy Beaumont couldn't even look at Maya. She continued trying to make conversation, even bringing up their mother, but their father kept focusing on football, as if dinner was just a continuation of his conversation with Colton.

When his attention turned to Landon's playing, Lucia tuned out for a moment, eyes drifting over Colton's hardened features as he ate. How much of what his father said had he internalized just then? How much of it had he internalized his entire life? How much of what he did was just his father's words in his head, telling him that's what he had to do for people to care about him? For people to love him?

When dinner was over, Lucia could tell Colton was ready to leave. Everyone but their father helped load the dishwasher, and Lucia and Colton hugged both of his siblings goodbye. Maya put Lucia's number in her phone, promising to keep in touch.

Maya and Landon would be staying the night since they both had to take a flight to get in and out of Charleston, so Lucia and Colton were the only ones to leave. At the door, Colton's father stood, still talking about football as Landon and Maya looked on solemnly.

"Don't forget to get in the gym more this week. You've got a big game, and you need to be stronger. You took too many sacks the game before last."

Colton sighed. "Yes, I will. Just like I have been."

"Well, clearly it hasn't been enough."

That was it. The words were bad enough, but the tone of them sent Lucia hurtling over whatever precipice she'd been standing on. She whirled around on him.

"Colton is one of the best, if not *the* best, quarterbacks in the NFL right now. Potentially ever. He's playing incredibly well compared to preseason, and he's on par with his performance from last year. He has professionals setting a schedule and training program for him, including myself. All he needs is your support. We can handle the rest."

Mr. Beaumont's face reddened, and she could see the impressed look from Landon and the open-mouthed shock from Maya over his shoulder.

She slid her hand into Colton's, weaving her fingers through his. They'd done so a couple of times for cameras over the past two months, but there was something different this time. This was for him, for them. This was to ground herself and to show her support for him.

Finally, his father spoke angrily, face completely red. "How *dare* you speak to me like that when I invited you into my home. You are a rude little—didn't your mother teach you any manners? I was nice to you as a courtesy, but you're ruining my son's game. The last thing he needs is an analyst as a girlfriend when he's playing the worst season of his life since joining the team."

At the mention of her mother, Lucia reeled back. Colton squeezed her hand, pulling her closer to him.

"Don't talk to her like that. She's the reason I'm playing as well as I am right now." He focused his eyes past his father, nodding at his siblings. "Goodnight."

Lucia followed him down the stairs, her hand still firmly tucked in his. She wasn't sure if he was upset at her for overstepping, but he didn't speak until they reached the sidewalk.

"Every damn year! He does this every fucking year. We can't just respect my mother for everything she did for us, for him. Everything she sacrificed and all that she dealt with near the end. Instead, we have to talk about the only thing he knows how to talk about. She's dead, and he acts like she never fucking existed."

When they reached his car, down the street and out of sight of his father's house, he leaned against it, his back against the driver-side door. "And you..."

"Colton, I'm so sorry. I shouldn't have said all of those things, it wasn't my place."

"Stop it. You were—god, you were..." He shook his head, running his hand through his hair. "You were fucking amazing. Phenomenal. I have never seen anybody take him on like that, and to do that for me?" His Adam's apple bobbed as if he were holding back a slew of emotions.

She placed a hand on his cheek to center him. Softly, she whispered, "You are worth so much more than a trophy or Super Bowl ring. There is far more substance to you than your father gives you credit for. More than even you give yourself credit for."

His eyes closed, and when they opened, the emotions swirling in them tugged at every part of her. She couldn't stop herself. She leaned forward and kissed him, softer than in her office. Soft and sweet. And he kissed her back just as softly, his arms wrapping around her.

What could've been seconds or minutes later, it became something needier, hungrier, hotter. Suddenly, the front of her dress was up around her waist, and she was about to beg him to take her right there on his father's dimly lit street. She pulled away, just barely, just enough to reach for the door to his backseat, but he caught her wrist, his jaw setting tightly, eyes closing.

"What?" she breathed out. She hated how whiny she sounded, but the sight of him in this button-down was doing unspeakable things to her.

Somberly, quietly, he said, "Luc, I have to take you home. You deserve to be worshiped, not taken roughly and clumsily in the back of my car." Her heart flip-flopped, and her stomach erupted with butterflies banging around all over her insides.

She knew it was a bad idea. Knew what Isa would tell her if she asked. But he'd been through so much, and the need to comfort him was overwhelming. She trusted her ability to have sex without letting feelings get in the way. If she thought of it as simply a perk of the relationship, there was really nothing wrong with it, right?

"Then take me to yours and worship me." His eyes looked back and forth between hers as if he couldn't believe he'd heard her correctly. She stared right back, confident in her decision.

And then they were in his car, racing back to his house.

They'd barely made it inside before they were on each other, Colton's right hand buried in her hair and his left holding her chin. He pulled away, hoisting her up so her legs wrapped around him, her heels digging into his ass. His thumb glided across her bottom lip.

"I used to think my favorite thing about your mouth was the smartass shit that it spouted when I pissed you off. Then I learned what it's like to kiss you." His eyes flicked up from her lips to her eyes. "Now, I'm thinking it's gonna be the way it makes me feel when I'm fucking it."

Her breath hitched, warmth flooding her entire body from her head to her toes, but most especially between her legs. Everything about this was better than in her office, better than she'd ever imagined. She was so shocked that she hadn't realized he'd already walked them into his bedroom. She didn't even have time to take in the fact that she was in *Colton Beaumont's bedroom* as he sat at the edge of his bed, her legs on either side of him and his mouth back on hers.

Her eyes stayed closed as she fumbled with the buttons on his shirt. She groaned as she struggled with one, and he chuckled deeply, helping her. When his bare chest was exposed to her, she stuck her hands under the material of the crisp shirt and pushed it off his shoulders.

They were godly. She had never seen such beautiful shoulders, and she was quickly beginning to wonder if she liked them more than his forearms she'd often caught herself nearly drooling over. His arms came out of the shirt slowly, and there he sat, naked from the waist up and absolutely glorious.

He kissed her neck, her head falling back as she pulled at the buckle of his belt. Suddenly, he flipped her around so that she was on her back, Colton standing above her. She opened her mouth to complain, but his lips were back on hers, his kiss biting as a finger trailed over the inside of her thigh, coming to rest at her panties.

His fingers stilled as his lips rested below her ear, nipping and sucking. He rubbed the lace of her panties as he asked, "Can I?"

Fuck, yes. "Please," she moaned, already needing the pressure of his fingers inside her. Her back arched as he brushed against her clit before his finger slipped under the lace.

"*Fuck,*" he choked out. "You always this wet for me?"

A moan was her only answer as his finger found her seam, rubbing what he found up to her clit and gently circling it. Lucia's whole body hummed to life, and her nails dug into his scalp as he bit softly down her throat. His nose traced down the middle of her body as he pressed light kisses through her dress.

"This," he mumbled gruffly, "needs to go." He slipped the straps of her dress over her shoulders and down her arms, kissing each inch of newly exposed skin until his breath warmed her bare breasts. His jaw tensed as he drank her in, and then he pulled the entire thing off, leaving her in only her panties and heels. Colton unbuckled the straps of her shoes, pulling them from her feet slowly and lightly brushing his fingertips up her legs in a way that had her practically shaking for him.

He moved up to kiss the hollow of her throat, then her chest, and then he was licking her left nipple, sucking it into his mouth as his hand played with the other. She gasped so loudly at the sensation that he chuckled.

Lucia had never been a fan of nipple play before, but now she knew it was because Max had been doing it *all* wrong. She wanted Colton to keep biting and twisting them as she writhed below him, wanted him to move lower and do the same to her clit.

"Please, Colton." Her words were more like a moan as his fingers dropped below her waist to play with her again.

"What do you want me to do to you, Moretti?" He kissed her stomach slowly, going lower and lower as he teased her entrance with his finger. Need filled her body, taut and painful.

"*Please.* I need you."

A moment later she looked down, and there he was, on his knees before her. He grinned. "I told you if you wanted me on my knees, all you had to do was ask."

Pulling aside her panties, he licked her clit once, twice, a third time, until she was pushing herself up into his face. He used his left forearm to press her body against the bed, his right middle finger circling her clit as his tongue dipped inside her.

She was vibrating, waves of pleasure taking over her body. She willed herself to slow down, to wait until Colton was inside of her to let go, but she was careening toward the edge, and she wasn't sure anything could stop her. He pushed his finger inside of her, and the size of it alone was enough for her whole world to shake. He curled it, hitting her in just the right place, and that was all it took for her to finish, dancing stars obscuring her vision.

When she could feel her body again, she found his face still buried in her. She tugged at his hair so he looked up at her, and when he saw the look on her face, he licked his way up her body, placing a kiss to her mouth, his hips tight against hers. She couldn't stop the moan that left her as he drove his hips into hers, her body coming alive again as it remembered what she'd almost had in her office.

She was frantic as she pulled at his pants, pouting when he moved away to take them off slowly. He gave her that grin that was branded in her mind.

"So impatient." He tsked, unbuckling his pants.

She would show him impatience. After pulling the lace off her body in one fluid motion, she stuck a finger in her mouth and used it to play with her clit while she watched him, and then the grin was gone, replaced with something much, much darker.

"Lucia..."

She closed her eyes and moaned, willing him to give her what she wanted. He was on her in an instant, his bare cock resting at her entrance. Her eyes opened wide, meeting his.

"I thought you wanted to fuck my mouth?" The words sounded absolutely filthy coming out of her, and she loved it, though she knew just by the feel of it against her leg that she'd never be able to take the whole thing in her mouth.

"Fuck that, I can't go another second without being inside of you." He rubbed his erection against her clit. "What do you want, Moretti? You want me inside of you as badly as I do?"

She reached down, smiling wide as he shuddered at her touch. "Fuck me like you mean it."

Chapter Sixteen

COLTON

Lucia lay on his bed, hair fanned out around her head, still panting from her orgasm, though she was smiling wide. She'd clearly liked the noise he'd made when she'd touched him, and he liked that she liked that.

In a voice that hardly sounded like him, Colton said, "I'm gonna make you come again and again until you're too tired to do anything but moan my name."

"Stop making promises you can't keep."

His whole body tensed at her words. He knew she'd just said it to rile him up, and it had worked. He pulled a condom from his nightstand, and in one fluid motion, he ripped it open with his teeth and pulled it over his erection, pumping over it once, then twice.

"Say that shit again, I fucking dare you." He leaned over her, his lips right above hers, his cock just barely touching her entrance. It took everything in him not to push inside her right then and there. She remained silent, though her lips were curved into a mischievous smile.

"That's what I thought," he grumbled before his lips found hers, and he kissed her hard, demanding. She dug her nails into his back, her hips shifting, begging to have him inside her.

Though his kiss was punishing, he pushed into her gently, his knees almost giving out at the feeling of being inside of her.

"*Yes*," she breathed.

His hands gripped her waist tightly, and her nails dug so deep, he would've been surprised if they didn't draw blood. "Holy fuck." She bucked her hips, pushing him further into her, and his eyes nearly rolled into the back of his head. "You feel fucking unreal, Moretti." His lips found hers again, and she bit his lip as he entered her fully.

Her moan was like music to his ears. She pulled away, eyes on his as she stuck that same finger from before back into her mouth and then used it to play with herself. He almost lost his hold on her at the sight, a noise halfway between a groan and a grunt leaving his throat. Any resistance her body had to him disappeared in seconds, and then he was all the way inside her, her cries and fluttering lashes encouraging him.

His lips captured hers again, his cock pumping into her rhythmically.

"Oh my god, Colton," she whimpered. He moved one of his hands from her waist to her shoulders, pushing even harder into her as they both gasped and moaned. She adjusted so his hand was around her throat, her eyes twinkling as his knees almost buckled for the second time that night.

His mouth dragged down to her neck, right above his hand, where he bit and sucked, her breathy moans spurring him forward. He felt his length start to tingle, but he needed her to come first.

"This is the best fucking pussy I've ever had." He wasn't even lying. She'd completely ruined him for any other woman. Her laugh, her intelligence, the way she could tell within seconds what was wrong with his game. It drove him out of his mind, and he would never recover if she didn't let him do this for the rest of his life. "You like that?"

"Mm-hmm," she moaned, her eyes shut tight, her fingers tugging at his hair.

"You're such a good girl just for me, aren't you?" He whispered it right below her ear. He'd correctly guessed about her praise kink and was rewarded with the feeling of her walls pulsing around him. She cried out, and he watched her face as pleasure overtook her. When he was sure she was there, he let himself go, kissing her hard as he came apart inside of her.

He knew he needed a minute before round two, but true to his word, he pulled out of her, threw out the condom, and dropped to his knees to worship her. And, just as he'd promised, all she could do by the end of the night was moan his name.

Practice flew by the next day, Colton's whole body twitching like he'd had seven Red Bulls. He'd overthrown Cooper at least four times, and Coach Turner was glaring at him like he knew *exactly* what his problem was. A shock, considering Colton didn't.

He thought lifting might help expend some of the extra energy that danced through his veins, but by the end of a warm-up run and four sets of squats and push-ups, he still felt shaky. His leg kept bouncing throughout the two hours of meetings, and even Cooper sent him a look as he stood and ran out of the room.

The wives and girlfriends of the team had planned a picnic for that afternoon. He'd planned to go home to change for it, thankful for the time alone to parse through his thoughts, but was met with the smell of Lucia's perfume in his car.

He groaned. He couldn't escape her no matter where he was. Worse, he wasn't sure he wanted to. Sure, he'd had many trysts with wonderful, beautiful women, but none of them had him wishing he could accidentally run into them in the halls of the facility like he was in high school. None of them had wound him so tightly around their finger that he might snap.

Until his eyes had opened and he'd realized she was gone, he hadn't known how badly he'd wanted her to be there when he woke up, wrapped in his arms. And that thought had haunted him all morning. He'd had to remind himself countless times that whatever had happened between them was strictly...what, exactly? He didn't quite know. They were attracted to each other, but they didn't—couldn't—have feelings for each other. They needed to be able to move forward and focus on the season.

Except he couldn't focus. He kept wondering why he couldn't have both the season *and* Lucia. Would a relationship really be so bad? He looked at Rudy, Chris, Sam, and all the rest of his teammates who had partners. If they could do it, why couldn't he?

Colton had always believed exhilaration was something he felt when he stepped into the end zone with the ball, or when he lobbed up a perfect pass to a receiver. That breathless feeling that accompanied a win? A hard-fought, well-deserved game ball? He'd thought those were the greatest feelings in the world. But Lucia set exhilaration to a higher standard, put it on a pedestal that only she could reach.

The problem? It was *fake*. She'd only agreed to the relationship to get the media off of her back and to get back at Clark. Which meant she probably wasn't having any of these concerns, exemplified by the fact that she'd left before he'd even woken up at five that morning.

He changed in record time and drove the few minutes to Lucia's house. She was already out on her porch, looking stunning in a long, floral dress similar to the one she'd worn the evening before. Colton shifted uncomfortably in his seat, hating how his dick had such a mind of its own.

"Hi," she chirped, a strange expression on her face.

"Hi."

Neither of them knew how to act, the car silent as he drove to Sabertooths Park. Finally, tired of the way she always closed in on herself after they'd shared a moment, he said, "Luc, we should talk."

Her head snapped to look at him. "Wha—what about?"

"Luc, it was one thing when you avoided me after what happened in your office, but this is different. We can't keep pretending these things aren't happening."

He pulled into the parking lot, seeing half his teammates already throwing a ball around, their children chasing after them.

She cleared her throat. "Okay, you're right. We should probably...I don't know. We probably should've set boundaries from the start. I just wasn't expecting to need to since we're...you know."

"We're what?"

"Us. We're us. Who, in a million years, could have seen yesterday coming?"

"Oh, right. 'Cause I'm *so* easy to resist."

She smacked his shoulder, chuckling.

He drew in a breath before saying the dreaded, "So, boundaries."

"Right, yes. We—we keep any hanging-outside-of-work time to a minimum. Just what we need to do to keep Tessa off our backs. We do nothing that could distract us or jeopardize our jobs."

Ouch. At least she'd confirmed what he'd known. He was a distraction to her. She didn't have the same war waging inside her that he'd had all day.

"Right. No distractions. Sounds good."

She smiled at him, getting ready to open her door. "Ready?"

"Moretti, if you open that door, I'm going to throw you back into your seat and close it on you just so I can open it again. As far as everyone else is concerned"—he nodded toward his teammates—"you're mine, and if I'm gonna be in a fake relationship, I'm gonna do it right."

He'd meant it as a joke. Kind of. But from the awestruck look on her face—whether good or bad—she hadn't taken it that way. Her hand slipped into her lap, and she cocked her head to the side.

"Alright, big boy. Let's see it."

He adjusted himself in his pants again, cursing as she snorted. He walked around the car and opened the door for her, extending his arm in a dramatic *this way* gesture and bowing.

"Princess..."

Before she could respond, Rudy was calling him over.

"Is holding hands within our boundaries?" He extended his hand toward her.

She slipped her hand into his. "Well, we're in public, so it's fine."

He smirked down at her. "Better be careful about making that the standard, Moretti."

She squeezed his hand tightly, a clear reprimand, as they walked toward the picnic tables. There weren't many people milling about who weren't with the team, but the ones who were had their phones out, taking pictures. Colton grimaced and pulled Lucia closer as they made their way to Jenna.

"Hey, Jen."

"Hi, honey. Rudy seems to need you over there." She inclined her head to where her husband was jumping up and down, trying to get his attention.

"Will you keep my dear Lucia safe if I leave her in your care?"

"Colton, I swear to god..."

Jenna was already laughing, holding her arms out to envelop Lucia. "I'll take good care of her."

He jogged over to where the team was passing footballs around. Before he could even hug Rudy, two of Rudy's three children were jumping on him. "Uncle Colt, Uncle Colt!"

"Hello, demons." He wrangled them so one was on his shoulders and the other hung like a bat from his arms.

"Alright, they're all yours. I'm going to have a conversation with your lovely girlfriend and my even lovelier wife." Rudy was gone faster than Colton could open his mouth to protest.

Cooper walked up with a grin. "I see Rudy roped you into babysitting. What a chump."

"Oliver, I'll give you ten dollars if you tackle Uncle Coop. Twenty between the two of you if you *and* James tackle him."

They jumped off him in an instant, Coop cursing as he ran halfway across the park before letting them corner him.

Colton turned to Hayley, Rudy's youngest. He sat down beside her. "Why so blue, Hayles?"

She shrugged. "I'm bored, and Oliver and James won't let me play with them again."

"Hmm. Let me think up some way to get them back."

"Who's that pretty lady that came with you?" She was pointing at Lucia, who was watching them as she spoke with Rudy and Jenna. She blushed at being caught but waved at Hayley.

"That's my girlfriend, Lucia."

"You have a girlfriend?"

"I do indeed. Don't worry though"—he tapped her nose—"you're still my favorite."

"What does she do? Does she play football too?"

Colton chuckled. "She certainly could if she wanted to. There'd be no stopping her if she got on the field. Luckily for me, she's a numbers girl, and she's making me a better player."

He watched Lucia laugh at Oliver and James as they terrorized half of the Sabertooths' offense. Finally, Jenna yelled to let everyone know it was time to eat. Everyone else formed a line beside the benches, and Colton chuckled at how the players dwarfed the little paper plates in their hands.

"You wanna eat?" he asked Hayley.

She only shrugged. Clearly, her brothers leaving her out of the game was still bothering her, so Colton tried another tactic.

"Hayles, I have an idea. Come with me? I know a game we can play with James and Oliver."

She stood and followed him to the table, an excited smile on her face. Colton pointed at Lucia. "You, me, and Hayley against the demon twins and a player of their choosing. Each."

"Dad! Dad! I call Dad!" Oliver shouted.

"And Uncle Coop! We'll take Uncle Coop!" James joined.

Cooper groaned. "Man, I was gonna eat."

Rudy set his plate beside Jenna's. "What are we playing to?"

"One possession each, end zone right where the field ends. Ladies first."

"Wow, Colton, I had no idea you were a lady."

Before he could respond, Lucia had sidled up to him, eyebrows scrunched. "Colton, I don't think I can—"

"It's decided, Moretti. Come join our huddle." Colton led Hayley and Lucia away from the picnic table and the rest of his teammates.

"Uncle Colt, how are we gonna beat them? They have an extra player."

"Great question. Lucia's gonna throw you the ball, and you're gonna run it all the way down to the edge of the field while Lucia and I guard you. Sound like a plan?"

Hayley thought for a moment. "Okay, but you can't let Oliver or James tackle me, they'll never let me play with them again."

"Hear that, Luc? Don't let the demon twins tackle Hayley."

"Worry about yourself, champ."

He grinned, glad things between them were back to normal. "Alright, then."

Colton grabbed a ball that'd been abandoned by the team at the mention of food. He lined Lucia and Hayley up, facing Cooper, Rudy, and the twins.

"Here you go, beautiful," he said loudly as he handed the ball to Lucia.

"Alright, hurry up. I'm hungry," Cooper called.

Lucia tossed the ball to Hayley and then moved to cover her right side. Colton followed her lead, covering Hayley's left. They moved as a unit toward the edge of the field. Rudy and Cooper didn't put much effort into catching them, but the twins were jumping around, yelling and screaming at their sister.

Just as Oliver broke through and closed in on Hayley, she threw the ball at Lucia's feet. "Ah!"

James moved toward it. In an instant, Colton picked up the ball, placed it in Lucia's hands, and threw her over his shoulder.

"Colton!" She laughed as he started to run with her. They weren't far from the arbitrary line they'd set as the end zone, so he tightened his grip on her legs. Five yards from the line, he felt little arms around his right leg, and then another set close around his left.

He pulled James and Oliver with him as he trudged closer and closer to the line. And then he was going down, Lucia with him. He turned so she'd land on top of him, her legs straddling his hips.

Lucia was laughing, holding the ball up in the air triumphantly. "We did it, Hayley! You beat the twins!" Colton looked around Lucia to see Hayley, a pleased smile on her face.

James snatched the ball from Lucia as Cooper yelled, "You can't call game when we haven't touched the ball!" Oliver ran after his brother, leaving Lucia on top of Colton in the grass.

She shifted, eyes widening as she felt him against her. She traced her finger down his chest, knowing exactly what she was doing to him. "At ease, soldier."

"If Luc says it's over, it's over." His voice came out gruff. He wasn't even sure if Cooper could hear him.

"Hey, man! This is a family picnic." Rudy was covering Hayley's eyes, turning her back toward the benches.

"Yeah, and it's still our turn." Damn Cooper. Best friend indeed. Colton made a note to ruin Cooper's next interaction with a woman.

He sighed, squeezing Lucia's waist once before releasing her. She rocked against him subtly enough to look like she was just shifting again before leaning down to whisper in his ear.

"That was for breaking your promise to not let the twins get to Hayley." She stood, motioning to the rest of their group.

"He's gonna need a minute." And then she was walking back to the center of the field.

He was going to have to break more of his promises if it meant she'd do that again.

Chapter Seventeen

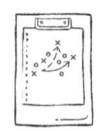

Lucia

Lucia wrapped herself in the hotel robe, hair tied up in her microfiber towel. She lay on her bed, looking up at the ceiling and pondering the fire she knew she was playing with. After her call with Isa, she'd sat in the shower, hoping to find answers in its scalding embrace.

Isa's words rang in her head. *"I just don't think you would've been intimate with him if you didn't have feelings for him,"* she'd said. *"Just be careful, okay?"*

Careful of what? She was happy with how things were. Teasing him at the picnic had been fun, and they'd set boundaries for the future. And honestly? If they slipped up again, she wasn't going to complain. Her pussy throbbed just thinking of their night together.

She let her hand drift lower absentmindedly, noticing how slick she'd become at the thought of him. Well, touching herself to thoughts of him wasn't off the table, was it? She parted herself, rubbing up and down slowly. She swirled her middle finger around her clit, the thought of Colton's body over hers encouraging her.

Her breaths became shaky and stilted. Just as she started to close in on her climax, her phone rang. She thought about letting it go to voicemail but decided against it. Her mood was further ruined when she saw who was calling.

"What do you want?" She sounded irate, but more than that, she knew she probably sounded seductive as hell.

"Been thinkin' about me?" She could hear his dumb grin from over the phone.

"I'm busy, Colton. What do you want?"

"Can't a guy check in on his girlfriend every once in a while?"

"Fake. Fake girlfriend."

"Fine. Fake. So what'cha doing?

She sighed, seeing her moment slip away. "Nothing anymore."

"Good, I love to hear it. Come hang out, I'm bored."

"That's anti-boundaries. We agreed not to hang out outside of work."

"Team bonding?" When she didn't respond, he continued. "Then bring your little tablet and tell me all the things I need to do better."

"On the field? Or do you need bedroom pointers?"

"You tell me, Luc. Anything you want me to do better?" Husky. His voice was oh-so-husky and she swallowed over the desire that grew inside her at the sound of it.

"What do I care? Won't benefit me."

"Just come, please. I'm bored." He didn't know how badly she'd *wanted* to come until he'd ruined it.

"I hate you."

"If you show up in a Vipers shirt, I'm ripping it off of you."

"I'd like to see you try."

He grunted. "Room 1524."

Lucia skipped the snacks, throwing on the Sabers sweatsuit she'd gotten her hands on. When the doors to the elevator opened, Cooper stood in the corner.

"Going up?" His smile was wide like he knew her secret.

"Oh, hi, Coop."

He tipped his cowboy hat in greeting.

She noticed that the button for the fifteenth floor was already lit up, so she cleared her throat and stared ahead. "How'd you get out of the door taping?"

He chuckled. "At this point, it's a joke. Coach Turner doesn't care, and he's realized adding more sprints or reps to practice won't stop us from doing what we like."

"It's so silly and outdated."

"Eh, it's tradition."

The elevator dinged and the doors opened. They both stepped out, and she took in the tall, glass window overlooking Dallas.

"Thank you." It was so quiet, she thought she'd imagined the words.

"Huh?" She stopped, scanning the hallway to figure out which of the many halls would take her to Colton's room.

"It's that way." He pointed to their left, his eyes crinkling with a smile. "I've never seen Colton like this. Goofy. Happy. Actually having fun during the season." He shrugged. "I don't know. He's normally so serious, sometimes even in offseason. It's different. So thank you."

"Oh, I don't think..." She didn't even know how to finish that thought.

He shrugged again. "All I'm saying is something about this is different for him. And I'm glad. It's about time." He turned, walking down the hall opposite where he'd pointed her. "See you around, Lucia."

Lucia tried not to read into his words. She knew Colton had only initially helped her out of a sense of obligation and pity. He'd felt bad that he'd gotten her into another sticky situation with the media. Still, Cooper's words were the validation she needed to know that she'd been doing something right. Maybe she'd been helping Colton in more ways than one.

His room wasn't far, and she knocked on the door, a little dazed from her conversation with Cooper. When he opened the door, he looked her up and down hungrily before his eyes turned worried as they landed on her face.

"What's wrong?"

"Huh? Oh, nothing." Unsurprisingly, he was wearing what had quickly become her favorite outfit on him. The white shirt and dark sweats slung low on his hips reignited the feeling she'd had in her room less than a half hour before.

She walked past him, trying to squash the thought of him pressing her against the wall. Instead, she focused on Cooper's words. "You didn't tell Cooper about us?"

"Us?" He closed the door, his head cocked slightly to the side.

"You know, us." She waved her hand between them. "The fact that this isn't real."

"Oh." His expression soured, and he walked past her to the bed. "I'm not much of a dater. I've had my share of"—he glanced at her before cutting his eyes away—"flings. But I haven't been in a relationship since college. I've been so focused on the game from the moment I turned pro. So, yeah, my friends are really happy for me that I have someone, and I don't want to take that away from them."

"Have you thought about a real girlfriend? I hear they're really easy to find for NFL quarterbacks. Especially Super Bowl-winning quarterbacks. They might even make you real happy. Make you more bearable."

The thought wasn't a pleasant one. She didn't like thinking of him dating someone else one bit. She wasn't even sure where the words had come from, but she almost wished she could take them back. Seeing Colton happy with someone else had the potential to hurt her feelings more than Max cheating on her, and that was an unsettling realization.

"'Real happy?' What does that mean?"

Lucia shrugged as she approached the desk, setting her tablet down.

"Do you think I'm faking happiness?" he probed.

"I don't know. I'm just saying...you're not horrible to look at. If you wanted a real girlfriend to, you know, fulfill your needs, make you happy, and be all the things you want, I'm sure you wouldn't have to look far." Now she was rambling and heading into territory she really didn't want to be in.

"Was that your twisted way of giving me a compliment?" He lay down, his hands behind his head, biceps bulging as he watched her at the desk.

"Shut up."

"For the record, I'm not really looking for a real girlfriend. I've got my hands full with you."

Her pulse hammered at his words, but she covered it with a roll of her eyes. "I mean when we break up. After the season."

"I don't know. I guess we'll see. I'm not sure it's in the cards until I'm done with the NFL. I can't really afford to be in a serious relationship when I have to spend as much time as I do training."

There was that nonsense again. He acted as if half of his friends weren't married with children. "What's your excuse for

Rudy? And Sam? And all the others who are on your Super Bowl-winning team with wives and children. Plenty of NFL players have partners."

"Yeah? And what about you? What are you going to do after the season?"

If he was asking about her love life, that would be a bust. "I sign a contract somewhere that will let me work with them until they're ready to promote me to head analyst."

"That's not what I meant, and you know it. And stop fiddling with the tablet. Come sit, we both know you didn't prep anything for us to work on."

She hadn't realized she was playing with the case of her tablet until he pointed it out. Just to spite him, she sat in the chair.

"Why aren't you looking for a real boyfriend?"

She'd known the question was coming, but hated that she couldn't sidestep this one. "After Max, they're not for me. I was already pretty sure I wasn't cut out for a relationship. He confirmed it."

His eyes darkened, his jaw set. Dangerous. This man was dangerous, and god, did she like it.

"Do you still have feelings for him?"

She scoffed, "Colton, we've talked about this. You know I don't. Love just hasn't worked in my favor.

He looked at her like he didn't believe her, so she continued, "I'm serious. So serious that I can honestly tell you I'm *glad* Max cheated on me."

She'd had inklings of that fact for a few months, maybe from the moment the news had come out, but it'd solidified when she'd realized that Colton cared more about her than Max ever had. It hurt, but she knew it was true. She just hadn't known it was something she was going to voice.

"What?" he asked incredulously.

"I'm not glad that it was so public or that it forced me to leave a job and friends I love. But I can't even begin to tell you the relief I felt at finally having an out. Our college years weren't so bad, other than around rivalry week. But once he got into the league, he changed. He's a good quarterback, and going in the first round proved it to him. He wasn't a very good boyfriend after that, but any time he thought I might be getting ready to leave him, he found a way to reel me back in. I won't bore you with specifics, but any time he did something wrong, he figured out how to fix it. He'd treat me the way I should've always been treated for a few days, and I'd give up on the notion of leaving him. He was all I knew, and to me, it just made sense to stay."

Whether good or bad, Max had been the constant that her father never had. In her mind, having him for as long as she had represented that she was doing everything right in her relationship.

"When he cheated on me, I finally had a valid reason to leave him. And I know that, to some, I had plenty of valid reasons before then, and I get that. But to me, at that time in my life, it wasn't so easy. So yeah, I'm glad he cheated on me. All I was in

Richmond was a numbers girl. The professional woman who worked hard, whose accomplishments had to remain quiet because Max couldn't handle being overshadowed. But here, I'm more than that. I have Jenna and Leigh. And you. And the team. And I can be whoever I want to be."

It felt good to get that off her chest. She hadn't told anybody, had hardly admitted it to herself, but she knew it down to the depths of her being that it was true. It was why she hadn't been able to voice her frustrations that first day to Isa when the news had broken and she'd been in a state of shock. She hadn't realized then that, in addition to feeling angry, she was *relieved*.

Colton had stilled as she spoke, his eyes on her, eyebrows drawn. In a pained voice, he whispered, "Of course you're more than numbers, Luc. You are the most intelligent person I have ever met, and that's in everything, not just football and data. You—" A strangled noise left him, and she wondered if he'd been about to say something he shouldn't. Something neither of them should have voiced.

Sensing that he needed comfort almost as much as she did, she stood and walked over to sit beside him on the bed. She kept her distance from him, but when he slid his hand across the bed toward her, she moved hers so that her pinky met his.

She hadn't realized that he'd put on *Pretty Woman* until she heard Julia Roberts telling the saleswomen what a huge mistake they'd made by not helping her the day before. Lucia smiled, knowing Colton had put the movie on for her before she'd even come into the room.

His bed was twenty times more comfortable than hers, and she sank into it happily. Around the time Richard Gere threw a wad of cash on the bed, Lucia's eyelids began to feel heavy, and her phone vibrated beside her. Colton was already glaring down at it, and before Lucia had decided whether to let it ring out or send it straight to voicemail, he'd picked it up.

"What are you *doing*?" she hissed at him.

"Lucia Moretti's phone." Colton's voice had an angry edge to it, but she was thankful he held his temper at bay.

She heard an angry male voice on the other end, and she jumped over him to try to grab the phone that was firmly locked in his hand.

"May I ask who's calling?" He paused. "Max?" Another pause. "Clark? Hmm, that doesn't sound familiar. Maybe you have the wrong number?"

"Colton!" Her whole body was on top of his as she grappled with him for the phone. He wrapped his free arm tightly around her, anchoring her to him and holding her arms down in the process. His entire body was solid muscle, hard like stone, and she wiggled against him to try to pry the phone from his grasp once again.

His pupils dilated as she rubbed against him in just the right way, his brows drawing together. When she realized the reason, she rubbed her hand against his hardening cock, a smirk on her face.

"Give me the phone, big boy," she whispered. The last thing she wanted was for Max to hear *that* little nickname. His arm slackened a bit, just enough for her to wiggle free and grab the phone.

"Hello," she said coolly.

"Lucia, what the fuck was that? You're screening my calls via that *asshole*? Are you blind?"

Colton's jaw was clenched like he'd heard the words Max was yelling at her. She walked into the bathroom, ignoring the embarrassment heating her insides. Colton was probably judging her for not having Max blocked, much less speaking to him. Especially after what she'd just admitted to him.

"I don't have him screening my calls, he's just being silly."

"He's being an asshole, is what he's doing."

"Can you blame him?" Her words were so sharp that she surprised even herself. She'd rarely stood up for herself in her relationship with Max, but she was tired of this game he was playing. She'd finally managed to escape him, and he just wouldn't leave her alone.

"The fuck does that mean?"

"It means, why the fuck are you calling me? Why are you still texting me? We're done. You made sure of that the minute you went out with that woman."

"Amelia has nothing to do with this."

Amelia. She had a name. And what a way to find it out. Like he still spoke with her, intimately. Sure, she could admit she was relieved that their relationship had ended, but that didn't change the sting of knowing that he'd preferred someone over her. Suddenly, her whole body felt heavy, drained and exhausted.

"Please stop calling me. Unless you have something important to say, please leave me alone." She hated how the words sounded so weak, like she was pleading with him. She *should've* blocked him, but even still, something inside of her wanted to give him the benefit of the doubt.

"Is this important enough? Your boyfriend is the biggest asshole on the face of the planet. He's going to ruin you. You'll come crawling back to me soon. And by the way, the next time my name comes out of his mouth, I'm serving his ass. You let him know that."

Tears pricked Lucia's eyes. She'd told Colton that the only valid reason she'd had to leave him was the infidelity, but more and more, she hated herself for not seeing the abuse as reason enough.

"Like I said, unless you have something important to say to *me*, please stop calling."

"Lu, I do. I do have something important to say to you, okay? I'm sorry, baby. Look, it was a mistake, and I know that. Let's talk it out. If it's what you want, I'll stop calling after you let me explain myself. When you're not with *him*."

She knew she should just say no. She knew she'd probably live to regret it, but wasn't this what she'd been waiting for? For him to want to talk it out and apologize? And she'd had enough realizations about her relationship with Max that she no longer felt like a conversation with him would lead to her going back to him. Even if she didn't necessarily believe he'd leave her alone, it was worth a try.

She dropped her voice, not wanting Colton to hear her relent. "Fine, but I'm busy with the season right now. I'll let you know when I have some time. Give me some space until then. And you and I will just be talking, Max. Nothing more than that."

"Of course, baby. Just tell me when."

The word, which used to be a comfort, only made her skin itch.

"Goodbye, Max." She clicked her phone off, walking back into Colton's room. His head turned from the TV, eyes fixed on her face, concern written in every groove of his face and every shift in his chest.

"Luc..." So oddly tender.

She shook her head, climbing onto the tall bed and sinking deep into the warmth of the sleek sheets. She felt a gentle hand trace up and down her waist, lulling her into sleep's clutches.

It was hours later when she awoke, the TV still humming softly, lights off, a strong, muscled arm tight around her, pressing her back into a solid chest. She thought about trying to leave but remembered the cold, depressing ride she would face to get to her floor and instead nestled closer, thankful for Colton's presence, more and more an anchor in the raging waters of her life.

Chapter Eighteen

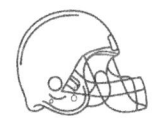

COLTON

There were a few NFL rules that Colton wasn't a fan of. But the one he truthfully didn't understand was the concept of being able to lose in overtime without his offense having the chance to touch the ball. His success on the field was ultimately a testament to how hard he worked, so to lose on the road to a team who'd started overtime with the ball simply because of a lucky coin toss? That just felt wrong. He hated how powerless it'd left him. At the end of a hard game, he didn't even have a chance to get on the field to try to win it. If he were a cartoon character, he'd have had smoke coming from his ears.

The moment the ball had found Dallas' wide receiver in the end zone and the stadium erupted in cheers, Colton had tossed his helmet to the ground. He'd tried so hard, and it felt like the loss erased the seven wins they'd managed.

He tried to be cordial as he shook the hands of each of his opponents, clapping some on the back who he was on semi-friendly terms with, but what he really wanted to do was take his anger out on the refs for enforcing a dumb rule. Yeah, he recognized it wasn't their fault, but all he had was the messenger.

The familiar tightness in his chest only tightened further as reporters swarmed around him like vultures in the tunnel. He could hardly hear them as they talked over each other, though none as loud as the disappointed voice in his head.

He had a few minutes to shower and change before the press conference, so he dodged the questions and ducked into the locker room. He let the steam clear his mind, scrubbing at his skin until it felt raw. Pulling on a Sabers sweatsuit, he tossed his stuff into his overnight bag and pushed his way out of the locker room. He wasn't in the mood to hear Coach Turner's lecture, as enlightening as it might've been.

He hadn't expected Lucia to be standing there in one of her sexy, green pantsuits he had started to love, nor had he expected the tension in his body to halve just by being in her presence.

"Moretti? What're you doing here?" Usually, the analysts packed up and hopped on the bus early. He knew because he always looked for her as he and his teammates filed into the big, air-conditioned units.

He hated the look of pity on her face but couldn't find it in himself to be upset with her for it.

"I...I just wanted to check on you before the press conference." She moved further down the hall, putting some distance between herself and the locker room, clearly wanting Colton to follow her.

When she turned back to him, her brows were knitted and she was wringing her hands. She didn't look away from his eyes, opening and closing her mouth as if figuring out how to say what she wanted.

"Overtime rules are fucking awful," he said, hoping it would help her find her words.

She laughed, nodding. "Yeah. They really are. Glad you're doing well enough to joke." She fiddled with her ring like she always did when she didn't know what to say, or when she was nervous. Colton reached a hand out to clasp hers.

She cleared her throat. "Just remember that a loss isn't just on you. That this season is still salvageable. But most importantly, remember that you're more than your team's record and your stats. Don't let them make you think otherwise, okay?" She squeezed his hand.

And just like that, the rest of the tension in his body was gone. It'd taken her a few sentences and a squeeze of his hand for her to ease the stress of the game. He couldn't believe she'd ever thought that she was *only* an analyst when her mere presence comforted him more than anything or anybody else.

He wanted to beg her to never leave so he could always feel so at peace.

Instead, he asked, "See you on the plane?"

"Can't very well stay here, can I?" She grinned, squeezing his hand once more before heading in the direction of the team busses.

When he'd asked Lucia to come over to hang out and watch a movie the next night, he'd thought he would get more resistance. He knew he had agreed with her stupid rule not to fraternize outside of work, but he didn't care for it one bit. He was chasing the feeling he'd had in his grasp that night with her at his house. Hell, he was chasing the high he had been feeling since the moment she'd walked into that damn boardroom.

He'd known he was attracted to her from the beginning. But this was something else entirely. This was making up reasons to see her. This was finding ways to touch her. This was trying to spend the little bit of free time that he had with her, even if it meant being more tired than he was used to the next morning. Though that could've been because of the thoughts about her that kept him up at night.

Having her pressed against him—like he had in his hotel room a few nights before, held tight to his chest until his coach had woken them with a loud bang on his hotel door—was decidedly his new favorite way to sleep.

He knew he was only digging himself a deeper hole, knew he was only biding his time until he inevitably got hurt, because she so obviously didn't feel as strongly for him as he did for her. But he couldn't bring himself to care. If this was all the time he'd get with her, just until the beginning of January, he would try to make it count as much as she'd let him.

His phone rang, and he answered, entering the pin to let Lucia up his driveway. His heart was beating faster than normal as he tidied around the couch Maya had helped him find, along with all the rest of his decor. He set out a blanket, trying to create the illusion of comfort his sister always seemed to talk about when she visited.

He walked to the tall door, taking a breath after the second knock before opening it. Lucia stood there in a pair of black sweatpants—likely from her time with the Vipers, but he had no way of confirming that—and the Sabers sweatshirt he'd given her. She was weighed down by two bags of...Were those groceries?

"I want to make it abundantly clear that, yes, I *am* breaking my rule about not hanging out with you outside of work, but it's only because I feel bad about the overtime rules and I know how grumpy you are about the loss. And there were reporters outside, so really, this is for Tessa. And also, you're my only friend here." A lie, but he'd let her get away with it. He was starting to think he'd let her get away with anything.

He took the heavy bags from her. "What's all this?"

"Oh. That. *That's* because I rarely see you eat anything but pizza, and I think it's high time you eat something healthy."

"You're...You're cooking for me?"

"Think of it as 'I'm here despite knowing I shouldn't be, and if I were home, like I'm *supposed* to be, I'd be making this for myself.' So you just happen to be with me on a day I'm actually cooking. But don't think you'll just be sitting around. I'm putting you to work."

And, boy, did she. He chopped all the vegetables for the salad as she worked on the pasta and chicken. He'd never had much time to learn how to cook, so he rarely did so for himself. Landon and Maya were the chefs of his family, and it was probably best that way.

They worked in silence, the sounds of chicken sizzling and water boiling mixing with the smells of Italian food.

After a while, she spoke. "Okay. In exchange for this lovely and delicious meal, you have to tell me something."

He chuckled. "I knew you weren't doing this out of the goodness of your heart."

"Never."

"Shoot."

"The first day I was here, you mentioned something about having my best friend sleep with your tight end to win our rivalry game. Explain."

Colton sighed. He didn't want to talk about it because he didn't even know what to believe. On the other hand, he owed her an explanation, especially if he'd been wrong.

"Isabella and Vinny were together around the time of our rivalry game."

"Yeah."

"After Lincoln won, Clark found me on the field. He told me about how Vinny had been talking to her about our plays, and that's how you guys beat us. I confronted Vinny, and he denied it, but I just thought he was trying to save his skin."

After a few years had passed, Colton didn't think too often about what'd happened. He had only relived the loss of the national title when the Sabers played the Vipers. But it had replayed more often in his mind when Lucia started working with him. Where before he'd felt angry and powerless thinking about it, he now only felt tired. It had been so long ago, and he didn't care as much, especially now that he'd learned it probably wasn't true.

Lucia set down the wooden spoon in her hand and turned to face Colton. "I can swear to you on my life that Isa was not interested in your playbook. She was just hooking up with Vinny. I..." She sighed. "I wouldn't be surprised if Max just said that to piss you off."

Colton nodded, having realized as much over the past few months. He owed Vinny an apology. "I think so too. But I didn't realize that until recently. I just believed him, and that fueled my hatred for him, and for you, for years."

"Well, you guys hated each other long before that game."

"Yeah, but not like that. I wanted to go to the board about it. I had never been so mad. We were supposed to make playoffs that year too."

"Yeah, I know. I'm sorry, Colton. I really am."

"I don't know what's worse: the fact that I was so sure of how good we were that I believed him, or the knowledge that you guys won because you were better."

She resumed stirring the pasta as it started to boil over the pot. "I know this might not be the right thing to say, but who cares? You won the Super Bowl last season. He has yet to do that. And if we're being honest, you're a far better quarterback than him."

His heart hammered in his ears. Lucia's compliments were only given when she felt they were worth giving, so his chest swelled.

"How have you been since he called?"

She strained the pasta and readied the chicken and sauce before she responded. "I'm okay. It definitely made me realize how much shit I took from him while we were together. I've been going through and analyzing it all, trying to figure out why I stayed for so long when he treated me like that. I had a lot of opportunities to leave, but he always found a way to keep me there."

She placed the pot in the sink and then added the sauce and pasta to a bowl. "I think I was always going to be his backup.

And that's why he's struggling so much with me moving on. I'm just glad I didn't marry him."

Me too.

Colton added all the parts of the salad into a bowl and mixed it, then walked the bowl to his dining table as he thought over her words. He couldn't imagine Lucia being anybody's backup. She was the most ambitious, intelligent, and beautiful person he'd ever met. He wondered if things would've been different if he and Lucia had gone to the same college. If he'd met her first.

"Abusive relationships are hard to navigate, especially when you don't recognize that you're in one." As he spoke, he thought about his parents and how much his mother suffered by staying with his father.

"You sound like you're talking from experience."

He shrugged, watching her dump the pasta into another big bowl before placing it on the dining table beside the salad. "My parents weren't happy together. My mom never said anything to me about it, but I think if she was guaranteed full custody of us, she would've left him."

For as long as he could remember, up until his mother got sick, his parents hadn't agreed on much. His father had always wanted him and Landon on the football field, and their mother had wanted them to go to school and have social lives. His father had wanted them to do drills and watch games, and their mother had wanted them to see her side of the family and learn her culture. She'd wanted to give them a well-rounded life filled with more than just football, but as with everything, their father had won.

"Will you tell me about your mom?"

Colton grabbed a set of plates and two sets of silverware as he thought about how he wanted to respond. "What about her?"

"What was she like?"

Lucia took the plates from him and began piling pasta and salad onto each before walking them into the living room. He followed her, mulling over her question as she set the food on the coffee table and sat on the ground in front of the couch. She took a bite of the food and hummed contentedly.

He sat beside her and finally answered her question. "She was...she was amazing. The funniest person you could ever meet. Even after she got sick, she was cracking jokes to try to make things easier for all of us. You know, my dad always talks about how he's been at all of my games since I started playing football, and that might be true, but my mom was there too, and she never expected anything from me for showing up. She was just happy I was having fun. Just happy to watch her children do what they loved."

"What was she like while you were growing up?"

That was a little tougher to answer. More complex. "I can't lie, it wasn't always easy. My mom was the best mom, truly, and she put her life on hold for us and my dad. She had three kids, all of whom played very high-level sports, and she was always the one to shuttle us to our many practices, feed us, and honestly, love us. But a part of me always resented that I'm half Indian."

Lucia's head whipped around to face him. At her questioning look, he continued. "It was hard to fit in, even in California. I went to a school with a lot of white people, and even if they didn't mean to make me feel that way, it was always clear that I wasn't one of them. My name may not sound ethnic, but one look at me, and you can tell I'm different. And, not that I had much contact with other Indians, but when I did, it was clear I wouldn't fit in there either. I didn't speak the language, didn't practice the religion, and barely knew anything about the culture.

"My mom tried to teach us, and our grandparents wanted to see us more and teach us all about our culture, but our dad was very strict with me and Landon growing up. We rarely had time to do anything outside of school and football. And football, it kind of took it all away. It didn't matter that I didn't fit in with any group of people, because the moment I got out on that field, it went away. People stopped caring as much when they saw what I could do with a ball. And I think, after a certain point, I just didn't really want to learn anymore because I'd found where I fit in. I was scared that learning about my culture had the potential to remove that for me and thrust me back into that same confusing place I'd grown up in."

He smiled sadly. "Now that she's gone, I regret that part of my childhood immensely, but as a kid, all I could see was the fact that others saw me outside of their predetermined boxes." He shrugged as he watched her hand hover dangerously close to his. "I rarely deal with anything like that anymore. But in high school, and college, and even when I first started in the league, everyone had something to say about my ethnicity. They love putting people in boxes, don't they?"

He was trying to lighten the mood after the surprisingly deep confession he'd made to Lucia, one he hadn't even talked through with his siblings, people who probably felt the same as him. But something about Lucia's question had seemed so genuine that he'd wanted to tell her how he'd felt all those years.

She lowered her voice to a whisper. "I'm sorry anybody ever made you feel that way. You deserve so much better than that. And if you ever decide you want to learn more about your culture, I'd love to learn, too."

Colton's cheeks burned at her words. "Thank you," he whispered back as he picked up the remote and clicked on the first streaming service that popped up. It'd been so long since Colton used his TV that he had to type in his login.

Before he pulled up a movie, he set the remote down and turned to her. "And I'm sorry about everything with Clark. I really am. You deserve so much better than what he gave you."

She shrugged, taking another bite of the food in front of her and refusing to meet his eyes. "Thank you. It sucks, but the whole thing just proved to me that love isn't real. Or if it is, it doesn't last."

"You really think that?"

"Tell me one relationship you know that's lasted, and not just out of convenience."

Immediately, he said, "Rudy and Jenna. Chris and Elaine. Sam and Kelly." Honestly, a lot of his teammates were in healthy, stable relationships. There'd only been a few who'd married women who may not have had the best of intentions.

"I guess time will tell, and maybe it works out for some people. But I was raised in a house with a single father whose heart had been broken by the woman he thought was the love of his life. A woman who couldn't stand the sight of him, and who *chose* to walk out on him and her child. And you know what my dad did? He kept trying. Kept looking for love everywhere he went, convinced he was gonna find someone someday. All that ended up happening was him jumping from one unfulfilling relationship to the next, and he never has found that soulmate he's been seeking."

Colton searched Lucia's face for a hint of what she was feeling. Sure, he'd lost his mother, but that had been due to illness. He couldn't imagine having a parent leave him by choice, and it made him angry to think of anybody leaving what he could only picture as a perfect, clever, and happy little Lucia.

"I'm sorry, Luc."

She shrugged again, this time meeting his eyes. "It is what it is. I've had a lot of time to deal with it and how it made us feel. I don't remember her a ton, but I know we were better off without her. My dad loved me the best that he could while dealing with his own demons."

Colton set his hand on her knee and squeezed gently. She gave him a small smile, grabbing the remote and clicking on a movie he'd never heard of while they ate the food they'd made together.

Chapter Nineteen

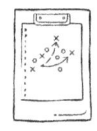

Lucia

Three days later, Lucia was still reeling from the conversation she'd had at Colton's house. She hadn't meant to tell him so much about her relationship with Max, and she certainly hadn't meant to explore her relationship with her parents any further, but something about the way he'd looked at her, like he'd wanted to know every little thing about her, had made her feel oddly seen.

She'd known his dad had messed him up pretty badly from past conversations with him and what she'd gathered at his family dinner. She'd known that he felt the only way people would love or care about him was if he kept winning because that's what his dad had conditioned him to believe. What she hadn't known was how hard he'd tried to fit himself into two different worlds that refused to let him in. Despite his best efforts to joke with her afterward, she could tell how heavily it weighed on him, and it hurt to know how poorly he'd been treated.

She wanted to show him that none of that mattered to her. While his culture and football were important parts of him, they weren't all of him, and they didn't define him. She wanted to make sure he knew that, no matter how their relationship ended.

Her eyes found him on the sidelines, sitting on a bench, head in his hands. Her heart hiccupped at the image, feeling an unusual need to go down onto the field and hug him. He'd played a pretty good game so far, helping the Sabers take an early three-score lead, but defense had started struggling during the second half, leaving them down by four points.

As defense got a stop and special teams ran out onto the field, Cooper walked up and patted Colton on the shoulder to tell him it was their turn to take the field. Colton stood, putting his helmet on and clapping his hands. They only had ten seconds left in the game, and they needed a Hail Mary if they wanted a serious shot at playoffs.

Lucia bit the tip of her pen cap anxiously, watching Colton get set up on the field. Any noise from the fans in the stands faded away, and she could hear her heart racing in her ears. For her, and Colton too, this was more than just the team winning. It was what they had been working toward all season. She knew he had it in him, had watched plenty of his film to know he could make it happen. It would be up to the o-line to keep him safe and up to his receivers to run their routes properly and get away from coverage.

Chris, the center, hiked the ball to Colton, and Lucia forgot how to breathe as he caught it and looked downfield. Cooper was struggling to get open with two defensive backs running alongside him, which left Devin, who wasn't doing much better. Tennessee had pushed all their backs to the end zone, knowing what the Sabers would try.

The analyst room was silent as Colton slapped the ball once and then sent it up toward the end zone. He'd chosen Cooper, and Lucia's heart stopped completely as the ball sailed toward the tight end.

She couldn't see the field well enough from their box, turning her attention to the TV just as Cooper jumped higher than a safety, and the ball landed squarely in his hands. Lucia jumped up with the rest of the analysts, screaming along with them as cords and papers were knocked from the tables.

She watched Colton jump up in the air, pumping a fist before lying on his back and looking up at the sky. The tension she'd seen in him just one play earlier was gone, and the TV showed how wide his smile was. When he stood back up to shake hands with the other team, she thought he turned to look at her in her box.

When he waved, she knew he had.

She waved back, grin wide. Wrapped up in the moment, she blew him a kiss, promising herself it was only because people were watching. She ignored the voice in her head that told her she was lying to herself, too excited to care. Her heart was so swollen with pride, she felt it beating out the craziest of rhythms.

Post-game moved quickly, and before Lucia knew it, she was being shepherded out onto the tarmac and into the private plane. She hadn't even had time to stop outside of the locker room but knew Colton probably wouldn't have had time to talk to her before the press conference anyway.

Lucia heard the players and coaches get on the plane, but the privacy curtain was closed so she couldn't see Colton. She settled into her seat, pulled out her tablet, and began going through the film she'd received from the game.

A few moments after they'd reached cruising altitude, her phone buzzed.

Colton

Come say hi.

She couldn't stop the smile that spread across her face as she responded.

Lucia

No <3

I don't want to walk by the whole team.

Colton: Not even for your boyfriend who had a very long day and deserves a hug?

Colton: I'll meet you halfway.

She sighed, closing her tablet and placing it in her purse.

Lucia: Fake. And fine, I'm coming.

When she walked past the privacy curtain, she entered the small, empty flight attendant area. A moment later, Colton walked through his own privacy curtain, a heart-stopping grin on his face as he scooped Lucia into his arms and twirled her around.

"Hi," he whispered.

"Congratulations, Superstar." Her grin matched his as she looked up at him. Something on his face changed at her words, and he set her down against the wall, his warm hands molding to her waist.

His eyes dropped to the new necklace she'd purchased during a late-night shopping spree a few days ago. He slid a finger underneath the pearl pendant. "This new?"

She nodded wordlessly, trying to calm the feeling his touch elicited inside her.

"I like it." His voice was husky, and there was that damn heart hiccup again. His hand dropped back down to her side as he said, "Thanks for being the best analyst a quarterback could ever ask for."

She scoffed, "Oh, please, Colton. You could've done that in your sleep. You were throwing like that long before I came along."

Her breath caught as his face dropped toward hers, his lips inches from hers. "No, Moretti. You were the only thing on my mind when I threw that pass. I heard your voice coaching me, not Turner or Fillmore. Not even my dad."

Her heart tripped at his words, and her body warmed at having him so close. His eyes dropped to her mouth, and they stayed there as his tongue slipped over his bottom lip. His gaze flicked back up to hers, pleading, a question clear as day in them.

She leaned forward and kissed him, expecting it to end with a light peck. She was pleasantly surprised when his tongue slipped between her lips and his kiss became deeper, needier.

She was panting when he pulled away, his left thumb finding her parted lips and running across them. His right hand, which had stayed anchored to her waist until then, drifted lower toward the warmest part of her.

"You soaked for me, baby?"

She sucked in a breath at his words but didn't respond, her brain practically short-circuiting.

"I just wanna make you feel as good as I feel right now. Let me do that for you." His finger lightly brushed against her inner thigh through the fabric of her pants.

"We ca—can't," she managed to stutter out. "Someone could walk in."

His lips dropped to the shell of her ear, even as his hand stilled against her. "Wasn't being in public the standard you set?"

She shivered at his breath on her ear, and god, she wanted it. She let her head fall back against the side of the plane where she rested, nodding once. She was strung so tight, want coiled so taut inside her, she was sure she would come within seconds. And something about letting him do something so filthy to her when the rest of their team was celebrating feet away excited her.

He flipped her so his back was against the plane and hers was against his hard chest. One rough hand held her to him by the center of her stomach, and the other pulled at the button of her pants, yanking down the zipper and slipping inside.

Her head fell back against him as his fingers slid under her lacy underwear, so far past caring whether or not someone might walk in on them. He rubbed the slickness around, the side of his thumb circling her clit. She was nearing the point of begging when his finger finally sank into her.

The hand that rested on her stomach flew to clamp over her mouth as a whimper left her. "Careful, sweetheart. I love it when you moan for me, but I'm not so sure the staff will feel the same." His warm breath heated her neck, and she bit down on her lip. He added another finger, pumping them inside of her slowly while he rubbed her clit.

Her hips bucked, begging for more. He chuckled, increasing the pace to match, and one of her hands came around to lace in his hair tightly. The feeling inside her continued to build, her hand tugging harder.

"That's right, ride my fingers, pretty girl. You wanna come for me? I want you to come for me." His words almost pushed her over the edge, but what finally did her in was the graze of his teeth against her neck.

Her hips moved again, and he held her tight as she began to shake, seeing stars. Every cell in her body spasmed, tingling and throbbing. Pleasure tore through her, and she was thankful his hand remained over her mouth. She choked on a moan as his fingers curled deep inside of her.

"That's right. Come all over my fingers, Moretti. They're all yours."

When she finished, her head turned to the side so she could look at him, feeling the flush of her cheeks. His grin was wicked, and he took the fingers that'd been inside of her and put them in his mouth, his eyes locked on hers.

Sex with Colton had been spectacular, by far the best she'd ever had. Had he placed himself in a prime position to have ruined all other men for her? Probably. Okay, definitely. But nothing put him firmly in first place more than the orgasm that'd just ripped through her as the entirety of the Sabertooths' staff, players, and coaches talked and laughed feet away.

"Come over later."

At her narrowed eyes, he laughed.

"Not like that. The media—and Tessa—will want to see you with me to celebrate this game, or they'll assume we've broken up."

She wasn't sure if her brain was just scrambled or if he was actually making sense, but she was thawing to the idea.

"Come on, it's Thanksgiving. We need to be with the ones we fake love. I'll be a perfect gentleman and keep my hands to myself." His voice dropped. "If that's what you really want."

She pulled away from him slightly, adjusting her pants and blazer and then running a hand through her hair. "Okay, for the media. But you better keep your hands to yourself."

As the final word left her mouth, TJ, a running back, walked into the little space. When he saw them, he grinned knowingly.

"Hey, Colt, Lucia. Didn't mean to interrupt." He continued walking back toward the staff section, likely to use the bathroom.

"A kiss goodbye?" Colton asked, laughing when Lucia smacked his shoulder. He opened the privacy curtain, waving his hand in the direction of her colleagues. "For the people?" he whispered.

She was going to kill him. She was going to kill him dead. Still, she pushed herself up using his shoulders and pecked his lips, hating the wide grin on his face.

When she returned to her seat, head spinning, heart racing, and feeling as though the eyes of the entire staff rested upon her, she found a new text message. In response to her last message about her coming, he'd responded:

> Colton
>
> Oh, you most certainly did.
>
> Meet me in the facility garage.

She resisted the urge to send a picture of herself childishly sticking her tongue out at him and shut off her phone.

Colton had been right. Four people were outside the gate of his house, snapping pictures of them as they drove up his driveway. Lucia rolled her eyes at his smug expression.

They'd grabbed snacks from the facility—most of which were gross protein shakes or protein bars, but Lucia was a beggar and therefore had lost her right to choose—and when they got to the living room, they laid them out on the coffee table.

"Do I get to pick the movie tonight?" Colton opened the box of pizza he'd conjured.

"Do you ever?" She watched his arm flex as he reached for the remote, her mind flashing back to the putty he'd turned her into on the plane. Shaking her head, she continued, "But I will give you options tonight. We can either watch *The Bachelor* or a romcom."

"Wow, you're so good to me."

Lucia swiped the pizza he'd lifted to his mouth, taking a bite. "I know."

Colton glared at her. "You'd think you'd be a little nicer to the man who had you clutching at him and practically moaning his name as you came a few hours ago."

Lucia gaped at him. "Wha—shut your mouth! Off limits! Anti-boundaries!"

"Oh, *now* it's off limits, but on the plane, it was all *'Colton, make me come'* and *'Colton, look at my bedroom eyes.'*" The pitch of his voice went up when he pretended to be her.

"I *never*—"

"*'Colton, your fingers feel so good inside of me.'*" He was laughing hard, his shoulders shaking at the look on her face. She turned the TV to an episode of *The Bachelor* to spite him, ignoring his offers of pizza and burrowing under a blanket that she'd found on his couch.

After the first episode, Colton pleaded with her, "Lucia, please. Tell me how to convince you to change it to anything else. I will proudly recite every line of *Pretty Woman* if you make it stop."

"Beg."

His pupils dilated. "What?"

"Beg for my forgiveness."

He tsked as he dropped to his knees in front of her. "I thought you wanted me to keep my hands to myself tonight."

"Yes, use your words."

"Not the kind of begging I hoped you meant, but fine." He clasped his hands together. "Lucia Middle Name Moretti, please forgive me for teasing you about how well I know your body. I will never mock you in that high-pitched voice ever again."

"Liar. And I don't have a middle name."

His eyes remained steadfastly on hers, and he stuck his bottom lip out, pretending he was about to cry.

She rolled her eyes. "Fine, we can switch it." She closed out of the reality TV show and searched for one of her beloved romcoms.

"You just like seeing me on my knees."

She absolutely did. She loved him on his knees in front of her. And while that thought in and of itself wasn't scary, the realization that came from it *was*. She actually *liked* Colton. Like, maybe less in a platonic *hey it's fun to spend time with you as a friend* way and more in a *shit I may be developing feelings for you that I don't comprehend but are definitely not okay* way. Every moment she'd spent with him, she learned something new and endearing, a puzzle piece to help her see the whole picture of Colton Beaumont.

And none of that boded well for her, because their end date was fast approaching, and he'd only ever agreed to this because he felt bad about the part he'd played in causing their...situation.

She made a point to remember to text Isa about their plans for her visit to Charleston. If there was anyone who could help her get her head on straight, it was Isa. And maybe she'd invite Jenna and Leigh just to prove to herself she had friends in Charleston who weren't her fake boyfriend. The fake boyfriend who she would only be seeing in professional settings after January.

She sank lower into the plush couch at the thought, wrapping the blanket tighter around herself and ignoring the concerned look Colton tossed her way as *You've Got Mail* began playing.

Chapter Twenty

COLTON

Colton didn't typically get to see his family for Thanksgiving since the chances of him, Landon or Maya playing on the day of were high, and without the support of his siblings, he wasn't really interested in having a tense dinner with his father.

Which meant he usually ended up at Rudy and Jenna's house for a slightly late Thanksgiving dinner, often with Cooper and some of their other teammates in tow. This year, Lucia's father was on a cruise for the weekend, so she'd agreed to accompany him to the Barrett household. He knew her only other option was to sit alone in her house all day, but he had still been ecstatic when she'd finally conceded.

Lucia had also asked him on several occasions if the reason he wasn't going to his father's house for the holiday was because of her outburst. To which he continued to respond honestly that, no, he just couldn't stand to be around his father for very long, especially if none of his siblings were there with him.

When he and Lucia arrived, Jenna immediately put them both to work mashing potatoes, making casseroles, and warming bread—notably passing the easier jobs to him, as she'd learned over the years that he wasn't the best in the kitchen.

Colton spent most of his time bothering Lucia, bumping into her, or rearranging the utensils she was using. When she got tired of his antics, a barely there smile pulling at the corners of her mouth, she banished him from the kitchen, telling him to make himself useful and play with the kids.

Cooper was already outside kicking a soccer ball around with the twins and Hayley. Cooper, Colton, and Lucia had all gotten there a bit earlier to help out where they could before Jenna's friends and more of the team showed up. The Barretts didn't usually host too many people, but every year, more and more showed up.

As couples and families trickled in, Colton split his time between playing with the kids, getting the adults drinks, and setting up the folding tables and chairs in Rudy's massive living room. Rudy was so busy helping Jenna that Colton was happy to take over hosting duties. Plus, setting up the living room meant being able to subtly glance over at Lucia as she helped in the kitchen.

After a couple of hours of letting people into the house, he opened the door to a very familiar and very distressed face.

"Mai? What're you doing here?"

Her eyebrows remained knitted even as she tried to smile at him. Voice raspy, like she'd been crying, she asked, "Does Rudy have room for one more?"

Colton wrapped an arm around her shoulders and walked her inside. "Of course," he said softly. He led her down a quieter hallway. "Tell me what happened."

Maya cleared her throat and shook her head. "I don't really feel like talking about it. I just—I needed to get away from my friend group, and you were the first person I could think of, and I knew you would probably be at Rudy's like you usually are for Saturday Thanksgiving, and..." She inhaled a shaky breath. "Is Lucia here? I'd like to pretend everything's okay. I don't want to talk about it," she reiterated.

Colton looked over her reddened cheeks and tired eyes, battling with himself on whether he should press her or not. He wasn't used to his vibrant and happy sister being so sad, and he felt his protective instinct increase. Still, he wanted to respect her wishes.

"Okay, that's okay. Let's go hang out with Lucia."

They walked back toward the kitchen, Lucia's worried glance finding them before it morphed into excitement at seeing his sister.

"Maya! It's so great to see you." Lucia's eyes found his, and without even meaning to, he seemed to communicate something to her that she understood. She approached them, putting her arms around his sister and taking her into the kitchen, chattering about how badly she needed to speak to *any* other Beaumont sibling. He was glad to see a genuine smile on his sister's face at that, gladder still to see how well Lucia and Maya got along.

He stood behind the couch as his teammates watched college games, keeping an eye on his sister and Lucia the entire time. When the food was ready, he helped carry the trays to the tables he'd set up.

"Time to eat. TV off," Jenna called. When a few of his teammates groaned, she glared at them. "Fine, leave it on, but turn it down so the people who actually like each other can talk amongst themselves."

They did as they were told, knowing better than to disobey Jenna Barrett twice in her own home. Cooper came inside, Oliver on his shoulders and James dragging from his leg. Hayley was talking to one of Sam's daughters, though Colton couldn't remember her name.

"Coop, could you make sure they wash their hands before they eat, please?" Jenna was already directing people as they grabbed plates and started piling food onto them.

When Maya heard Jenna, her widening eyes landed on Cooper, mouth slightly open like she wanted to say something. Cooper's expression mirrored hers when he saw Maya beside Lucia.

"Mai, what are you—when did you get here?" Colton was surprised at his friend's concerned tone, eyes flicking between his best friend and his sister.

"I—I missed Colton."

Hayley tugged Cooper toward the hallway with the guest bathroom, and he followed her reluctantly. Colton's phone rang, his father's name popping up on his screen. He groaned but answered it, walking out the door Cooper had just brought the kids in through.

"Dad."

"I've called you twice today. We need to go over the game."

"Dad, I'm busy right now. Can we talk about this later?"

"Busy? Do you even care about playoffs? Your focus is being pulled, that much is clear."

"What does that mean?"

"It means your incredibly rude girlfriend is distracting you from your game and may very well ruin your chances at getting through to playoffs this season."

He ignored his father's words, tired of the variations of the same conversation over and over again. His father had been warning him a minimum of twice a week since meeting her that Lucia was going to be the reason he lost out on another chance at the Super Bowl. As if the woman who'd single-handedly saved his game could ever be the cause. If anything, like he'd told her on the plane, she was now the voice in his head that reminded him about the best way to scramble, not to release the ball too early, not to slap the ball the same way before he threw the same pass. Knowing she was in that analyst box watching him each game lit a fire under him like nothing else ever had.

His eyes watched her through the screen door, a glass of wine in her hand as she spoke with Maya. While the tired conversation with his father wouldn't end productively, it did remind him that this was temporary. After January, she may very well never speak to these people outside of the game-day environment again, and that thought had him swallowing over a rock. No matter how much she seemed to genuinely enjoy everyone, this was a duty for her, a way to ensure she got to keep her job and stay ahead of the media.

"Dad, is Maya staying with you while she's here?"

"The last time I heard from Maya, she was in Asia. What does that have to do with playoffs?"

Colton held back a scoff. Maya had come back from the Open in Hong Kong three weeks ago, and he was sure she'd tried calling their father since then. He probably hadn't answered his only daughter's calls.

He was glad Maya was in town, even if it wasn't necessarily under pleasant circumstances. He rarely got to spend time with her, and having her stay with him would make his often-lonely house feel more like a home. The way that Lucia had started to over the past few weeks. He grimaced when he realized where his thoughts were heading once again.

"Dad, I'm gonna have to call you back. I'm at a team event." And for the first time in as long as he could remember, he hung up on his father before he'd even had a chance to tell Colton that his call was more important than any team event, a line Colton had heard plenty of times over the years.

When he was back inside the house, he piled some food onto his plate and sat beside Lucia.

"Everything okay?" she asked him softly, her eyes trained on Leigh and the conversation she'd been a part of with Jenna and Maya before. Her hand moved closer to him on the table, though she stopped before she reached his.

"Yeah, just my dad."

Her eyes snapped to him. "Is he upset with you for missing Thanksgiving with him?"

Colton scoffed, "Right, that would be the normal parental response during the holidays, but no. He just wanted to tell me, once again, that I'm too preoccupied to get through to playoffs."

Lucia rolled her eyes. "He needs a life." She smacked a hand over her mouth, her eyes wide. "Oh my god, I'm sorry Colton. That wasn't an appropriate thing for me to say. I should probably slow it down with the wine."

He knocked her shoulder with his as he started eating. "I'm in complete agreement, don't worry."

After a couple hours of mingling with the team and their families, and with most of the food gone, groups of them began leaving, either to enjoy the rest of the night together or in some cases, to hit King Street for the evening.

Once Maya seemed more like herself again, he agreed to leave her side. He went to the kitchen to help Jenna put up some of the casserole dishes and place pieces of pie on paper plates for those who were staying for football and trivia, when Jenna said, "Tell me you're staying for trivia this year."

He hadn't thought much of it, but Lucia had been enjoying herself so much, he wondered if she'd want to stay. "If Lucia and Maya want to stay, I'll be glad to."

Jenna's smile was wide as she set the last casserole dish in the sink. "You like her a lot."

"Maya? Well, I'd hope so."

"Colton."

He sighed. "Fine, yes. I do. I like her a lot."

It was hard to admit it out loud. He'd admitted it to himself, and it was difficult enough knowing that she wouldn't be in his life as much soon, but telling Jenna only made the thought of that harder to digest.

"Do you lo—"

"Do you need any help?"

Colton was glad for the interruption, not sure of the answer to the question Jenna had been about to ask. Though, when he realized it was Lucia doing the interrupting, his heartbeat picked up, worried she'd heard his confession.

"Nope, we're just finishing up. Thanks, sweetie."

Colton smiled at Lucia before asking, "Do you want to stay for trivia?"

She blinked at him.

He chuckled. "Think of it as a knockoff of Trivial Pursuit, but all the questions are about the NFL."

"Oh, absolutely. Get ready to get your ass kicked."

Jenna snorted beside him. He turned to her solemnly. "She's not kidding. She's a four-time fantasy football champion, Jenna. She's insane."

Lucia walked out laughing, and Jenna sent him a knowing smile. "Right. Well, we'd better set up trivia in front of one of the thousands of TVs we don't need in this house."

Lucia was in the bathroom while they set up the table, and they seemed to be missing a chair for her. He'd just stood to grab another when she walked out. The thought vanished when he saw her hair was down, out of the clutches of the clip she always wore. His heart stuttered, not for the first time that night, taking in the way her long dress hugged her body.

She looked alarmed at the lack of seats, so he sat back down and patted his leg. "Come on, Moretti. I've got a perfectly good seat right here."

He probably shouldn't have offered, but he'd barely talked to her all day. There had been so many people during the meal, and so many conversations, they'd hardly said more than a few words to each other here and there. Having her close to him, right in his lap, was something he couldn't deprive himself of. Not when they were so close to January.

She moved closer, a frown marring her beautiful features. "I hardly think your friends are interested in playing trivia with the Disgustingtons."

Jenna shuffled the cards before placing them and the other pieces out on the board. "We're your friends too, and we don't care as long as Colton's here. He usually leaves early. Actually, he leaves every function before the fun starts, so we don't care."

Rudy, Cooper, Chris, and Sam all nodded their heads in agreement, so Lucia perched on his knee tentatively. Colton placed a hand on her torso, his fingers splayed across her abdomen, scooting her closer to his body. She made a noise as she moved up his leg, but their friends were already setting up their pieces on the board and didn't seem to notice.

"Okay, let's just do couples as teams," Jenna announced. "Coop, you and Maya can team up."

They were already sitting next to each other, so they nodded, not making eye contact with each other. Lucia looked back at Colton questioningly, mirroring his own confusion.

Each team rolled the die, and Lucia rolled a six, allowing them to go first. Jenna read off their first card. "Who was the first player to rush for two thousand yards in a single NFL season, and what team did he play for?"

Lucia didn't even consult him before she responded, "OJ with the Bills." She smiled wide, confident in her answer. Jenna nodded, and everybody around the table groaned.

"This doesn't seem fair. Lucia's whole job is to know random facts like these."

Colton glared at Sam. "Don't be a sore loser. We're all in the league, we should all know these things."

Sam continued grumbling but took his turn. Each team continued around the table, and before Maya and Cooper rolled their die, Lucia's phone lit up in her hand. "Asshole Clark" flashed across the screen, and Colton wasn't sure whether to laugh at the contact name or be pissed that Clark was still bothering her.

He sat up slightly so his lips were against her ear, tightening his hand on her stomach as she shivered. "If you don't block his ass, I swear to god, I will."

Lucia elbowed him, though she ignored the call, shoving the phone into her bra.

"You're crazy if you think I won't go in there."

He got a sharper, more painful elbow for that one.

The couples continued taking their turns, and as more drinks flowed, everyone struggled a bit more with the questions, except Lucia. No matter how much wine she knocked back over the two hours, she was as sharp as a tack, rarely even checking for Colton's input before answering the questions.

Lucia leaned closer and closer to his chest with every round of laughter at Rudy or Chris answering completely incorrectly, and Colton realized how fucked he was because Jenna might not have been so far off. He knew it was wrong, but when she met his eyes before laughing at something Rudy said or smiled wide at him because she'd answered correctly, he pretended those smiles were just for him, and that they meant something.

If Lucia wanted to use him, he'd let her, even if it ripped his heart into a million little pieces that might never fit back together.

Chapter Twenty-One

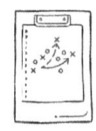

Lucia

Lucia didn't want to talk to Max. She really didn't. But she'd told herself she would allow him to apologize. Plus, if it meant never having his contact flash across her screen again, she'd be thankful, though she couldn't be sure it was true. No matter the outcome, she could feel this would be the last time she talked to him. She wouldn't be falling back into his trap ever again.

He'd done a surprisingly good job of not contacting her until Thanksgiving dinner at Jenna's, but whether that was because he thought they would be getting back together during this call, she didn't know.

Her phone buzzed.

Isa

> You got this! You are so strong.

> And also I love you! Remember you deserve the world :)

Lucia chuckled, though it came out shaky. She struggled with confrontation of this nature, and it was clear from her breathing and the nausea in her stomach that this wouldn't be different. She'd memorized a script of points to hit on, but she knew Max would probably find a way to derail it.

Her laptop signaled a video call. She took a few centering breaths, touched her new lucky pearl necklace, and answered.

Max sat in the dining room of a house that used to be hers. In a chair that she'd picked out. In front of a painting she'd found at a flea market. She hadn't even thought to take it and the other art when she'd left, only grabbing the essentials.

"Hi, Max."

"Hi, baby. I've missed you."

A year ago, those words would've given her butterflies and set her heart alight. Now, they were just words, ones that actually made her a little uncomfortable.

"I know you said you had something important to tell me. I wanted to give you an opportunity to do that."

So far, so good. The script was doing her well.

"Lu, come on. It's us. I know it looked bad, but you didn't have to start hooking up with Beaumont to make your point. I got it, loud and clear. Just come back to me."

And there it was. He hadn't even attempted to start the conversation with an apology and had completely ignored the glaring fact that she'd lost her job in Richmond because of him.

"Max, I thought you might apologize. I was trying to give you the benefit of the doubt, but at this point—"

"I'm sorry, okay? I am. I'm really sorry that it happened. You were working so hard, and we hadn't been together in a while, and I thought I'd get away with it."

Lucia scoffed, "You're sorry you didn't get away with it? You can't even apologize for cheating?"

"What does it sound like I'm trying to do? I said I'm sorry. I shouldn't have done it. I love you so much, baby. We were a perfect fit. Do you remember our anniversary trip to Greece? We spent a week in paradise together, and it was perfect. The sex on the beach? All the sunset dinners? And remember how we talked about going there for our honeymoon? Let's do that, baby. Let's get married and go to Greece. Right when the season's over."

She remembered Greece. It had been beautiful and just what she'd needed. He'd whisked her away for their anniversary, putting in a good word with her bosses who gave her a week and a half off during offseason.

What he failed to mention was that it'd been a spontaneous trip because he'd gone days without responding to her. She'd been with the Cardinals for a brief time, helping them with a training program for their quarterback, and had planned to fly out to Richmond to spend their anniversary with him. For the three days leading up to her flight, she hadn't heard anything from him. Radio silence.

It was only as she got on the plane that he'd texted her that he was looking forward to seeing her. She'd been uncertain about whether to even go, not sure where they stood or if Max had forgotten their anniversary, but then she'd gotten that text, and everything was okay again. She hadn't yet gotten to the point in their relationship where she realized how shitty it was for him to spend days at a time without so much as a hello, especially during the offseason when he wasn't nearly as busy.

He'd surprised her with tickets when she'd landed in Virginia, and they'd left the next day. He'd flirted with the flight attendant the entire flight, but then they'd touched down in Greece, and it had all gone away. He'd treated her like a queen the entire week, taking her to expensive dinners and flying them to the islands for clubbing. Buying her presents and telling her how much he loved her, how much he couldn't wait to marry her so they could honeymoon there.

She had let him get away with so much because he'd always known when she'd been thinking about leaving, and he'd found a way to fix it. It hurt to know that she'd spent such a long time allowing herself to be wrapped up in a relationship like that, but if there was something she could take from this experience, and from what Colton had taught her, it was that it was time to forgive herself.

Forgive herself for allowing Max to sweet talk her into staying in a relationship in college. For not seeing the toxicity and abuse the longer she stayed with him, even when it meant getting hurt. For not listening when Isa told her she could do so much better.

The point of life was to learn. She hadn't learned from her father's mistakes, so she'd had to live through the experience herself. And now that she had, she knew that love just simply wasn't for her. Maybe she'd get a dog and become Auntie Lucia to her friends' children.

She smiled sadly. "I remember, but I'm not in that place anymore, Max. I'm not in love with you, and haven't been for a while."

There was a loud thud as Max slammed a hand on the dining table, his phone shaking at the impact. "Bullshit, Lu. Bullshit. Is this because of Beaumont? I'm going to crush him the next time I see him. Had you already started seeing him before you took the job? Is that how you got the job?"

Lucia sighed exasperatedly, her eyes closing. Leave it to Max to believe she couldn't get a job on her own. "I never so much as looked at anyone else when we were together, and I think you know that. Colton and I...it just kind of happened."

Colton's timing was impeccable, a text vibrating her phone.

Colton

> Cooper is annoying the shit out of me. I've never wished to be free of team bonding more.

Lucia let out a small giggle before she looked back at her laptop screen, noting Max's pinched brows. She set her phone back down.

"He's playing like shit."

"Colton's been steadily improving to his best performance all season, which is more than I can say about some people." Namely him, but she was trying to be mature. "He's talented and a hard worker and already doing so much better than he was. He's an amazing quarterback, and I can't wait to see where he goes from here."

"Didn't help him when we beat his ass during rivalry week junior year. And I'll do it again if you guys somehow manage to get to divisionals."

Lucia rolled her eyes. The Sabertooths had more of a chance of getting to divisionals than the Vipers. Then, she remembered what he'd told Colton after the game, "I can't believe you told him Isa took his playbook."

He grinned slyly. "Genius, right? If only I knew someone who could help me actually pull that off this year."

She scoffed at the insinuation. "Yeah, I'm gonna give you our plays. You jeopardized my career, and now I'm going to end it entirely so that you can cheat your way through playoffs? No, thank you. I'm gonna help Colton make sure you lose."

She couldn't believe he'd even thought she'd be on board with that. "Is that why you called? Because you thought I'd give you their game plans?"

"Of course not. It would've just been a bonus."

"I can't believe you." But honestly, she could. This was absolutely something Max would do.

"What do you see in that asshole, anyway? You know what he was like in college. He was the scum of the earth. What does he give you that I haven't?"

Lucia could think of a lot of things Colton had given her that Max never had. Even though it was just pretend, he found ways to make her smile whenever he could. He didn't act like a childish asshole when he lost games, punching walls around her and yelling in the way that Max used to in college. He'd introduced her to his friends so that she could have a community in a new place. He'd offered to help her when she was at her lowest point. He treated her like a person, made her feel heard, and listened to her when she gave him feedback. He celebrated her achievements. He didn't expect her to give him other teams' playbooks.

He'd made her come. *Many* times.

"Colton cares about my feelings. Not just when he wants something from me, but all the time. You spent our entire relationship putting in just enough effort to keep me around. Right when you could see I was on my way out, you started giving me the love I needed the entire time. I deserve more than that. I deserve someone who makes an effort to talk to me, even when they're busy, even if it's just a 'hi, I miss you.' I deserve someone who wants to spend time with me. I deserve someone who can see that I'm an intelligent person with thoughts and insights that matter beyond stroking their ego."

"Come on, Lu. I can be that person for you. Let's talk through this. We can make this work. You're right. I've made a lot of mistakes, but I can fix them. Just be patient with me and I can be who you need me to be."

"No, Max. No. There's nothing you can say to me to change my mind. I've been plenty patient. I waited seven years for you to figure your shit out and treat me right. I have no patience left to give. I appreciate everything our relationship taught me. We had some good times, and I'm thankful for that."

"Lu, plea—"

"I'm not done. I forgive you for cheating. A few months ago, I might've wanted to know everything about it. Why did you do it? Why her? What was I doing wrong? But I don't care now. I forgive you, and I thank you. Because of what you did, I have Colton and the Sabers. I'm finally happy. Can't you just let me be happy?"

"We were happy."

"Maybe you were. But I wasn't." He didn't respond immediately to that, so she continued, "You promised you wouldn't call or text me anymore, so please don't. I won't respond."

She ended the call, having gotten as much from the conversation as she could. She went to Max's contact, and after only a moment's hesitation, she blocked him.

Chapter Twenty-Two

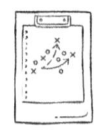

Lucia

Lucia was beyond excited when she saw Isa bounding out of the airport toward her, dark hair flying. She'd missed her best friend immensely, and she needed her now more than ever. Luckily, both their bosses had let them take that Monday and Tuesday off so they could discover the beauty of Charleston together.

Isa jumped into Lucia's arms, nearly knocking them both over. "You have no idea how horrible that flight was. I swear, the kid behind me wanted to be smacked upside the head." She sighed, squeezing Lucia.

"I'm so glad you're here. I've missed you so much."

Isa pulled away, tossing her bag into the back of Lucia's car. "I need to shower and change, and then I'm ready for drinks and views. I might need a nap, but we can remedy that with an energy drink."

Lucia laughed as they got into the car. "We'll stop to get some on the way home. How's Abby?" she asked, referring to Isa's girlfriend.

"Good. She was thinking about joining, but couldn't get time off from work. Plus, I wanted you all to myself."

Lucia pulled out of the pickup area. "Well, Jenna and Leigh will be meeting us later in the evening, if that's okay. And Maya too, if her dinner with Colton and their father finishes early."

"Good. I need to meet these new friends who are trying to take over my job as best friend. And what's this nonsense about hanging out with Colton's sister?"

"Nobody could ever replace you as my best friend, Is. And Maya's a few years younger than us, but she's in town for the week and wanted to come out. She's sweet, you'll like her."

Isa grumbled something under her breath that sounded like "we'll just see about that" before watching out the window, taking in Charleston. Isa had nothing to worry about on that front. No matter how many friends Lucia made, Isa would always be her oldest and closest friend.

"How has this city been treating you? How've you been feeling about the new team?" Lucia felt her friend's concerned eyes on her. They'd tried to talk once a week since she'd left but had rarely been able to stay on for longer than a few minutes, which meant Isa only knew the highlights. Such was the way of the season.

"I—okay, honestly I like it a lot. There's something about this place that makes me wish they'd sign me for longer than the season."

"Mm-hmm, or someone."

Lucia forced out a scoff, though it sounded weak even to her own ears. "Please."

Isa let her drop the subject for the time being. When they reached Lucia's house, she showed Isa around the few rooms and gave her what she'd need for a shower.

While her friend got ready for the evening, Lucia picked out a tight, black dress, clipping some of her hair into a small claw clip and pulling pieces out to frame her face. She did her makeup quickly, hoping to get an hour or so to go through some statistics from their previous game for a report for Tim.

She'd only managed half an hour before Isa was ready, sporting a similar dress but in dark green. When Lucia pointed out the color, which was unlike Isa's typical palette of blacks, reds, and blues, Isa shrugged. "I figured I'd try to fit into the Sabertooths' culture. Wouldn't want anyone here thinking their top analyst is hanging with a Vipers athletic trainer."

"Please, as if anybody knows who I am." Lucia called a car with a drop-off on King Street.

"In case you haven't noticed, you've been getting some serious exposure since you started this whole thing with Beaumont. People most definitely know who you are, especially around here. Half the internet wants to be you."

Lucia grimaced. She'd tried to stay off news sites and social media since the story had broken, not interested in seeing the sordid things reporters would come up with about their relationship. She wanted to inspire people because of her career, not the man they thought she was dating.

"I try not to focus too much on it."

The car was outside her house quickly, and they spent the ride whispering about the posts Isa kept pulling up on Lucia's relationship. Lucia kept telling her to *stop* because the number of people talking about how badly they wanted to be her was incredibly off-putting. When they reached their destination, Lucia thanked the driver, and the pair located an open spot at the bar.

The marble top was cool to the touch, and Lucia rested a hand atop it as she glanced around. Jenna's recommendation had been spot on; this place was exactly what she had been looking for. Black accented with gold everywhere she looked, even on the bar menus. Behind her was a wall of booth seating in front of small circular tables and cute, felt chairs, all of which were occupied by couples and groups of friends.

When they'd ordered—red wine for her, New York Sour for Isa, and a petite cheese platter to split—Isa turned to Lucia.

"Max has been a raging lunatic since you blocked him. He's come in needing treatment a couple of times because he's playing too aggressively."

Lucia took a sip of her wine. "I don't want to talk about Max. How's Charlotte? How are the analysts?"

Isa shrugged. "The analyst team is definitely lacking without you, and they know it. Charlotte asks me how you are about once a week. You can tell she's pissed at John and the rest of the suits for making her almost fire you."

That was gratifying. A part of her was glad to hear that they were struggling without her. She wished Charlotte didn't have to suffer as a consequence, but she hoped John saw what a mistake he'd made.

Lucia sighed. "I'm just thankful she had the foresight to look for other jobs when she heard what happened. I didn't even think about that when I saw the news."

"Yeah, Luc, but I think you had other things to worry about. Nobody faults you for that. Speaking of which, if you wanna hop back on the dating roller coaster, that cute guy over there hasn't stopped looking over at you." She inclined her head to point at a man who was indeed looking at her, a smile flashing as he raised his glass in greeting. "You should go talk to him."

He was cute, Lucia supposed, but a far cry from the dark-haired quarterback who drove her crazy. Who, she'd begun to realize, she wanted to *keep* driving her crazy.

"I'm here to hang out with you, not trap a man. Plus, I have a..." She stopped herself before she called him her boyfriend. "Colton."

"Right. Let's talk about that absolute dumpster fire of an idea, shall we?"

"I don't know what you're talking about." She smiled at the bartender as she set their drinks in front of them.

Isa's voice dropped to a whisper. "Okay, so let's just imagine for a minute that sleeping with someone you're pretending to date has never, in history, ended poorly. What's going to happen when playoffs start?"

Lucia matched the volume of Isa's voice. "First of all, it was one time. Second of all, we're going to break up, end of story. We'll be friends, probably."

She hoped they would be. Colton had quickly become an incredibly important person to her, and she couldn't imagine what her life would look like if they went back to a strictly analyst-player relationship. It would break her heart to lose him, and the thought of only seeing him during their sessions had her taking a bigger sip of wine.

"Oh, are we just ignoring the time he wrecked you on the plane?"

Lucia slapped a hand over her friend's mouth, a laugh bubbling out of her. "Isa! Shh, I don't need strangers knowing more about my life than they already do. Keep whispering."

Isa rolled her eyes but listened. "This is a bad idea, *osita*. What is he gaining from this? I'm suspicious. He has to have agreed to this for some reason, something to benefit him."

The thought was a shot to Lucia's chest, but she tried to play it off, not wanting Isa to see how it'd affected her. "I think he's just a nice guy. He originally did it to help me because I was distraught when the news came out. And I think he likes that it gets Max mad. But, I don't know, something's been different recently. It feels like he *wants* to spend time with me, even when cameras aren't on us." She hadn't told Isa about the night they'd cuddled. Sheepishly, she continued, "I even go to see him in his hotel room at away games."

Isa sipped her drink. "Well, are you getting dicked down?"

Lucia sputtered, choking down her wine. "Not outside of the time I told you about. We just talk and watch movies and...enjoy each other's company?" She noted the incredulous look on her friend's face. "I don't know, it's weird to conceptualize, but it's true."

Isa just hummed.

Lucia took a bite of the cheese that'd been set down between them, savoring the flavor on her tongue. "Obviously my luck with relationships has run out, but that doesn't mean I can't have fun. So what if he's just using me? Who's to say I'm not using him too?" She wasn't sure the words were true as they left her, but something inside her wanted to convince Isa that it was all just harmless fun.

"Just don't get caught up in the process. Remember why you're here. This is the job that boosts you to head analyst."

Isa was right. Lucia had to focus on her end goal. The last thing she needed was for her relationship to become a complication.

The mildly intoxicated pair wandered down the street to Marion Square, at which point Isa tutted playfully, talking about how Richmond would always be better. They were fast approaching the time they'd agreed to meet Jenna, Leigh, and Maya at a cute little bar inside Hotel Bennett, another recommendation from Jenna.

Lucia felt warm and bubbly as they walked into the hotel, happy to be out for a night with a group of friends for the first time in a long time. When they finally made it into the bar, Lucia and Isa both looked up in awe at the crystal chandelier, marveling at the pink chairs, pink tables, pink everything.

"This may be the only champagne bar I've ever been to, but it's certainly my favorite."

Lucia smiled at that. Her smile widened when she saw her friends already seated at a table. She was excited for Isa to meet them, even if she wasn't certain they would get along. She'd made Isa promise to be nice, especially to Maya, but nobody could get Isa to do anything she didn't want to do.

"Hi! This is Isa." She then pointed at each of her friends. "Jenna, Leigh, Maya." They all exchanged hugs before sitting down.

"We ordered first rounds for you guys, hope that's okay." Jenna smiled pleasantly at Isa. "How're you liking Charleston? How long are you in town?"

"It's nice, though I've only really been on King Street. We're going to Saltwater Cowboys tomorrow, hanging by the water, and then I leave late tomorrow evening."

"Oh, Rudy and Colton love Saltwater Cowboys. I think it's Colton's favorite place to be, on the rare occasions he isn't in football mode."

Maya laughed quietly beside Lucia, though it sounded forced. When Lucia looked at her closer, she could see the sadness that'd been there at Jenna's house still lining her face, and she wondered what might still be weighing on her.

Just as their champagne arrived, her phone buzzed. When she saw who'd texted her, the warmth from the alcohol spread through her whole body, those pesky butterflies fluttering around again.

Colton

> Take care of Maya, I think she's upset.

> I'm sure dinner with our father didn't help, even if it was her idea, but something's been wrong since she got here.

Lucia

> Always.

"Lucia?" Jenna had been talking to her and she hadn't even realized.

"Huh?"

"I was asking how things have been with you and Colton. I remember the beginning stages with Rudy, especially with the spotlight, though I bet there's a bit more of that for you two."

Lucia stowed her phone, not wanting to get caught texting the very man they were talking about.

"Oh, good, good. We're really good."

A mischievous grin spread across Leigh's face. "Do you get to see him when you travel with the team?"

Lucia chuckled, not sure why Leigh looked so impish. "Yes, if we get time, we try to see each other."

"And the sex?"

For the second time that night, Lucia choked on her drink, not quite certain why her friends were so interested in her sex life.

"Ugh, gross. That's my brother." Lucia stifled a laugh at Maya's words.

Jenna leaned forward toward Maya, her cheeks rosy like she hadn't had an opportunity to talk like this for years. "What's up with you and Cooper, anyway?"

Maya went rigid as four pairs of eyes fell on her. She downed her glass of champagne and then cleared her throat. "Nothing. He's Colton's best friend, and he's like a brother to me."

Lucia was having a hard time believing that, but if Maya wanted to pretend, she wasn't going to out her. Later, she would try to talk to her separately.

Jenna looked unconvinced as well. "He looks at you like you put stars in the sky. The same way Colton looks at Luc."

Lucia was startled at that. Isa tensed beside her, like she, too, wasn't sure what to make of the comment. Did Colton look at her a certain way when they were around others? She certainly hadn't noticed, but if Jenna thought so, he was doing a great job of acting. All those Redditors who'd made fun of his sandwich commercials were seemingly wrong about his skills.

Her phone buzzed against her chest, and she pulled it out as stealthily as she could. Which was not at all stealthy, if the displeased look on Isa's face told her anything.

Colton
> You never take care of me when I'm upset, what's that about?

Lucia
> I've taken care of you plenty.

Colton
> Like when?

Lucia
> How about the night after I met your family?

She felt her cheeks pink at the memory, knowing the alcohol was making her overconfident. She deleted the text she'd started writing, which detailed their night a bit *too* clearly.

Colton
> Jesus.

> How is that not anti-boundaries?

She smiled at his use of her words. Her friends' laughter reminded her where she was, and she tucked the phone back into her dress.

Her friends continued talking about everything from the season to Jenna's precious children to Devin's wild parties—at which point Isa promised she would try to make the next one. Lucia was glad Isa was getting along with her other friends, her chest aching as she remembered that she only had her for a day.

After they'd had perhaps too many glasses of champagne, they staggered out of the pretty bar as a group.

"Everybody have a ride? Rudy's coming to get me and Leigh if anybody needs to be dropped off."

"Colton's getting me," Maya responded sleepily.

Lucia frowned a little, worried about her. Maya had barely smiled all night, and toward the end, she'd had a couple more glasses than the rest of them, her eyes closing and her head resting on Lucia's shoulder until they'd gotten up.

"We'll order a car," Lucia added.

That seemed to wake Maya up. "Colton won't like that at all. You can come with us."

"Oh, no, it's okay. We don't mind."

Maya shook her head. "Yeah, that's not gonna work. I feel like you know my brother well enough to know he's not gonna go for that."

Lucia sighed, exchanging a glance with Isa, knowing Maya was right. "Okay, I guess we're going with Colton, then."

Jenna clapped her hands together happily. "Great! Rudy will be thrilled to see how absolutely wasted his wife is."

"You deserve it. You take care of the munchkins more than anybody." Leigh patted her best friend's shoulder, though the motion was awkward since they were leaning against each other for support.

Jenna sighed happily, a loving smile on her face. "True."

Rudy was there quickly, helping his alcohol-addled wife into his passenger seat and Leigh into the back simultaneously. He'd sat in his car until Colton's ridiculously overpriced car found them.

If Lucia thought the alcohol had warmed her against the December chill, the feeling that flooded her as Colton's eyes looked her up and down set her ablaze. She watched him swallow as they landed on the slit of the dress that exposed her leg, made longer by her tallest heels. The feeling that was beginning to become far too familiar found its way behind her navel, desire to feel his warm, calloused hands all over her body, caressing her in places she hadn't even known she'd liked until him.

Isa nudged her, and Lucia realized Maya was already in the back of his car. Colton tried to help Isa into the back, but her best friend nearly snarled at him as he opened the door for her.

"I see Isa's still not my biggest fan," he whispered to Lucia as he helped her into his passenger seat, his hands warm on her waist, searing through the fabric of the dress.

She tried to think of something clever to respond but found herself giggling instead. Perfect. Colton had once said she and alcohol and heels didn't mix well, but she was starting to wonder if it was actually her and alcohol and *his presence* that rendered her brain into mush.

The car was quiet as he drove them to her house, the only noise coming from a snoring Maya.

Finally, Colton broke the silence. "Did she seem okay? I'm really worried about her, but she won't tell me what's going on. And she never drinks like this."

Lucia remembered the forlorn expression on Maya's face at their Thanksgiving dinner, which had only seemed to vanish when she'd been near Cooper. It'd been there, subtler, all night tonight, and she wondered if maybe she *did* know why.

"We didn't get to talk about it, but something tells me it's got something to do with a guy."

Colton's hands tightened on the wheel, his veins becoming more prominent, sending Lucia's heart into a jackhammer. They didn't speak for the rest of the ride, and Lucia felt Isa's eyes flicking between the two of them.

When they reached Lucia's house, Colton walked them both to the door, keeping his hands on or near Lucia at all times. When she finally managed to get the door unlocked and open, Isa said, "Luc, I'll meet you inside."

"Huh?"

"Go inside, *osita*. I need to talk to Colton."

Isa shoved her into the house. Then, Lucia watched, stunned as her friend closed her door, pushing her out of the conversation with Colton.

She heard Isa talking to him quietly. When she tried to wrench open the door to chide her best friend, she found it held tight.

When did Isa get so strong? she wondered.

Colton's response was low, muffled completely by the door. They continued in that fashion for a few minutes, though Isa's tone seemed to shift as the conversation went on. Finally, the door opened, knocking Lucia back.

His eyes found hers, and the sweet smile he gave her had her own lips inching up. He walked away, and Lucia closed the door and whirled on her best friend.

"Isa, what did you say? He's doing something nice for me because he's secretly a sweetheart. He doesn't deserve to be ripped to metaphorical shreds for that."

Isa wouldn't meet her eyes as Lucia locked the door.

"You're right." Finally, her eyes met Lucia's. "But *I'm* not the one who's going to rip him to shreds."

Chapter Twenty-Three

COLTON

Something had changed between Colton and Lucia since Thanksgiving, and he couldn't be sure if he was the only one who felt it. By the end of the evening, he'd known he was screwed, but he hadn't known the extent. Then, later, when Isa had told him he needed to leave Lucia alone because she deserved better than to be used as a pawn in his game against Clark, he'd snapped. He'd confessed feelings he hadn't even had an opportunity to work through on his own.

"Lucia has divided the timeline of my life in two: before she came to Charleston, and after," he'd said. *"Nothing has been clearer to me than the fact that she deserves far better than I could ever give her."* He cringed at the memory, remembering how he'd quieted his words so Lucia wouldn't overhear. Who was he kidding? Isa had most definitely told her every ill-conceived

word of his admission, and clearly, she didn't feel the same way because she hadn't made any mention of it since.

And that was okay. He was content with whatever she was willing to give him, even if the thought of their imminent breakup made his hands sweat and his heart splinter. But they'd agreed to the break up because it was what was best for their careers, and he needed to get on board. The Sabers had enough wins to go to the playoffs, and if he wanted another chance at the Super Bowl, he needed to prevent any and all distractions. Especially beautiful, brunette ones who he would willingly give up football for so he could spend the rest of his lifetime worshiping at her feet.

Regardless of her feelings, to keep up appearances, they continued their outings together. Cooper had invited them to double date, stating that he felt he hadn't hung out with Colton as much as they usually did during the season. Colton had given Lucia an out—many, actually, because he really didn't want to go—but she'd convinced him it would be fun.

Unsurprisingly, Cooper had pulled out all the stops. When he wanted to enjoy a night out, he truly made sure he did. The restaurant he'd chosen was completely empty, and at Colton's questioning look, his best friend admitted that he'd reserved it for the evening so they wouldn't have to deal with any press or fans.

Colton refrained from reminding Cooper that the woman on his arm was, in fact, a fan. Colton had no idea where his friend found these women, but this one hardly spoke, eyes sparkling and grin wide like she'd won the lottery.

Lucia smiled over at her as they looked through the menu, their very excited server standing a few feet away. "Have you lived in Charleston long?"

The woman—whom Colton referred to in his mind as Bouncy because he'd been too busy watching Lucia smile when she'd introduced herself—clapped her hands together.

"Since college! I decided to stay when I got a job here."

"Oh, what do you do?"

"I work in advertising."

Lucia set her menu down, and Colton noticed the way her finger stayed pointed at what he assumed she wanted to order. He smiled.

"Do you like it?"

"It's okay. It gets really fun around the Super Bowl when everybody wants ads with the Sabers." She patted Cooper's hand. "That's how we first met, actually. My agency had a client who wanted Cooper here for an insurance ad."

Cooper grinned at Lucia. "Not looking into a new profession, I hope. Colton won't survive if you leave the Sabers. He needs his emotional support Lucia."

Colton kicked his friend under the table. "Dick," he muttered.

Lucia's laugh was melodic, echoing around the empty restaurant. She inched slightly closer to him, her leg resting against his in the booth. "I don't know why everybody says that. Colton is the most capable quarterback in the league right now, he doesn't need me anymore. I'm not sure he's needed me since the third or fourth regular season game. All he needs to remember is to scramble his feet a little better and not release the ball early."

Colton whipped his head to look at her, frowning. "That's ridiculous. You've helped me through every single game this season." He didn't know how many times he'd told her so, not sure why she was selling herself short. He'd tell her for as long as it took for her to understand that he was being honest.

Cooper all but guffawed. "See? I told you. This guy's life just flashed before his eyes at the thought of you leaving."

Colton was going to kill his best friend. For real.

Lucia rolled her eyes like she didn't believe it, turning back to Bouncy. "How fun about the ads, though! I bet they're gonna have a lot of calls asking for them after the Super Bowl this year." Colton's heart soared to hear she believed in him and his team enough to place them back in the Super Bowl this season.

"Actually, yeah, I heard that after last season, there were a lot of calls asking for Cooper and Colton to shoot together."

Their overzealous server walked over and asked for their orders. When he'd taken them down in his little pad, he grabbed their dinner menus and set a beverage and dessert menu in front of them.

Colton tensed when Lucia's hand found his thigh, his dick shooting up to attention at her touch. She stifled a giggle when she noticed the way he shifted. He knew she loved torturing him, especially in public, and dinner with his best friend and his date was no different.

"So, is it true you guys got together in college?"

Lucia stiffened at Bouncy's question. "Uh, what?"

Even Cooper seemed to have tensed. "You shouldn't listen to everything you hear, Liv."

"Where did you hear that?" Colton asked.

Bouncy—Liv—seemed less sure of herself as she responded to Colton. "Oh, people at the agency were talking about it. All of those silly news articles talk about how you guys both went to school in Los Angeles."

Lucia shook her head, and Colton's heart sank as she removed her hand from his leg. "Um, no. We didn't know each other very well back then. Different colleges."

Colton knew the topic was sensitive because she'd been with Clark in college, and obviously, those memories were still bothering her. But he wondered if there was more. If she was still upset about his accusations that Isa had slept with Vinny, used his friend to get information.

How miserable had he made her life back then? Everything he'd done and said in the name of school spirit and rivalry had been aimed at Max, but he wondered how much of it had affected her, too.

A hand reached inside him and squeezed his heart tightly. He'd have to talk to her about that, because the last thing he wanted was for him to still be the cause of any strife for her.

A few minutes of silence later, Lucia seemingly still inside of her head, Liv reached over to her. "I'm sorry I said anything. I'll be sure to straighten out the story at work. How did you two get together, then?"

Colton jumped in, hoping to save Lucia. "We were spending a lot of time together for work, and we started to realize..." What had they started to realize? That they didn't actually have any reason to hate each other? That they were uncontrollably attracted to each other? He didn't know how to end the sentence, but luckily, Lucia did.

"We liked each other. And then the media was all over it even though we wanted to keep it silent, and now here we are."

Liv nodded somberly. "Yeah, unfortunately Colton and Cooper are far too important in this city for any gossip to fly under the radar." That was an understatement.

Their food arrived quickly, and they remained mostly silent as they ate besides the occasional question from Lucia, who tried her hardest to make Cooper's date feel welcome and included.

When their waiter came back to ask if they wanted dessert, Liv whispered to Cooper, who shook his head once. "I don't know about y'all, but we're gonna head out."

Colton took in Lucia's barely slumped shoulders and the sad look in her eyes which had lingered there since the topic of Max had come up, even as she did her best to smile at Cooper and his date. Colton shook his head as well. "No, we're ready to head out too."

The waiter deflated but smiled as he brought them the check and thanked them for the night.

The car ride from the restaurant to Lucia's house was silent. He wasn't sure if she was thinking or angry with him, but he wanted to make sure they talked through it. It wasn't until they reached her porch, his body shielding her from the guy who seemed to stand outside of her house perpetually with a camera, that he spoke.

"Can we talk about what happened?"

Her eyes searched his face, and he hated the pained look in them. She nodded wordlessly, and he followed her inside her house for the first time.

He knew her house was a haven of sorts for her, which is why they were always at his, and he was thankful they were finally at the point where she trusted him enough to let him in.

It was decorated exactly the way he'd imagined it would be, whites and tans and browns with greens splashed here and there. It was very her, down to the wine bottle open on the counter and the blue-light glasses resting next to her tablet.

She sat on her couch, and the look she gave him seemed to ask him to join her. He sat beside her, giving her some room in case she wanted distance.

"Luc?" he asked uncertainly.

"I'm sorry that you…that you felt like we cheated you out of your senior season. But sometimes, I remember how horrible you were to Max, and how he'd—" She sniffled, swiping at her face angrily. "How he'd react to it. And I know he was just as bad, maybe worse, toward you. And I know he probably deserved it. But I was always stuck dealing with the consequences."

Blood rushed into his ears at her words, wanting so badly to reach out and comfort her. His jaw tightened. "What do you mean 'how he'd react to it'?"

She shrugged. "Sometimes, when you said something particularly nasty on TV or your team fucked up our practice field or our mascot statue...he got really angry. But he usually couldn't rage at you, so he raged at me and kind of...I don't know. He'd get loud, and it was just hard. He'd be in a mood for days. Weeks, even. And I had to just pretend everything was good, but I was honestly scared sometimes."

Colton closed his eyes, trying to gather his bearings before he said or did something impulsive. "Did he ever...hurt you? Did he ever put his hands on you?" He only realized his fists were balled at his sides when he felt the bite of his nails in his palms. He opened his eyes at the sting.

She shook her head. "He never did anything physical. But if I was late to see him or did anything that even kind of bothered him in that time, he'd scream at me, and sometimes I thought he might." She wiped at her face again. "I sometimes struggle to understand how that Colton and this Colton are both you. I know you were younger and you've matured. And it's not like you did anything to hurt *me*. How could you have known what was going on?"

"Luc..."

"I don't blame you, not really. It was Max. But when I first came here, it was on my mind. And then we had fun together and I realized I *liked* you and you weren't this horrible person Max had made you out to be. And I kind of just forgot about it, you know? We spend so much time together that all I usually see is this side of you. This great guy who obviously cares about me in some capacity if he's willing to put his love life on hold to date me and save me the humiliation of...I don't even know what." She sighed heavily.

Put his love life on hold? He hadn't had a love life before her. He hadn't cared about anyone the way he cared about her. The fact that he had ever, even indirectly, been the cause of her pain made him want to go back in time and change everything. He swallowed over the stone in his throat, trying to formulate a coherent thought, wanting nothing more than to take her in his arms.

"And normally, I can compartmentalize. Separate that time from whatever it is we've been doing recently. But when she said that, for some reason, I just couldn't. I remembered it all, the way it felt in college, and it just...it just came crashing down on me that it had been you. And that it really did happen."

He couldn't hold himself back any longer, not when she was sitting so close to him, her head in her hands. He moved closer to her on the couch, his arms inches from picking her up.

"Luc, can I...?"

She looked up, realizing his closeness, eyed his arms, and then nodded slowly. He picked her up, setting her on his lap and wrapping a blanket around them. He pressed her head to his chest, his cheek resting on top as he ran a soothing hand through her hair.

"Luc, I don't think there are words in this world that can express how sorry I am that you got caught in the crossfire of our shitfest. If I'd known—*god*, Luc, if I'd known, I would've called a ceasefire so fast. I never would've done anything to piss him off ever again. If I could go back in time and change it all, I would."

If he could go back in time, he'd have found her first and made her his. Because she should have had someone infinitely better than Max Clark.

"Luc, you have to know that you deserved so much better than that. That you *deserve* so much better than that. The next time I see him, it's going to be tough not to beat him until I'm behind bars for assault, because the thought of him yelling at you? Of him taking any of his anger out on you? Makes me want to sink my fist into his face until he can't smirk anymore. Nobody should ever be treated that way, especially not you, Luc. God, you..." He sighed, pulling her tighter to his chest, trying to rein in the anger coursing through his veins. "You are"—*Intoxicating. Exquisite. Perfect*—"amazing."

She wrapped an arm around his neck as she snuggled closer to him. "This is exactly what I meant. I can't understand how you could be so kind now but also have done all those things back then."

He continued running his fingers through her hair soothingly. "I'm sorry," he whispered again.

She sniffled. "You're forgiven...if you put *The Bachelor* on until I fall asleep."

He held her even as he reached for the remote, clicking on the show. He wondered if, after everything, he should come clean to her about how he really felt. About how his heart couldn't rest in her presence. About how his body ached to have her against him, warm and cuddled up in his clothes. About how every second he'd spent with her since she'd joined the Sabers had been exceptional. About how she'd changed his life so much, all for the better.

"Luc, I—" He cut himself off when he realized she was already sleeping in his arms, almost thankful that his bravery would have to wait for another day.

Chapter Twenty-Four

COLTON

The last time Colton had seen Lucia outside of work had been that night he'd held her on her couch until they both fell asleep. The closest he'd gotten to her since then, besides sitting in the chair next to her in her office, were their two pre-game kisses in the end zone, both of which felt different, more real than before. They'd both been so busy with the season that most of December had flown by, and while they still talked a lot during their sessions, she was hyper-focused on his game. Thankfully, they hadn't had any more losses and had gotten through their Christmas Eve game with flying colors, leaving them with twelve wins.

He wished he had more time with her, knowing their deadline was imminent. Even if they could find a way to be friends after everything, he'd be left in pieces. He just hoped it wouldn't affect his game. Otherwise, he'd never forgive himself. And he would never hear the end of it from his father.

Speaking of the man, Colton stood outside the door of his father's Charleston house, dread once again filling his body. And once again, just like during the dinner with his father and Maya, he didn't have Lucia by his side to serve as a buffer. He couldn't be sure what awaited him, but he knew that the holiday meant nothing to the cold-hearted man who had shaped him.

He took a breath and rang the doorbell before he could convince himself not to. Liliana, his father's housekeeper and chef, opened the door with a smile, beckoning him in. Colton noticed the shoes in the foyer, and he toed his own off, glad Maya was back in town. He'd let her know she could stay with him again rather than deal with their father and his coldness, but she hadn't wanted to bother him after the game the night before. Not that he would've been bothered. The only other person he would've cared to have at his house had been on a plane to Philadelphia right after the game.

Maya came into view, jumping into Colton's outstretched arms. "Colt! Thank god you're here. Landon is driving me insane."

Colton smiled, thankful that his father wasn't the first person he had to deal with. When he walked into the living room with Maya, he saw Landon sitting on the couch, eyes focused on the TV, which Colton realized was playing *Home Alone*.

"Wow, really taking it back, aren't we?"

Landon turned to look at Colton, an impish grin on his face. "What's wrong with *Home Alone*? It's a classic."

"I wanted to watch *The Grinch*," Maya said, pouting.

"Maya, please. If you don't even know the full name of the movie you can't pick it. It's called *How The Grinch Stole Christmas*, not *The Grinch*."

Maya waved her hand at him while she looked at Colton, as if to say, "See?" Colton was too tired to play TV politics with his siblings, so he threw himself onto the couch beside his brother.

"Sorry, Mai. We can watch it after *Home Alone*."

She looked at him, faux-betrayal on her face. "You? My greatest ally? You're dead to me," she said as she walked out of the room.

Colton sank into the couch as he asked, "Where's Dad?"

Landon shrugged, tension immediately seeping into his posture. "Who knows? He left as soon as I got here."

"And here I was thinking I played well."

Landon laughed. "Well, we can't all be as perfect as Dad thinks he would have been."

Colton remembered what Lucia had said about him overshadowing his brother. His relationship with Landon had been strained for as long as he could remember. Maybe when they'd been little, they'd been able to get along, but the minute Landon had been old enough to start learning football, their father had pitted them against each other. Their relationship had never stood a chance. Now he wondered if Lucia had been right, and maybe the reason it'd always been difficult between them was because Landon resented him for their childhood.

"You've been doing really well this season. I know it's impossible to get Dad to say anything nice. But if there's a team I'd want to end up in the Super Bowl other than us, I'd want it to be you guys." An olive branch. Something about this season made him want to remedy the relationships in his life. At least the ones that *could* be remedied. He was tired of feeling tense around most of his family members.

Landon's eyebrows shot up. "Thanks, man. And Dad's a dick if he says anything to you about yesterday, you've been playing better every game since preseason." He gave Colton a genuine smile. "Lucia certainly deserves a raise and a permanent position with the Sabers."

That sentiment was absolutely true, and Colton wanted to shout it from the rooftops of King Street for anybody who would listen. Instead, he smiled back and said, "Yeah, she really does."

Colton watched the movie for a while, his mind swirling with thoughts of Lucia. As the kitchen scene began, Colton stood, going in search of Maya.

"Mai?" he called up the stairs as he climbed them. "I'm sorry I let Landon win this time. I promise we'll watch *The Grinch* as soon as it's over."

He found her sitting on the bed of her guest bedroom. The house was so large that they each had their own guest room, in addition to a couple of extra rooms that were never used because nobody but them visited. When he walked closer, he saw her eyes rimmed with red.

"Mai? What's wrong? If I'd known you were this upset about it, I would've put my foot down with Landon about the movie."

She sniffled, a half-hearted laugh falling from her. She shook her head, wiping at her eyes angrily. Colton sat beside her, pulling her into him. She rested her head on his shoulder.

"What's going on? You haven't been yourself since Thanksgiving. Even Lucia's been worried."

Maya heaved a sigh. She didn't respond for a moment, as if collecting her thoughts, and Colton sat in quiet support of her.

"I was sort of seeing someone. He's on the pro circuit with me. Might even say he's a part of my friend group. We'd sort of been..." She pulled away, a torn expression on her face. "It feels weird talking to you about my...endeavors."

Colton coughed. After the initial shock, he said softly, "I can't promise I won't kill him, but I promise I'll try not to if you don't want me to."

That got a real laugh. "I wasn't even worried about that! No killing. Can't have my favorite oldest brother in prison. Anyway, he's not worth it, and he really didn't do anything wrong."

"What happened?"

She raised her shoulder in a half-shrug. "We'd been hooking up for a few months. And since we were always at the same tournaments, always hanging with the same people, it felt longer. We've been friends for a few years, you know?"

He nodded.

"We decided to do Friendsgiving together since some of us chose not to go home and a few of my friends aren't even American. We were all hanging out, and he pulled me aside and said that he'd been developing feelings for me. Great, right? Because as he said that, I realized I'd developed feelings for him, too. Or, honestly, that I'd had feelings for him since the beginning."

Again, Colton nodded, though this time, it was more strained as he guessed where her story was headed.

"Except when I told him I was into him too, he told me he isn't ready to be in a relationship. He said we had to stop hooking up and go back to being friends. And I agreed because I didn't want to try to fight it. Booked the first flight I could find out of there, and I've been avoiding him since."

"Mai, I'm so sorry."

She collapsed onto her bed, groaning. "Damn you, Colt. I'd just stopped crying about it when you came up. Tell me something happy now. Tell me about you and Lucia."

He cleared his throat, wanting so badly to come clean to her about his situation but knowing it wasn't the time. "What do you want to know?"

"How did you know you wanted to be with her?"

Colton thought for a moment. Maybe it was the text she'd sent him of The Abominable Snowmonster of the North, with just three words: *look, it's you*. Maybe it was the way she stood in a room full of men—no, in a profession full of men—confident and self-assured. Maybe it was the fact that she was quite possibly the most intelligent person he'd ever met. Maybe it was those damn pantsuits and heels he loved seeing her in so much, her hair tumbling over her shoulders. Maybe it was the noises that left her beautiful mouth as he fucked her. Maybe it was every little thing about her.

"I don't know, really. I've never felt about anyone the way I feel about her. My whole life—I mean, shit, you know how it was with Dad. My whole life, I thought the only way people would ever love me was if I was the best at something. And with football, I *was* the best. I was the best, and everyone in high school and college loved me because of it. Everybody in South Carolina has loved me since I came here, especially last year. Because I *won*. And then I met Lucia, and she showed me that not everything is about winning."

He shrugged, meeting Maya's eyes. "She was the first person who made me believe that I could be cared for even if I'm not the best quarterback in the league. Even if I never play again. She makes me think that there are others in the world who might like me for me. She made me feel like I'm enough as I am. And that's not something I've ever believed. So, yeah, I guess I realized how I felt about her when I realized how important and cared for she made me feel."

It was all true. Every word of it was true. She'd planted roots in his heart, deep and unrelenting, and every beat was a reminder that she was there. That his heart now beat for her. It was a terrifying thought, especially because he knew it was entirely unrequited. But there was nothing he could do except love her completely, utterly, unequivocally, irrevocably.

Maya's arms wrapped around him, squeezing him tightly. "I love you, football or not, Just so you know. So, there are at least two of us."

He leaned against her. "Thanks, Mai. I'm not sure Luc loves me." When he felt her looking at him questioningly, he continued, "Not yet, at least." And likely not ever. She'd said as much in his house when she'd told him relationships weren't for her. Not after Clark and her mother ruined love for her.

Turning away the painful thought, he asked, "So what's his name, where does he live, and what does he love most in the world?"

Chapter Twenty-Five

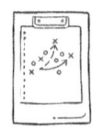

Lucia

Lucia had never minded spending the holidays with only her father. It'd been years since she'd even *seen* her mother, and she'd long since forgotten what it was like to spend Christmas with both of them. Her father's parents were somewhere in Italy, so they were usually unavailable as well.

This year wasn't especially different, though she hated seeing that look in his eyes that accompanied yet another heartbreak. He'd gotten back from his cruise, tan, happy, and in love. Then, apparently, only days later, the woman he'd gone with had decided she no longer wanted to be with him.

Lucia hadn't seen him in so long that she hadn't expected the first thing she saw to be the lowered shoulders, knitted brows, and deep sadness in his eyes. It wasn't new, though. This was how he'd been for the nearly twenty years her mother had been out of their lives. Strung along by woman after woman, heartbreak after heartbreak. He never seemed to take the hint that the universe hadn't forecasted love for him.

But Lucia did. It was all the confirmation she needed to remind herself to rip out the butterflies that kept flitting around in her stomach, throw them in the trash, and set them on fire. She wasn't about to play the fool again.

Her dad had tried to tell her that frozen meals were satisfactory for Christmas, and she'd gasped comically. She went to the store and picked up ingredients for a salad and her dad's favorite pasta. She was sure all he had been eating were frozen meals, casseroles, and lasagnas his neighbors brought him every once in a while. She wondered when he'd last eaten a vegetable.

She got to work cooking for him as he lay on his couch, staring at the ceiling blankly. She hated to say that this was standard, too. How many times had she had to find her own way in elementary and middle school because he'd been so focused on his pain? How many times had she asked him to come to her track meets in high school, only to find him on the couch, blankly staring at the ceiling when she got home? It was like she'd gone back in time to when she was still a kid looking for guidance. Any indication of where she should go, what she should do next.

"Dad, come help me. It'll be a good distraction, I promise. We can talk about whatever you want." She was only home for three nights, and she couldn't stand the thought of them spending the rest of their time together in this tragic silence.

He stood like a zombie, grabbing the peeler she handed him and getting to work on the potato. She willed him to say something, anything. Another moment of silence and she might've combusted.

Finally, he spoke. "What've you been up to, sweetie? I feel like we've hardly spoken these past few months." She heard the hurt in his voice and knew she should've called him more. She'd thought about it, had really wanted to, but every time she'd picked up the phone to do it, she'd remembered this. The way he stood, bent over like everything good in the world was gone. The permanent crease between his eyebrows. The unkempt stubble along his jawline. And then she'd gotten mad and put her phone away.

"I've been working really hard for the Sabertooths. I'm hoping if they do well during playoffs, they'll sign me for a few years. I might be able to work my way up to head analyst if I'm in one place for a while."

"Have you thought about trying to work with the Eagles?"

There it was. The dreaded question. *Why don't you move back to Philly? Be nearby?* She didn't want to be in Philly. She'd had a hard enough time trying to get *out* of Philly. The moment she'd set foot in California, she was a new person. All of her past hardships had been shed, and the Philadelphia Lucia was gone. Life had almost been easy.

She didn't want to become Philadelphia Lucia again. But she couldn't say that. So, instead, she said, "Maybe. But I have a reason to be in Charleston now."

"Right. I saw that in the news, about you and the Sabertooths' quarterback. Why didn't you tell me about him?" She'd been talking about her new friends and the fact that the other analysts were finally listening to her, finally recognizing what an asset she was. But she supposed Colton fit into the equation somewhere. As a friend.

"We were trying to keep it quiet," she lied. "I wanted to wait until there was something to tell before I let you know. Didn't want you to get your hopes up."

He peeled the potato and set it down on the cutting board, going back to lie on the couch. She sighed, too tired to try to coax him back off. When she finished cooking the meal, she put a plate out for him, then watched it get cold as she ate. She washed her dish, set it on the drying rack, and watched the rise and fall of her father's chest a few more times before she trudged to her childhood bedroom.

She loved her father, but this was not the future she saw for herself. She had plans for her career. Lying on the couch and wallowing for months at a time, ignoring all life's responsibilities, was not in the cards. She would not make the same mistakes as her father.

Texts between her and Colton had been sparse since she'd left Charleston. They'd taken to sending pictures of unusual things to each other and writing "look, it's you." It'd been a good way to pull her from the intense sadness that seemed to overwhelm her every time she went back to the house she'd grown up in.

She'd spent most of her time so far cooking healthier meals for her father and cleaning up the house. She didn't really have friends in the area anymore, and she felt itchy sitting around and doing nothing. Like an idiot, she'd decided to leave her tablet in Charleston, thinking it'd be good to get away for a couple of days and spend quality time with her father. But that had been a bust, and her hands were twitching, begging for something to do.

Her flight the next day was only two hours, and then she'd be back in her cozy house that she now realized had transformed into a home. A home she missed dearly.

In the meantime, she finally decided to doom scroll through all of the posts about her and Colton. Curiosity and boredom won, and she found herself scanning the headlines that appeared when she searched their names together. There was one new one which didn't feature her at all. She clicked on it, stomach already twisting into knots.

It was a picture of Colton, Maya, and another woman, and it'd just been posted. The woman was beautiful and tall, just like Maya, and probably about Maya's age too. She looked like she could've been a model. Her eyes were fixed on Colton, whose face was stoic, like an unbothered statue. He didn't appear to be looking at the woman, but the feeling in Lucia's stomach still moved to her chest, impeding her ability to breathe.

As if he'd been inside of her head, her phone vibrated with a text from him.

Colton

> If you see the picture that was just posted with me, Maya, and another girl, that's just Maya's friend.

> Not pictured: Landon, whose tongue was down her throat moments before the photo was taken.

She wondered why she cared so much. Why that green fist of jealousy squeezed her heart so tightly, so painfully. Perhaps it was because of how natural the woman looked beside him. How right it seemed for her to be there, standing beside him, gazing up at him like he was the answer to all of her problems. Maybe she'd been there with Landon, but the photo was a reminder that Colton was one of the best quarterbacks in the league. He could have had any woman he wanted, and she was sure this beautiful woman was far more his type than she was.

That was okay. She'd agreed to a January break up, and at some point after that, she was certain he would realize his feelings for someone who looked as perfect as this woman. And their relationship would be a distant memory. Three months wasn't very long anyway.

Lucia sent back a thumbs up. Then, not caring that it was dumb and childish, she responded:

> **Lucia**
> You don't owe me an explanation.

> **Colton**
> Just never want you to feel an inkling of what you felt with Clark.

Her heart did that dumb hiccup again. The one that made her wonder how much of her soul she'd given up for this agreement. How could this man who'd been so hell-bent on making Max's life so miserable for so long, indirectly doing the same to her, also be the man who'd taken her face in his warm hands and wiped her tears, offering himself up to fix everything? How could he be the man who'd made every effort to ensure she had friends in a new place? How could he be the man who'd made sure she got home safely every day?

She didn't know how to reconcile the two versions of him. Max had grossly overexaggerated Colton Beaumont's cruelty. Colton had never been the terrible villain Max had made him out to be.

She brushed off the thought as she typed out her next text.

> **Lucia**
> Thank you.

Almost immediately, he responded.

Colton

> See you tomorrow?

Lucia

> Yes.

> Shouldn't you be off your phone and enjoying a night out with your siblings?

Colton

> Always gotta check on my girl.

Her chest tightened, and her fingers ached to respond. To clarify what he could possibly mean by that. Why he would call her that when nobody else could see or hear.

And then it hit her like a freight train. All of her suppressed feelings came flying out as she realized why she cared so much, why she'd been so jealous at the sight of the picture.

She had feelings for him that went far deeper than friendship. Feelings that were deeper than a casual hookup, and terrifyingly enough, deeper than anything she'd felt for Max. Increasingly, she was beginning to understand the difference between the coldness of her first love and real, heartwarming love.

This relationship, whatever it was, had the potential to hurt her far more than she'd ever been hurt. Maybe even more than all of her father's heartbreaks. And that was far too scary a thought to entertain. She wouldn't let herself get hurt ever again. She needed to look out for herself, even if it meant losing someone who'd become so important to her. Because if she waited any longer, she might hit the point of no return, and she wasn't sure she could handle that.

I will not play the fool, she reminded herself. She repeated the mantra until she fell asleep. *I will not play the fool. I will not be my father. I will not play the fool. I will not be my father.*

Chapter Twenty-Six

COLTON

Colton had arrived early to Lucia's house, and she'd texted him to come inside. They had an hour or so before they had to be at Devin's for his New Year's party, and Colton was excited to start the year with Lucia at his side. He walked up to her door and knocked, wishing he'd had the foresight to bring her flowers. She'd been distant since returning from Philadelphia a week earlier, more pensive. Maybe she needed a sign that things were going to be okay. More than okay, actually, since they'd clinched the top seed for the playoffs.

All those thoughts left him as the door swung open. Lucia stood in front of him in yoga pants and his Sabers sweatshirt, her hair in a messy bun—absolutely breathtaking. But what stood out the most to him were her eyes. They were red, and the minute he realized it was because she'd been crying, he stepped inside her house, shut her door, and placed his hands on either side of her face, taking in everything from her hair down to her toes to figure out what was wrong.

"What happened, pretty girl?" he asked, worry lacing every word.

Lucia closed her eyes, leaning into his touch. After a moment, she moved away from him, and something like foreboding swirled in his stomach.

"I just wanted to tell you how much I've appreciated you. Everything you've done for me. I know it was because you wanted to get back at Max, but it's been"—she stifled a sob—"a pleasure to pretend to date you, Colton Beaumont."

His heart stopped. Nothing she'd just said made sense. There was a disconnect between her words and her demeanor, and Colton was struggling to put it all together. He used his thumbs to swipe the tears from under her eyes.

"It wasn't just because I wanted to get back at Max, Luc. It hasn't been about that for a while."

He'd apparently said the wrong thing, because she only sobbed harder. He didn't know how to help, so he gathered her in his arms and held her close to him, the strawberry scent of her shampoo calming him. She didn't pull away, her arms locking around him as she cried into his dress shirt.

"Tell me what's wrong, Luc. *Please*."

She pulled back from his arms, walking toward her kitchen. The space between them felt like an ocean that Colton couldn't cross, no matter how hard he might've tried. She rested her hands on her kitchen counter, her back to him.

"I can't keep doing it. I'm sorry, Colton. I really am. But I can't go until playoffs. It's too hard."

Colton felt sandpaper grating in the back of his throat. He tried to clear it, but nothing helped.

"What are you saying?"

Even though his body seemed to comprehend what she had said, his mind was moving too slowly. Hadn't they agreed to January? He'd thought he had at least another week or two. What had changed? And if this was something she wanted, why did she seem so *sad*?

She didn't respond.

"Luc, what are you saying? I thought we agreed to playoffs. Where is this coming from?"

Her body shook, and the effort it took not to follow her into the kitchen and gather her in his arms again almost broke him, but he was trying to respect the distance she seemed desperate to put between them.

"I just went home, and I saw my dad, and I remembered everything with Max, and I just can't. I can't do it. I can't do it, Colt. I don't want to lose you, and if I continue to try to keep it together, I know I will. I can't let myself hurt like that again." Her voice was strangled, and her body was wracked with sobs.

Lose him? She could never lose him. She could do almost anything to him and she wouldn't lose him. A life without Lucia didn't make sense to Colton.

"Lose me? Sweet girl, you could never lose me. I'll always be here for whatever you need. You have to know that."

She was silent for a few moments before turning around and facing him, tears still streaming down her face. She shook her head once.

"I have to do what's best for us. We blurred the lines too much. It's only a week sooner than we said, right? Wasn't this always the plan?"

Screw the plan. He didn't care about the dumb parameters they'd set. He didn't care about any of it if it meant not keeping her in his life.

She continued, "We can continue doing our sessions like normal, but no need to keep going out and doing stuff together. The press will figure it out sooner or later, but for now, they'll just assume we're too busy with playoffs."

Despite the heater that hummed to life, Colton felt oddly cold. He couldn't find the words to express to her that this wasn't what he wanted. Not at all.

Instead, he pleaded, "Give me one more night. Please. Just let me have one more night."

Maybe taking the night would give him enough time to process and figure out the right thing to say to her. He needed to. He couldn't go back to seeing her as just an analyst that was there to help his game.

Lucia's eyes met his. She wiped the tears from her face, patting her cheeks and under her eyes a few times before she nodded. "Okay. We agreed to be there, so one more night. I'll get ready to go to Devin's," she whispered.

He nodded, and even though he should've, he didn't feel victorious in the slightest. "I'm gonna take a drive. I'll be back in thirty."

The drive hadn't cleared his head, and the short, sparkly, silver dress Lucia chose to wear wasn't helping one bit. That fucking dress. It was absolutely going to be his undoing.

All he'd wanted was to take her back into her house and talk to her, make her see that she was making a mistake. But that probably wouldn't have done anything since he still couldn't formulate a coherent thought to explain his feelings. So instead, he'd driven them to Devin's house and parked himself beside Rudy and Cooper, his eyes never straying from Lucia for long.

Lucia laughed at something Jenna said as they danced together, and Colton could hardly pay attention to what Cooper and Rudy were talking about beside him as he watched her smile light up her whole face. That tug on his chest that he felt any time she was near made an appearance, and he tried to breathe through it, rubbing two knuckles over his sternum.

"Do you feel ready for playoffs, Colt?" Cooper looked over his beer at him.

"About as ready as we can be, I think," he answered distractedly.

Cooper and Rudy exchanged a surprised look, which pulled Colton's attention back to them. "What?"

Coop shrugged. "Nothing, man. That's just...I never thought I'd hear you say we're ready for any game, let alone a playoff game. You're Mr. We-can-always-be-better." Rudy raised an eyebrow at Colton like he agreed with Cooper.

"Well, of course we can always be better. But if we beat Tampa Bay next week, we have a bye for Wildcard week, which we always utilize well. Don't you agree we've found our rhythm? We're playing like last year."

His friends still looked unconvinced, but Colton's mind was already off football. Of course he was excited for playoffs and for what the rest of the season might bring them. They were right on the cusp of what they'd all been hungry for: a chance at another Super Bowl ring. That didn't change the fact that being separated from Lucia for those three days when she was in Philadelphia had been agonizing. His fingers had itched to text her about every minute detail of his life, from his pizza leftovers to the horrible bars Maya and Landon had dragged him to. He'd wanted to tell her everything but had settled for little daily check-ins, even when she seemed distant. And now, without understanding why, he was about to have to say goodbye to their quality time together. To their texts. To his safe space. All he would have of her would be their sessions after practice.

"You know how much I love the game, but let me tell you, I'm so glad the season's gonna be over soon. I'm tired of the road. I just wanna be home with Jen and the kids, man."

Cooper set a hand on Rudy's shoulder. "That sounds like a personal problem, my friend."

"Nobody's managed to seduce Cooper Hayes' heart, then? You'd think with all the women who throw themselves at you, you'd have found somebody you like enough."

Cooper's eyes flicked to Colton briefly before going back to Rudy. "Nah, I'm not really interested in settling down like y'all two. I've got a few years before I gotta worry about that. If I ever do."

"I never thought I'd see the day that Colton would be out so often, and it's for a woman. So who knows what might happen, Coop."

Colton frowned. "What does that mean?"

Rudy put his hands up in surrender before taking a swig of his beer. "You never came to parties for more than an hour or so. Same with Thanksgiving at our house and any other team event. You'd come, show your face, and go home to watch film or lift like a masochist." He shrugged. "It's just nice to see that Lucia has gotten you to relax a little. Shown you that there's more to life than a pigskin."

Colton's eyes slid back to the woman in question. Devin's house had never been so packed, people crushed together body to body like the parties back in college. Still, he could make out the wide grin on Lucia's face as she moved her hips to the music, her hair wild and free, cheeks flushed from the heat of the house and the alcohol that was surely in her system. He was glad she was feeling better. The sight of her crying had destroyed him, and he'd hated every second of it. Just watching her made his lips twitch up into a smile, despite the pain he felt knowing it might be the last time they were together in this way. He vowed he would do everything he could to ensure she had a good night, even if it killed him. Even if it meant pretending it didn't.

"See? I've never seen you like this."

"Huh?"

Rudy just smiled at him, genuineness lining his features. "I'm happy for you, man."

"Alright, this is getting to be a bit sappy for me, so I'm gonna go find a sexy and willing woman to satisfy my many desires. Catch y'all tomorrow." Cooper headed outside where a large group of women danced together. Colton was sure Coop would have no trouble finding what he was looking for, knowing his friend really did have women throwing themselves at him in droves.

"I'm gonna go get another beer. Do you need one?" Rudy eyed Colton's nearly full beer.

"No, I'm set for now, thanks." His eyes, drawn like a magnet to Lucia, found her again. Leigh had joined them, along with another couple of women.

A group of men Colton didn't know had been circling the girls most of the night as if waiting for the right moment to approach. Colton tensed as a guy moved toward Lucia and whispered in her ear, a grin on his face. He hadn't touched her yet, but Colton's hand still tightened around the bottle in his hand. He watched as the guy danced at a surprisingly respectful distance from her, even as she stopped paying him any mind and resumed dancing with Jenna.

They continued like that for a few minutes, Colton's eyes never leaving them. The guy talked to his friend, watching the girls dance with a look on his face that made Colton's blood boil. Then the song changed, and the guy's hands landed on Lucia's waist.

Colton's mind emptied, and he was across the room in seconds.

Chapter Twenty-Seven

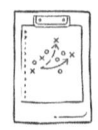

Lucia

Lucia felt the man's hands on her waist, disappearing after only a second or two. She whirled around to yell at him, but Colton was already gripping him by his collar, whispering something in his ear that had the guy paling. Lucia's heartbeat ratcheted at the sight, reminded once again of what she was about to give up.

Colton dropped him as he spoke, quiet but dangerous. "Go. Away." He took a step closer to Lucia, his voice falling to a whisper for only her ears. "You okay?"

Her whole body erupted with warmth at the sound of his deep voice, strained as if he were trying to hold himself back from something. She took a step toward him, placing a hand on his cheek.

"I'm okay."

She'd had plenty to drink, and she knew it was making her do things she shouldn't, but if this was the last night she had with him, she wanted it all. She'd made her peace with their time coming to an end—or at least she was trying to—but why shouldn't she let herself enjoy the night they had left?

What she wanted was his hands on her, his lips on her, his everything on her. She felt hot, hot, hot and she wanted *him*. She grabbed his hands and placed them on her waist, swaying with the music until he loosened up and watched her, seemingly entranced. She turned around in his arms, allowing her hips and ass to rub up against him in a way that brought her body to life. Luckily, Jenna and Leigh didn't seem to mind.

Lucia had been to plenty of New Year's Eve parties when she'd been with Max, but she'd always been the stuffy analyst at those parties. She'd stood beside Max in her work-appropriate dress and chatted quietly with some of the team wives. The only time she'd really been able to let loose was when she and Isa had gone out, away from Max.

Being there in Charleston with Colton and the Sabers, she basked in the fact that there were no expectations, no arbitrary rules she had to follow. She could dance and laugh and yell and drink and smile as much as she wanted, and she loved every second of it.

The volume of the music lowered as they moved closer to midnight, and her heartbeat started to slow while she and Colton chatted with their friends about the season and the new year, his hands placed somewhere on her at all times. It made her wonder if maybe he was struggling with this as much as she was. Did he feel that twist in his stomach the way that she did? Did he feel the sandpaper in his mouth and throat like she did? Based on his reaction at her house, she thought it was possible.

Two minutes before midnight, when the countdown on Devin's TV began, she turned, placing her hands around Colton's neck and playing with the hair at its nape. Their eyes met, tinged with a sadness that only they understood, but the moment that grin found his face, the whole world disappeared. She could almost imagine they were really together and in love. There was only Colton. Bright, beautiful, goofy-only-for-her Colton. She grinned right back, wanting him to smile at her like that forever, despite knowing she shouldn't and that he wouldn't.

"What're your resolutions for the new year, Moretti?"

She hadn't had time to think about her resolutions much, though honestly, when had she ever?

"Wouldn't you like to know?"

He squeezed her waist tightly, chiding her, but the feeling of his hands tight around her only served to fuel the desire that'd been simmering below the surface. His eyes dropped to her lips like he knew exactly where her mind was.

"I suppose my top resolution will be to help the Sabers get another Super Bowl win." She didn't voice the first one that came to her: finding a hobby that made her as giddy as being in his arms. She was too scared to tell anyone, knowing the chances of her finding anything remotely close were unlikely.

Something like sadness flickered in his eyes for a second before everyone in Devin's house began shouting down from ten. She closed her eyes as they reached one, pulling him close to her and kissing him deeply, turning into putty as one of his hands slid up to cup her face. He pulled away much too quickly, and she pouted, opening her eyes as everyone around them cheered.

"Happy New Year, Moretti," he whispered, pained.

He didn't pull away entirely, and her eyes searched his face before she asked, "What about your resolutions?"

"I suspect those will be broken soon enough. Probably better if I don't tell you."

"Colton."

"Lucia."

She huffed. "That's not fair. I told you mine." Even if she'd bent the truth a little.

She was startled when he bent closer to her, his hand still cupping her chin, his lips against the shell of her ear in a way that made her shiver.

"Fine. I told myself that I'd fight every single urge I have around you until, inevitably, you're no longer mine. I promised myself that I'd keep my hands off the curve of this waist that I love so much. That I'd stop thinking about tasting you every time you glare at me. That I'd stop thinking about the way you moan when I'm fucking you. I promised myself that I'd find something else to occupy myself with, ideally football, because the fantasies I keep having about you *can't* be healthy. But above all, I promised myself that I'd find the strength to walk away from you after the Tampa Bay game, because if not, I'll never be able to get you out of my head. And I'm starting to think that one's been broken long before now."

Her breath had caught at his first words, and she'd held it until he finished, heat pooling between her thighs. She didn't know when her eyes had closed, but she was acutely aware of her other senses, the feeling of his breath on her ear, the sounds of Devin's music getting louder now that the new year had begun, the smell of sweat and beer and longing. The taste of him, minty, with a hint of beer, still sat on her tongue.

She was confused. So fucking confused. His words were a confession that neither of them seemed prepared for, especially not now. Not after what she'd said at her house. Why hadn't he said something like this when they'd been talking then? She knew she had moved away from him, trying to find the courage to tell him that they needed to stop, but she also knew that if he would have pulled her into his arms again, she might've given up on all of it. Why hadn't he tried to comfort her with these words if he felt the same way?

Because he was good. So good, and so sweet. The sweetest man she'd ever met. He cared about her feelings and respected her boundaries, always making sure he wasn't overstepping. And now he was telling her that he wasn't going to be able to get her out of his head, and she didn't know what to make of it, even as she felt her heart splinter.

Tears pricked her eyes, but all she could say was, "Colt…"

He pressed a kiss to her forehead, his lips brushing against her skin as he spoke. "Please don't cry, sweet girl. I didn't mean to make you cry."

She hiccuped as she tried pushing back the tears. "No, no. I'm okay. I just…I didn't realize you felt that way about me."

"Does it change anything?" he asked hopefully.

Lucia imagined for a minute what a life with Colton could have looked like. More sessions in her office. More movie nights in his hotel rooms, cuddled up against him. More waving like a buffoon from the analyst box when he turned to look at her after a spectacular play. More Thanksgivings where she felt free and happy. A lifetime of texts that made her smile.

And then she remembered the little girl who'd waited at the bus stop all alone because her father hadn't been able to get out of bed. The little girl who'd fallen off a stool and cracked a tooth while trying to cook herself dinner because she'd been tired of eating frozen macaroni and cheese. The woman who'd taken a chance on a man who'd only pretended he wanted a wife who loved football, when in reality, all he'd wanted was a trophy wife who kept quiet. The woman who'd continued to give someone the chance to prove her wrong, while persistently being proven right.

She cursed the universe for making the mistake of giving her Max when she'd needed Colton. But it was too late for her.

She shook her head. "It can't. It can't change anything."

Colton moved away from her, eyes closing as he let out a breath. He nodded once. "Okay. Then let's do our last night right. Let's go home."

Home. She liked the sound of that too much. To cover up that fact, she whispered, "Only if you promise not to be nice."

Surprise registered on his face only briefly before they said goodbye to their friends and left the party. The silence between them in the car was tense, full of anticipation. At her request, they went to her house, and he helped her out of the car, taking her keys from her and unlocking her door.

And then he was closing it and pressing her against it, his kiss sweet and delicious, a hand on her waist and the other pushing against the door right beside her head. She bit his lower lip, sucking on it gently before letting it go, and then he groaned, and the kiss became something else entirely.

He picked her up and walked her to her kitchen, all the while keeping his lips on hers. When he set her down and backed away from her, she frowned.

"What happened?"

"Luc, how much have you had to drink tonight?"

"Barely anything." A lie, but despite the two or three drinks, she felt surprisingly sober.

"Liar."

She crossed her arms, hoping it pushed her tits up, the silver sparkles of her dress sending light all around them. She grinned when his eyes fell to them.

"Colton"—she drew out the last letter—"I know you wanna fuck me."

He swallowed, his eyes flicking back up to her eyes. "I want to do unfathomable things to you, Moretti. But I won't unless I know you're sober enough to remember tomorrow how hard I make you come tonight."

She could feel herself getting wet at the thought of what he might do to her. "What do you want me to do? You want me to walk a straight line while tapping my nose with each pointer finger at intervals? Want me to breathe into a breathalyzer? How can I prove to you that I'm sober enough for you to ruin me tonight, officer?" In a way she wasn't certain made her seem less drunk, she continued, "Z, Y, X, W, V, U, T—"

"Luc," he groaned. His hand ran over the bulge in his pants, and Lucia wanted that honor.

"Come ruin me, Superstar," she purred. Her confidence astounded even her, but Colton did something to her that no other man had been able to.

He must've decided that she was sober enough, because he was on her in an instant, a strong hand cupping her face and a finger dropping down, down, down until her legs were widening and a whimper left her mouth.

"I want you to wear this dress while you come all over my cock." He buried a hand in her hair, pulling her head back to expose her neck. His breath swirled against the column of her throat before he pressed kisses to it.

Lucia slid a hand down his toned chest and stomach before she landed on that bulge. She fumbled with his belt, frustrated. When she finally got him free of his pants, he hissed at her touch. She smiled innocently at him, batting her eyelashes as she pulled him to rest at her entrance.

His body stilled. "You're not wearing anything underneath this dress?" The noise he made was primal. He kissed her hard, rubbing himself against her. Her eyes fluttered closed and she moaned, needing him inside of her.

She heard the sound of foil ripping, and her eyebrows came together, even as she continued enjoying the feel of him pressed against her. "You had a condom in your pocket? You knew this was gonna happen?"

"Car. Grabbed it before we came in." He grunted the words out as he pumped the condom over his erection and placed it back at her entrance. His hand palmed her body until it reached her ass, and he picked her up easily.

He slipped into her, his hands on her hips, holding her up. For a second, she marveled at the strength it must've taken to hold her up with just his arms, and then she was digging her nails into well-muscled shoulders and moaning.

"Yes, Colton, *please*."

"Please what, Moretti? What do you want?"

"God—" She choked as he slammed in and out of her. She couldn't believe she'd been wet enough that he'd slipped right in without any resistance. She loved the feeling of him moving inside of her, loved how deep he hit her, but she knew she needed *more*. "I want you to lean me over this—*fuck*."

She swallowed as he kept pumping in and out of her.

"What was that?" he asked her smugly, a smirk on his beautiful face.

"Lean—lean me over this counter and rail me, *please*."

He cursed, setting her back down on the counter for half a second before turning her around. Her body pressed into the cool marble of her kitchen countertop, feeling the chill spread through the fabric of her dress.

Colton's hands drifted underneath her dress and up until they gripped her hips tightly. She grabbed onto the bar top in front of her, and this time when he slid into her, she cried out. He was deeper than anybody had ever been, and she finally knew what it meant to be completely full.

"Oh my god, Colt, *yes*."

"You like that?" Yes. She loved it. She never wanted it to stop. "So fucking good, Moretti. You feel so fucking good."

The sounds of him slapping against her were pushing her toward her climax, and she felt her ass bouncing at every thrust.

Colton slid an arm up out of her dress and placed it lightly against her throat, pulling her against him as he continued thrusting. "Hold onto me, Luc." She pulled her hand from the counter and placed it around the back of his neck. The hand on her hip gripped her tighter before sliding down to her clit and rubbing her in circles. Over and over, he filled her from behind, his lips pressed to her ear, whispering all kinds of dirty things.

"Oh my—*fuck*, Colton. I'm gonna come."

"Yeah, you fuckin' are. Come all over my cock, pretty girl." His tempo inside of her and against her core picked up until she was screaming his name. The earth fractured, and she felt herself tightening around him, her body nearly giving out from the pleasure.

The hand that had been playing with her clit flattened against her stomach, anchoring her to him. His other remained around her throat, and she loved the feel of his large hand there. He'd learned from their first time how she liked it. She leaned further into him, her hand fisting into his hair the way it had on the plane.

"Such a good girl. I love when you listen to me." She tugged at his hair a little, just to spite him, and a garbled cry left his mouth. He used the hand that was around her throat to push her face to the side and kiss her mouth. He thrust into her twice more, the arm around her stomach tightening as he came hard, moaning deeply into her mouth.

She enjoyed the feeling of his body shaking with his orgasm. And though she knew it was stupid, she pulled herself from him, turned around, put her arms around his neck, and kissed him deeply. If it was going to be her last time feeling this way, she needed it all.

Which is why she took his hand and led him into her bedroom, her silent question already answered as he walked behind her. After helping her take off her makeup and change, he slipped into her bed and held her close, his warmth enveloping her like a shield from the reality she'd be faced with the next morning.

Chapter Twenty-Eight

COLTON

Colton took a hit, grunting as he landed underneath one of his defensive linemen. He helped Colton up, apologizing profusely, but Colton shook it off.

"No worries, I'm all good. My fault." He'd barely been paying attention to practice and hadn't realized how much time had passed since Chris had snapped the ball to him.

Focusing on football was a nearly impossible task. Colton's thoughts hadn't left Lucia for a moment, not even when he was on the field. He was so far gone. He'd known spending that last night with her would only hurt him more in the long run, but he hadn't realized the depth of his feelings until he'd spent a week away from her. She had called out sick for their sessions the week following their night, and the distance hadn't done him any good. If anything, it'd just proven to him how in love with her he was. Still, he hadn't contacted her, trying to respect her wishes.

Colton's performance had been subpar at best in the last game of the regular season. The Sabers only barely managed to beat Tampa Bay, a team they'd been projected to beat by miles. Lucia had steered clear of him both on the plane and once the team was back in Charleston.

Now, during a Wednesday practice of bye week, he couldn't even throw one solid pass. It'd been nine days since he'd seen her, spoken to her, held her, and all he could think about was the feeling of her wrapped in his arms. He was sure Coach Turner was one bad throw away from pulling him and putting in their second string, but he couldn't help that his thoughts were elsewhere, no matter how hard he tried to concentrate.

As if Coach could read Colton's mind, he yelled, "Beaumont, get the hell off my field!"

Colton's head snapped to Coach Turner. He jogged over, pulling his helmet from his head. "Coach—"

"I don't want to hear it. If you can't make basic passes to your receivers, you're out for divisionals." The divisional round of playoffs was only eleven days away. Worse, it was against Max Clark and the Richmond Vipers. He *needed* to play in that game.

"Coach, I promise I can do this. I'm just in my head. I'll stay late. I'll do whatever you need me to do. I promise I can do this. I *need* to do this."

Coach Turner's eyes were already sweeping the field before he said, "Go shower and cool down. I need to think."

Colton's heart jumped into his throat as he nodded. He ran off the field, ignoring the looks of his closest friends. Cooper had asked him a few times what'd been going on with him, as had Rudy, but he'd been too embarrassed to explain that his relationship with Lucia had never been real, and yet he'd fallen for her harder than he knew possible.

He breathed in and out quickly, trying to relax even as his mind ran a hundred miles a minute. He needed to find a way to prove to Coach that he could do what needed to be done for the Vipers game.

He took a quick shower, hardly noticing the way the water scalded his skin, and threw on a pair of sweatpants. He couldn't find the sweatshirt he'd left in his locker, and then remembered it was one of the ones he'd let Lucia have. His chest grew heavy at the reminder.

She'd been the last person he expected to see as he walked out into the facility, and yet there she stood, a white, long-sleeved button-down tucked into a pencil skirt that grazed the tops of her knees. Her eyes drank in the upper body he'd worked so hard for, and then her eyes met his and he stopped breathing. She opened her mouth to speak, then closed it.

I think I might be in love with you, he thought. *And I think that even though that scares the shit out of me, even though I've been convinced my whole life that I can't have a girlfriend* and *this career, I can't bear to be without you.*

He opened his mouth, but the stricken look on her face and subtle shake of her head made him close it. He didn't voice his thoughts, and she appeared relieved as she hurried past him to the elevator, his arms aching to reach out to hold her again long after the doors closed. At least her being at the facility meant their sessions would continue.

He walked to his car, trying to understand the look on her face when he'd been about to speak. He located a shirt and threw it on, then went up to her office. He stepped inside, ready to ask how she was feeling, when he noticed Tim standing beside her.

Lucia wouldn't even meet Colton's eyes as Tim looked between the two of them. Finally, Tim spoke.

"Today will be a joint session. I'll be supervising Lucia, but you can continue as if this were a normal session."

"Why?"

"Lucia wants to make sure you're getting all the help you need as we go into playoffs." Colton had been asking Lucia but Tim responded.

Colton's eyes hadn't left Lucia. She still refused to look at him. Why was she making this so hard? Why had she called backup, especially when it was at the expense of her independence? She hated people believing she couldn't do her job, so why would she invite someone into their session as if she wasn't capable?

And then it all came crashing down on him as he realized why.

She'd sobbed as she'd told him she wanted to end things. She'd let him take her in his arms, let him comfort her, even as she told him she didn't want to continue their relationship. She hadn't wanted him to talk when they were alone together. She'd asked someone to come and sit with them through sessions so they would have to keep things professional. She'd agreed to go with him to Devin's, and then when he'd confessed his feelings to her, she hadn't said she didn't feel the same way.

When he'd asked if it'd changed anything, she hadn't said "no" but "it can't." *It* can't *change anything.*

All of this had arisen from her seeing her father for the holidays, a man Colton knew had spent a lifetime getting his heart broken. The man whose experiences had convinced Lucia that she wasn't built for love.

And it all came together. Maybe she didn't feel about him exactly how he felt about her, but she was struggling too. She didn't want this, maybe as badly as he didn't want this. She was pushing him away because she was scared about her feelings for him. Because she'd felt that thing between them go from a tentative friendship to something entirely different. He hadn't been faking it for a while, and now he knew she felt the same way.

He wasn't going to let her push him away. He wasn't Max Clark, and he wasn't any of the women who broke her father's heart. He wasn't going to give up on them just because she was scared. Things were different for them, and he was going to show her that. Because even if it took him a lifetime to prove it to her, he loved her.

He sat through the session, providing responses only when asked, his head in an entirely other space. And when the session was over, he watched her shoot up and leave with Tim like she knew being alone with him had the potential to change her mind. For the first time in a week and a half, Colton had hope.

January 11th

Colton

> If you can honestly say you don't have feelings for me, then I'll leave you be. But you have to swear on your fantasy football team or it doesn't count.

January 12th

Colton

> I know what you're doing. You're pushing me away because you care about me too. So here's me refusing to let you.

January 13th

Colton

> You can keep having Tim in our sessions, but it won't change how I feel about you. And how you feel about me. Eventually, we're probably gonna end up alone in your office or the hall, and then you're gonna have to face what this is.

January 13th

Colton

> Don't give up on us, Luc. We both know this is different.

January 14th

Colton

> I can do this forever. You not responding won't stop me from texting you. We both know how stubborn I am.

January 15th

Colton

> Stop running, Luc. I won't stop texting you, finding ways to see you at the facility, telling you how I feel. I won't give up on this, no matter how long you ignore me.

Once he'd learned what was really going on with Lucia, he'd gotten his shit together on the field. Now, only three days from the game, he felt certain in his abilities. He would do everything it took to bury Clark and the Vipers. Not for himself, not for a ring, not even for the team. For Lucia.

His father had invited him over after practice, and it'd been a few weeks since he'd been at the house, so he'd agreed. He stood outside, taking in the perfectly manicured shrubs and greenery that lined the stairs of the house, something he was sure his father had nothing to do with, other than perhaps handing someone cash.

That itchy and tense feeling that always accompanied meetings with his father was there beneath his Sabers sweatsuit. He saw a flash in his periphery but paid it no mind. He climbed the steps up to the front door and rang the doorbell, half-hoping the man wouldn't come to the door.

He was not so lucky. His father opened the door, a suit on that told Colton he'd been working from home. Rather than speak, his father turned on his heel and walked inside the house, leaving the front door open.

Colton stepped inside, respecting his mother's wishes by removing his shoes, and closed the door. He followed his father toward his study, taking in the bare walls for the first time. No pictures of the family, or of his deceased wife, or even photos of nature. The walls were just bare.

"Hey, Dad."

"I'm glad you and that girl broke up. She was ruining your chances at another Super Bowl."

Colton's legs almost gave out at the words.

"What?" he asked, his voice breaking on the word. How would he know about that? Had the media reported on it just because they hadn't been seen together outside of the facility for a couple of weeks?

"You haven't heard? It just came out that she's been talking to Max Clark the whole time she's been in Charleston. You wasted your season chasing that girl. That woman was a Viper through and through. I can't believe you trusted her. I knew from the moment she walked through this door that she was no good."

Colton had to place a hand on the wall beside him to steady himself.

"That can't be true. Lucia wouldn't do something like that." She wouldn't, he knew that. He'd learned about her relationship with Max over their past few months together, and there was no way she'd been lying to him about that. The agony in her voice and the sadness that took over her body when she'd talked about it couldn't have been faked.

His father shoved his phone into Colton's hand. On the screen, *The Richmond Herald* claimed to have insider information about the torrid affair between Lucia and Max. About how Lucia was taking information from her work with the Sabers to the Vipers.

It had to be Max's doing. It had to be. He scrolled down, looking for any proof. There were pictures of Lucia and Max together, but none of them looked recent. Then, Colton's finger stilled over an image.

In it, Lucia and Max were on some kind of video call, and Lucia was looking down, smiling. Colton would've waved it off, but sitting around her neck was a necklace with a pearl pendant. The necklace that she'd told him was new after their Thanksgiving win.

Colton's heart hammered in his chest, blood rushing in his ears. It didn't make sense. Why would she have called Max? And if it hadn't been anything bad, why hadn't she told Colton? He was sure there was an explanation for all of this. There had to be.

Before he handed the phone back to his father, he saw a video. The hammering in his chest increased as he hovered over it and then finally clicked it open.

"Yeah. I'm gonna give you our plays." The voice was unmistakably Lucia's, and she was talking to Max. And wearing that necklace. Which meant that this conversation, whatever it was between them, had happened after Thanksgiving, months after she'd left the Vipers.

Colton looked back at his father in disbelief.

"Are you crying? Christ, you're such a girl. This is why you should've been at the gym more this season. Look at you! Clark's bigger than you and probably faster too."

When Colton didn't respond, his father continued, "I hope you now realize that she was a waste of your time and that your focus should remain on the game. Women and children come after the glory."

Colton had heard his father talk down about women in the past, but this was different. He hated to hear him talk about Lucia in that manner. Despite that, he bit his tongue, as he always did. He might have been a coward, but he couldn't bring himself to say something to the man who'd practically built his career. At least the lecture was over.

Colton opened his mouth to speak, but it seemed his father wasn't done. "If I could've had you and Landon on my own, I would have. Your mother only babied you and slowed me down."

Colton shut his mouth. He was still reeling from the article, but he'd snapped to attention at his father's words. For him to disrespect Colton's mom in such a way—the woman who'd loved them and nurtured them the way their father should have, the woman who'd been there for all his practices and games, who'd loved him unconditionally—outraged him. No, it was more than rage. There was no word to describe the eerie tendrils that wrapped themselves around Colton's insides and pulsed through him as his father shattered any resolve he'd had to keep his mouth shut.

"How fucking *dare* you. How dare you talk about Mom like that. Mom was the only good part of our childhood. All you did was take away our chances of being actual children, ruined my relationship with Landon, and ensured I never spent time with the family who actually cared about me. I have grandparents who've wanted to be a part of my life, *our* lives, since long before Mom died. But I've felt so guilty about how you made us shut them out, especially after Mom got sick, that I've stayed away, kept them locked out for so fucking long. I'm fucking tired of your self-serving bullshit. I'm tired of your lectures. I'm tired of letting you tell me how to play football like I'm not already a thousand times more successful than you ever were. I'm tired of you treating Landon like he's second best and Maya like she just doesn't *exist*. And I'm tired of you talking shit about the woman I love because you're so emotionally stunted that you've never successfully shown anybody love."

Colton turned on his heel, stomping out of a house he was sure he would never see again. He pulled his phone from his pocket as he got in and started his car, noticing a text from Lucia for the first time in nearly two weeks.

Lucia

> It's not true. I swear it isn't. Please don't believe it.

> I would never do something like that.

Colton wanted to believe her, but her words from the video kept ringing in his head. *I'm gonna give you our plays.* Why would she have said that? It felt like college all over again.

He raced to the facility, searching everywhere for Lucia. When he got to her office, Coach Turner and Tim stood outside, somber looks on their faces.

"Is it true?" Colton asked.

Coach Turner's face didn't change as Tim spoke. "We can't say for certain. She's on temporary probation. You can't speak to her until she's been cleared. We don't know if she's been feeding the Vipers information about the team."

At the last sentence, Coach turned a disapproving glare onto Tim before looking back at Colton. "We don't believe she has been, but we're taking all necessary precautions. As you know, this is an important game, and we need to be sure no information was exchanged before she can be reinstated."

Despite the eyes of the two men on him, Colton's back hit the wall, and he sank to the ground. Betrayal sat heavy in his chest, and as soon as Coach Turner and Tim walked away, Colton opened his texts and read and re-read Lucia's last message.

Chapter Twenty-Nine

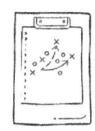

Lucia

The moment Lucia saw the news article, she texted Colton. While she'd been the one to end things between them, her feelings for him hadn't changed in the slightest, and the idea that he might have seen and believed the news threatened to break her into little pieces. Especially after she'd had to spend over a week without his jokes and laughter to make her feel better.

The article itself was so stupid. How unfulfilled were the people at *The Richmond Herald* that they had to keep finding things in her life to talk about? She knew this was Max's doing, felt the heat of rage build in her when she saw the quote taken out of context from their last conversation. He'd screen recorded it, as if he'd planned this from the start. Like if the conversation hadn't gone his way, he'd have the recording as some kind of leverage. She wouldn't be surprised if this was his way of getting back at her for blocking him. It had probably been an added bonus that it would get in Colton's head three days before the game.

Max was pathetic. He knew he wasn't as good as Colton, so he'd turned to psychological techniques to win. What a piece of shit. She wasn't sure whether the tears she held back were due to her anger at him or frustration at the possibility that Colton might not believe her. Might never want to speak to her again. Especially not when this had been his fear from the moment she'd joined the Sabers.

She wasn't surprised when only moments after she'd composed herself, Tim and Coach Turner stepped into her office, mixed expressions of pity and anger on their faces.

She steeled herself for a lecture, or worse, to lose her job. She knew fighting tooth and nail to keep this job wouldn't work. For this, she would *beg*.

"Before you say anything, none of it is true. All of those pictures were taken before we'd broken up except for the phone call. That phone call was our breakup call and the quote in the video was taken out of context. I was being sarcastic. I didn't tell him anything about the Sabers, and I haven't talked to him since." She said it all in one breath, and she came up for air at the end of it.

"We're putting you on probation until further notice. We obviously need to get to the bottom of these allegations. We will have to pursue legal action if it's determined that you've been conspiring with the Vipers," Tim responded, words clipped.

Lucia willed the tears away. Coach Turner's face softened when he saw the look on her face. "Our hands are tied here. We know you're a professional and a great analyst. *When* we determine you didn't conspire with the Vipers, the Sabers' legal team will look into a defamation suit. For now, it's probably best if you leave your equipment and go home. We'll try to have a decision for you before the game on Sunday."

Lucia looked down and nodded. Her hand automatically reached for her tablet, but she set it down a second later. She grabbed her purse, keeping her head down as she left them in her office, praying as she walked to the elevator and down to the facility garage that she didn't run into anybody else. She could only imagine what the team and staff thought of her.

Lucia lay on her couch, wrapped in one of Colton's sweatshirts and yoga pants, unwashed hair in a bun with light-brown strands hanging around her face haphazardly. She hadn't left the comfort of her couch in over a day, glued to an old season of *The Bachelor*. She couldn't even bring herself to eat anything other than her mini ice cream cones, the empty box abandoned at her feet.

Isa had called a couple of times to check on her, but she didn't answer, texting her that she wasn't up for talking about the article. Her father had tried to call once too, and she wanted to speak with him even less.

Her phone lit up with another call from Isa. When Lucia didn't pick up, Isa texted her twice in quick succession.

Isa

> Do you have Tim's phone number? Send it to me.

> This is serious. Call me! Or send me his number.

Lucia's eyebrows knitted together as she saw the attachment Isa sent her. It was a video, and when she clicked it open, it was the screen recording Max had taken of their conversation.

She called Isa immediately.

When she picked up, Lucia said, "How did you get that?"

"The short version is that I went into the locker room during practice. Figured out his password—he's so pathetic, it was the date Lincoln beat Crestview our junior year. Sent it to myself. Now you have it."

Lucia sat on her couch, mouth open in shock. "That's..." She didn't know how to finish the thought.

"Brilliant? I know. I finally found a way to exact my revenge. Well, part of it at least. Anyway, get that to Tim and Coach

Turner. And Colton. He needs his head clear if he's gonna win."

Lucia wasn't sure she wanted to text the video to Colton. It was one of those things that needed to be shown to him in person. But she had no idea if she'd be given that opportunity before the game.

"Isa...I can't even tell you how thankful I am for you. I really am."

"Don't you get sentimental on me now, *osita*. Get that to the Sabers so you can get cleared to work. I want to see you after the game on Sunday."

She'd been so caught up in everything, she'd forgotten that her best friend would be in Charleston for the game. Vipers trainers always traveled with the team.

Isa clicked off the call before Lucia could say anything else. She forwarded the video to Tim and sat on the edge of her couch with bated breath.

Forty-five minutes later, Lucia's ringer echoed around her house, breaking the silence that she'd been sitting in, staring blankly at the wall. She answered it on the second ring.

"Lucia Moretti speaking."

Coach Turner's kind voice answered. "Hi, Lucia. Glad I caught you. I just wanted to let you know that, as expected, you've been cleared to continue working. Legal will be in touch about a defamation suit in the case that *The Richmond Herald* doesn't remove the article."

She thought she'd be happier to hear the words, but she still felt the hole in her chest. She hadn't heard anything from Colton, and she wasn't sure if that was because he didn't want to talk to her or because he wasn't allowed to.

"Thank you so much. I'll be in tomorrow morning before the game."

She thought that would be the end of the conversation, but Coach Turner asked, "Do you know who might have leaked this information to the press?"

It seemed like the answer was obvious. Why was he asking something he knew the answer to?

Then, she realized. "No," she lied.

A beat of silence. "You know that if you give me his name, it'll make all of this go smoother. Legal action may be taken against him specifically, by us and the Vipers, and he'll be formally reprimanded, potentially taking him out of the game."

She shook her head despite knowing he couldn't see the motion, certain of herself. Even if Colton had given up on her, she wouldn't give up on him.

"Colton needs to beat him on the field Sunday. Anything else won't be enough for him. He needs to prove to himself that he deserves to win. That he's the best. I won't take that from him."

He sounded proud as he said, "See you tomorrow."

She thanked him again. Just as she hit the sleep button, her phone buzzed.

Colton: I shouldn't be texting you, but I can't help myself. We should talk after the game.

She smiled softly, tension leaving her body. She knew it didn't mean all was forgiven, but at least he was talking to her. Regardless of where their relationship stood, the last thing she wanted was for him to believe she would have done something that horrible.

Lucia: Whenever you want, I'll be there.

And for good measure, she typed out one more.

Lucia: Good luck, Superstar. Kick his ass for me.

Chapter Thirty

Lucia

It was the first home game Lucia had worked since the fake relationship started where she wasn't standing in the end zone, waiting for a kiss. Just the thought of Colton running out onto the field and not having someone there for him made her chest tighten painfully.

The stadium erupted with screaming and cheering as the Sabers ran out onto the field, Colton leading the charge as usual. The lights shut off momentarily as green, firework-like sparks leaped into the sky. The sounds of 80,000 fans doing the Sabers roar put a small smile on her face, and Blade the Sabertooth ran up and down the field, jumping for joy near the loudest sections.

Boos rang out when the Vipers came onto the field, and she had to ignore the looks from her colleagues when Max's face appeared on the screen above their windows. Despite the allegations clearly being false, since she'd obviously been cleared to continue her work, they'd become cold toward her once again. Not that she was surprised. Nothing the men in her life did surprised her anymore.

After the national anthem, Colton went to the center of the field for the coin toss, a grim expression on his face. His glare was leveled at a grinning Max, who looked like he'd already gotten everything he'd ever wanted. A jolt of electricity shot up her spine as the corner of Colton's mouth lifted a fraction when he won the toss, electing to defer.

Max's first drive was sloppy, and the Sabers' offense was on the field quickly. Unfortunately, they didn't do much better.

The teams traded three and outs before each kicked a field goal. The game was much slower than everybody had hoped. Colton and the offense went back onto the field for a final drive before the end of the half, with a minute and a half and two timeouts left. They'd been able to accomplish much wilder feats, so she had faith that they could do it.

On first down, TJ, the Sabers' first-string running back, got three yards. On second down, Colton faked to TJ and then ran the ball another three. She could see Coach Turner gesturing at Colton from the sidelines, likely changing the play call. They wouldn't get the remaining four yards they needed if they kept rushing.

On third down, Chris hiked the ball to Colton, who looked downfield for an open receiver. Two defensive backs were covering Cooper, and Devin's route looked busted. The offensive line was struggling to keep the Vipers at bay, and in the blink of an eye, two of them were on Colton. He tried to evade, but there was nothing he could do, and then he went down. Hard.

She hadn't realized the gasp had left her mouth until her coworkers looked at her. She stood, walking toward the tall, glass windows of the box as if getting closer would provide him the support he needed to get up.

Get up. Get up. Get up. Why wasn't he getting up? The Vipers' linemen were already standing, high-fiving each other and gesturing at the crowd, but Colton remained on the ground. Lucia didn't so much as breathe as her eyes flicked from the field below to the screen, trying to make out if Colton was moving at all.

"Come on, Colt. Get up," she whispered pleadingly. "Please, get up." Her eyes began filling with tears as trainers came out onto the field and rolled him over. He moved a little, but needed help getting up.

A golf cart came out onto the field, and the trainers loaded him onto it, something clearly wrong with his leg. Lucia's heart beat in her ears as her eyes followed him until he disappeared inside the tunnels. Was she allowed to go see him? Would she get in trouble for leaving the box? Did he even want to see her?

She stood still, body pressed close to the glass of the box, ignoring the odd looks she was getting. Elijah went out onto the field and tried to gain more yardage, but only brought them close enough for another field goal.

The moment the half was over, Lucia ran out of the analyst box, her lungs on the verge of collapse as the walls began closing in on her. She didn't care what the rest of the analysts thought of her, everything was getting to be a bit too much.

She paced the hallway outside the box, warmth licking down her cheeks. She realized she had been crying when her face grew tight as the tears dried. She walked into the bathroom, splashing water on her face as she tried to breathe through her anxiety.

She was sure he would be okay. Being taken off on a cart didn't necessarily mean anything was wrong. He could've just been in shock or rolled his ankle a little. He might have already been up and moving. She needed to stay positive or she would lose her mind.

Still, her thoughts kept straying to the moment he'd gone down, trying to figure out what might have been wrong. Why hadn't he moved? Why hadn't he been able to get up on his own? She rolled her shoulders to loosen the tension building there.

When she walked out of the bathroom, she was surprised to see Isa standing outside the analyst box, eyes scanning the hallway.

"Isa?" she asked like she wasn't sure if it was a dream, like she needed someone to pinch her hard to confirm everything was real.

The moment Isa's eyes locked on hers, a look of sympathy washed over Isa's face, and she rushed over, throwing her arms around Lucia. Lucia melted into the embrace, resting her head on her friend's shoulder.

"Hi, *mi cielo*. It's okay, it's gonna be okay."

At the words laced with comfort, Lucia began sobbing again. "What if something is seriously wrong with him? What if he can never stand again? What if he can never play football, or do anything he loves, ever again?" Her words were smashed together, and it was a wonder Isa could understand anything that came out of her mouth.

But it was her best friend, so of course she did. "I saw him. I wanted to check on him before I came up to see you because I knew you were going to be worried. He's okay, *osita*. I promise. He's banged up, and they're doing some x-rays on his left knee and ankle, but it'll take an entire legion of soldiers to keep him from getting back on that field. He's a fighter."

For the first time in ten minutes, Lucia let out a relieved breath. Then another, and another. She pulled away from Isa, searching her friend's face to confirm that the words were true. Her tears stopped as she wrapped her arms around her torso, looking away from Isa.

"I know what you're going to say. I did what you told me not to. I got attached. And I know it was—"

"Luc, no. I would never say that." Isa sighed, pulling Lucia by the hand until they were against the wall. Only when her friend lowered her voice did Lucia realize how many other staff members filled the hallway around them.

"He cares about you, Luc. It's about time you find someone who'll treat you right, and Colton will."

A harsh breath left Lucia. "It doesn't matter how we feel. He's upset with me after the shit with Max, and even if that weren't true, I can't do this again, Isa. I can't."

"What the hell are you talking about?"

"With the news article that came out. He thinks it's true and—"

"Not that. He's not so dense to believe the Sabers would've kept you if it was true. What do you mean you can't?"

Lucia hadn't told Isa about what had happened on New Year's Eve. She'd been too embarrassed that Isa had been right, because she *had* been hurt by everything, just like Isa'd said she would.

"Come on, Isa. You've seen it. You've seen my dad, you've seen how his life has been for years, ever since my mom left us. I won't let someone do to me what my mom did to my dad. The breakup with Max wasn't so bad, but I just know it would be worse with Colton. Even this weird fake breakup we're going through is harder."

Isa looked at her sympathetically. "You love him?"

She surprised herself with her quick reply. "Yes."

Of course she did. If she hadn't known it by the emptiness in her chest for the past two weeks, she'd known it the moment Colton had gone down on the field.

"Then tell him that. You can't let fear rule you for the rest of your life. I know you're scared of getting hurt, but Colton has never treated you like Max did, right?"

Lucia shook her head.

"Don't let Max ruin your chance at happiness. If you keep pushing Colton away, Max wins. You'd be a fool to let him go."

Isa's wording was like a smack to the face. This whole time, she'd been worried about Colton hurting her and her becoming the fool once again. Did Isa really think she was being foolish *for* sticking to her beliefs and trying to move past her feelings? How could Lucia or Isa or anyone be sure she wouldn't get hurt if she told him how she felt?

She thought about him in the training room, pissed off, in pain, and potentially alone. Or at least without somebody who cared about him as much as she did. She couldn't believe she'd waited so long to go see him. She could only hope she'd have enough time before the end of halftime.

"Isa, can you get me into the training area?"

Her best friend beamed at her, taking her hand and dragging her down to find Colton. It only took a few minutes of wading through Sabers' staff before she was outside the room. Isa nodded at her encouragingly, and Lucia opened the door.

He was facing away from her, lying on his back with his left ankle taped and raised. She could only see the side of his face, but she could tell he was brooding. He must've seen her in his periphery because he turned his head, his eyes landing on her.

She couldn't decipher the look on his face. Was he happy to see her? Did he want her to leave? How much time did she have to tell him how she felt before he had to go?

The trainer who was working with him moved toward her. "You can't be in here."

"It's fine," Colton spoke quietly.

Lucia moved so she was close enough to touch him, her eyes scanning him from head to toe. Just seeing him all beat up brought tears to her eyes, and she couldn't believe the number of times she'd cried in the past two weeks. She'd turned into a weepy mess.

He didn't shy away when she set her hand on his shoulder.

"Are you okay?"

He nodded, but she could tell he was in a lot of pain.

"Is it true? I can't imagine they would have let you work today if it were, but…"

Lucia sucked in a breath. It hurt that he didn't trust her, but she also understood. It was her fault for not telling him about the call with Max.

"The call happened, yes. But nothing else was true. I didn't want to tell you because I was so embarrassed that I gave him a chance to apologize. I didn't want you to think less of me."

"I never would have thought less of you." His voice was gravelly. "So you really said that to him? That you would give him our plays?"

Betrayal was clear in his every word, and for the hundredth time in two days, Lucia wished she'd told Colton about the call.

She closed her eyes, nodding. "I did, but it was taken out of context. It was sarcastic. I have the video of the whole thing I wanted to show you, but that should probably wait until after the game. Isa got her hands on it for me, and it helped me clear my name with Tim and Coach Turner."

He nodded once, still no semblance of a smile on his face. "Okay."

Okay? Okay like he believed her? Or okay like he would decide how he felt after he saw the whole video?

"Okay," she echoed. "I guess I should go."

"Why'd you come down here, Lucia?"

"I wanted to see if you were okay. I was worried about you."

He looked at her incredulously. "That's the only reason?"

Lucia glanced at the trainer, who'd been standing awkwardly behind her the entire time. He took the hint, walking out of the room quickly.

"I wanted...I *want* to tell you that I'm sorry. About New Year's Eve." She let out a breath, her hand sliding down to clasp his. "I was scared. I had just been in Philadelphia watching my dad deal with another heartbreak, having to cook and clean for him because he'd hardly left the couch the whole time, and it scared me. Because I realized how much I care about you. How much of it wasn't pretend for me."

She wasn't ready to tell him she loved him yet, but she was trying her best.

"I realized that it was more than I've ever cared about anyone, including Max. And that scared me. Because if Max was able to hurt me the way he did, then if anything ever happened between you and me, I knew it would be so much worse. And I don't think I could handle that."

She felt a tear slide down her cheek, her pulse jumping when Colton wiped it from her face gently. "I'm so scared of being my father, Colt. I don't want to end up like that. It hurt me so much to say goodbye, and every single time I saw you afterward was like a punch right to the gut. When you came into the facility and started to say something to me, I knew if you spoke, I'd lose all my resolve. So I ran away like a coward and asked Tim to join our sessions." She rested her right palm on his cheek, her thumb brushing over his cheekbone. "I'm done running now. If you still want me."

The door opened and Lucia started to move her hand away, but Colton placed his hand over it, keeping her anchored to him. "Of course I still want you, Luc. I told you as much in my texts."

Lucia dropped her eyes, embarrassed that she hadn't responded to any of them. She hadn't been able to swear on her fantasy football team, and she hadn't wanted to lie to him. "I know, but after the news, I wasn't sure."

"One minute before you need to be on the field, Colton," the trainer said. Lucia huffed out an annoyed breath, wanting nothing more than to keep talking.

He grimaced as he pulled himself up into a sitting position, Lucia helping him.

"I didn't believe it until I saw the screenshot of you on the phone with him. Even that, I wasn't sure about, but then I saw the necklace and I knew it was recent, and I didn't know what to think." Finally, he smiled softly. "But I trust you. We'll recover from the game tonight and talk about it tomorrow, okay?"

Lucia contained the urge to throw her arms around him, especially since the look on his face as he lowered himself to the ground told her how much pain he was really in.

"Are you going to play?" She couldn't help the worry that tinged her voice as she asked.

"Coach will have to wrestle me to the ground if he thinks I'm not gonna go out there and kick Max's ass. We can win this game, I know we can. And I want to be the one who helps us do that."

Lucia didn't want to tell him what to do, even if she was worried about him. She nodded, happy to hear him talk like he was a part of the team, rather than the only person on the team.

"Be safe." *I love you*, she thought.

Then Colton was being ushered out of the room, limping toward the tunnel that would take him out to the field. Lucia turned down the hallway in the other direction and headed to the analyst box. Isa had already gone out onto the field.

After she closed the door and sat down, she watched him limp onto the field, suited up and ready to start the second half. Her heart trampled over itself at the determination on his face, and she said a prayer to a god she'd forsaken a long time ago to keep him safe.

The second half was similar to the first, except that every time Colton went down, he took longer and longer to get back up. She was ready for Coach Turner to make the call to bench him and put Elijah in. She knew it would metaphorically kill Colton not to play to the end, but she was worried playing to the end would *actually* kill him.

By the end of the third quarter, the Vipers were up by a touchdown, and very few of Colton's drives had looked like they would result in points. The fourth quarter was more of the same, and even Coach Turner looked torn, a green-looking Elijah beside him. As they neared the end, she watched Colton and Coach Turner exchange a few words before he patted Colton's shoulder and sent Colton back in. It could've very well been their last drive, and once again, Lucia found herself standing beside her table, biting the top of her pen.

She could tell from their formation that he was going to try for a long pass. He moved his feet after the snap, just like they'd practiced, and let a beautiful ball sail toward Devin who caught it on his way out of bounds. Thirty yards. She let out a small sigh of relief, but they were far from being able to celebrate.

The Sabers tried running the ball on the first two downs, but then on third down, Colton let the ball fly as he took a hit, Cooper jumping over a defensive back to catch it in the end zone. Colton stayed on the ground, but he pumped his fist before one of the Vipers' players helped him up.

She looked over at Coach to see if he'd try for two or go for the extra point. When their kicking unit didn't move, she bit down on the pen harder. Coach was putting an enormous amount of pressure on Colton to get this win.

They were going for two points. Their last attempt to take the lead and leave the Vipers with forty-five seconds. She could practically hear the entire stadium inhale as Chris snapped the ball to Colton. The Vipers' secondary was doing a good job of keeping Colton's receivers covered, and Colton evaded one lineman and then another, limp-running laterally across the field until it seemed the attempt would end with a sack. Instead, Colton limped quickly through a hole in the defense toward the end zone and leaped into the air, arms extended and ball knocking over the pylon.

Lucia jumped to her feet, letting out a squeal that was drowned out by the rest of the analysts cheering. Her heart tried to go back to normal but sped up again when she saw the look on Colton's face. His smile was wide, as the adoration of nearly 80,000 fans washed over him, his name chanted all around the stadium. Even Coach Turner was jumping up and down with the offensive coordinator, a huge smile on his face and his clipboard abandoned on the sidelines.

Colton had gotten what he wanted, what he needed, to convince himself he deserved to be where he was. All Lucia could do was smile.

Chapter Thirty-One

COLTON

Colton shifted in his bed, looking for some relief for his aching left leg. The tape around his ankle had only been able to stop the swelling so much. His entire body felt like it'd been put through a meat grinder, and yet he hadn't stopped smiling all evening.

Most would have assumed that was because of the win. He'd held his breath until the last second ticked off the clock, but beating the Vipers out of the playoffs had been the second-best reward for playing through his pain.

The real reason he couldn't stop smiling was because of the woman who was curled beside him in his bed like she was his missing puzzle piece, brown hair tossed across the pillow on her side. They had a lot they needed to work through, but they'd agreed to set it aside for the night, too exhausted to try to talk through everything.

He needed a little more of an explanation from her, but the moment the game was won, he'd known he wanted her to stay the night. The win had been exhilarating, but it was nothing if he couldn't celebrate it with her. Winning didn't matter if Lucia wasn't a part of it.

Before her, that certainly wouldn't have been true. He'd never needed anyone besides his teammates to celebrate with, but clearly, things had changed. Lucia had changed everything for him.

He'd spent his entire life believing that winning was the only way for people to love and respect him, but Lucia didn't care about any of that. She'd told him countless times that he mattered regardless. That he was important whether he quit the NFL right now or waited years to retire.

So while he knew there would be a lot to talk through in the morning, words couldn't express his happiness at having her in his bed beside him, clothed in his t-shirt and sweatpants.

His movements must've woken her because she groaned. "Is it time to get up?"

He chuckled. "Nope. Go back to sleep, pretty girl."

A second later, her breathing evened out again. His phone lighting up on his nightstand reminded him of what he needed to be looking out for before their talk.

After the game, Colton had hobbled over to Clark and had told him in no uncertain terms that if he didn't apologize publicly and ensure *The Richmond Herald* retracted the story in the next twelve hours, news would spread about the woman he'd impregnated and swept under the rug only months before he'd started dating Lucia in college. He had his agent and the Sabertooths' PR team to thank for that tidbit of information. The girl had been trying to get in contact with Max for years, only thinking of approaching the media once Colton's team had asked about her willingness. Max had paled at the threat, the sneer on his face disappearing instantaneously.

Scrolling through all of Max's social media profiles and *The Richmond Herald's* website, Colton found that neither had been done. He set his phone back down, making a note to himself to check again in the morning. He wanted to make sure he could show it to her when they talked.

Colton rolled over, slinging an arm over Lucia and closing his eyes, hoping his body would relax enough to let him sleep.

Colton woke to the smell of pancakes and bacon, his stomach growling. He was thankful he didn't have to be at the facility until the afternoon, especially since sleep didn't appear to have helped his body's healing at all.

He walked into his kitchen, the sight of Lucia whisking something in a bowl making him wish he could wake up to this every day.

"What are you doing?" he asked, unable to keep the smile from his face.

"I'm terrified by the number of pizza boxes in your fridge. I genuinely don't know how you look as hot as you do when you eat like this."

"But you don't need to cook. I could've ordered us something."

"What, breakfast pizza?" She laughed at her own joke. "I like cooking for you. Plus, think of it as a part of my apology." Her smile tipped down at the corners.

He wouldn't tell her because he wanted to hear what she had to say, but she was already practically forgiven in his eyes.

"Do you need any help?"

"Nope. You can just sit and watch. You don't really look like you should be moving around anyway." Her eyebrows furrowed as she took in the way his body was overcompensating for his many injuries.

"I'll be fine. I'm always a little beat up after games."

Lucia turned around, her back facing him as she cut up some potatoes. She was going all out for this apology breakfast.

"I know I could've sent it to you, but I wanted to be here with you when you watched the video of the call. My phone's on the counter if you want to pull it up. Password is zero-eight-two-three."

Colton's stomach turned at the thought of having to listen to her talk to Max, but he brought the phone closer to him, typed in the password, and opened the app. He played the video, turning up the volume.

His heart ached at the shakiness of her voice as she spoke to Max. He cringed at the mention of her having sex on the beach with him, pushing the image out of his head as fast as it had entered. His jaw clenched as he heard Max slam something after she'd told him she wasn't in love with him and clenched harder at the insinuation that Lucia couldn't have gotten her job with the Sabers on merit alone. He bristled at Max's mention of him.

By the end, all he felt was pride. He was so proud of her for holding her own against Max and finally telling him what needed to be said. When the video ended, Lucia turned to look at him, her bottom lip tucked under her teeth.

He walked to where she stood in front of the stove, wrapping his arms around her. "You okay?"

"Of course I am. Are you?"

"I'm proud of you for not backing down. And thank you for saying all that about me to him. Standing up for me."

The sounds of sizzling had her turning in his arms as she scrambled the eggs in the pan along with the diced potatoes. She leaned back against his chest, her left hand resting on top of the arms wrapped around her stomach.

"I'm sorry that I didn't tell you about the call. Like I said, I was so embarrassed that I agreed to even take the call since I'd given him so many other chances. And then he said that thing about the Sabers' playbook, and I was even more embarrassed because not only did he not redeem himself, but he tried to take advantage of me. Again."

Colton settled his head on her shoulder, watching her cook. "It's okay. I think I was hurt by it mostly because you didn't tell me that you were gonna talk to him. I know we weren't really together then, but it'd felt like we were. And seeing you with that necklace, smiling while talking to him…It broke something inside of me."

Lucia turned the heat down on the food, setting the spatula down and placing her other hand on top of his too. "I know. I should've told you all of it, especially since Thanksgiving was so amazing. I had the best time with you and everyone, but it was something I wanted to do alone, and then when it was over, I didn't want to think about it anymore." She paused, her head turning to the side and resting against his chest.

"And the reason I was smiling in that picture was because you texted me about team bonding. You could probably see that Max was pissed because that little laugh was me giggling at your message. That was the only time I smiled, and he screenshotted that part on purpose. I'm so sorry you found out the way you did."

At the mention of her laughing at his text, he squeezed her waist. "Forgiven."

He kissed her cheek, then her neck, then let her go, sitting on the bar stool across the counter once more.

She began moving stuff from the pan onto plates, so he opened his phone to check if Clark had done what he was supposed to. When he found no mention of the pictures or video clip and saw a new post on Max's Instagram, he turned the phone so she could see it.

"Look."

She turned to him, grabbing the phone with a questioning look. He stood and took over for her, putting a couple of pancakes, bacon, eggs, and potatoes on two plates and setting them on his counter side by side.

"I don't understand. He's apologizing for leaking the video and pictures? Why would he do that?"

Colton shrugged, guiding her to a bar stool gently with a hand on her back. "Maybe he was worried about a lawsuit."

Lucia looked at him through narrowed eyes, setting his phone down. "You did this, didn't you? You convinced him to do this. And got the article taken down." She didn't wait for confirmation before she asked, "How?"

He grinned. "I have my ways." A well-paid woman who he'd gladly given Max's contact information.

He thought Lucia would have been happy, but she began moving food around her plate, her shoulders slumped.

"Luc? What's wrong?"

She turned to him, eyes shining. "Nothing's wrong. It's perfect. You're perfect. I—I'm just so sorry." She sighed. "I'm sorry that I ended things the way I did. That I ran away from this because I was scared it would end with me hurt like it did with Max. I'm sorry I ever compared you to him. You are wonderful and sweet and caring. These past few months with you have been better than anything I've ever experienced. There's no comparison. You make me feel cared for, even when you're busy with football."

She looked down at her lap as if embarrassed. "I can't focus on work when I know you're in the building or out on the field. I can't imagine not watching romcoms with you in your hotel rooms, or not forcing you to do agility training on the field after everybody else has left." They chuckled together at that.

"The thought of being away from you makes my stomach churn. These past few weeks without you have been torture. And watching you go down on the field almost killed me. I was so worried about you, Colt, you don't even know. When I saw you in the training room, I tried to hold it together, but…"

Colton couldn't take it. He took her hands and pulled her toward his couch. He sat her down, dropping to his knees between her legs and placing his hands on her waist. "Luc, you are the reason that I love football again. I've been going through the motions for the adoration of the fans for who knows how long. For the first time since—god—flag football? I love it again. And that's because of you. You were the first person in my life to make me feel worthy, even without winning. Like I matter regardless of my stats."

Her lips parted, and he ran a thumb over them. "Wait, let me finish, sweet girl. I'm sorry I didn't tell you how I felt sooner. I don't know if it would've changed things, but I was scared. So scared to fully admit it to even myself because…god, if you knew how I feel about you, you'd have the power to end me completely.

She made a noise that sounded like surprise and something else. "Colt..."

"You've lived under my skin for so long, put roots down inside of me that don't want to move. I can't go a minute without thinking about you. When I'm in meetings, lifting, practicing, even during games, you consume my every waking thought, even when you shouldn't. I can't even pinpoint when it all changed for me, not really. All I know is that I...fuck, Moretti. I love you. I love your little skirts and those ridiculous heels. I love that you have ten different green pantsuits for game day. I love that you know more about football than me. I love that you know how to fix my game with just a glance at my film. I love how good you are at football trivia. I love that little groove between your eyebrows that you reserve for me, mostly." He placed his thumb between her brows where he usually found that groove, though it wasn't there now.

"I love that you came here and made friends with my friends so fast, and that you made my sister feel so welcome when she visited. I love your strength, and how brave you are after everything you've been through. And most of all, I love the feeling I get when I run out on that field and get to kiss you in the end zone like I'm a giddy teenager during homecoming. You've changed my life immensely over the last five months, and I'm so grateful to know and love you. You've made me better in every single way." He chuckled, remembering his conversation with his father. "Hell, I finally stood up to my father because of you."

Her eyebrows shot up at his last sentence. "You did?"

He nodded, a wide smile on his face. "I did."

She looked like she was still processing his rambling, so he added one last thought. "I've spent my whole life only caring about one thing: how I can get my next win, my next championship, my next Super Bowl ring. And for the first time in my life, I realized at the game that none of that shit matters if you're not there. If I can't smile up at you as you jump up and down in the analyst box, if I can't celebrate with you, what's the point?"

Tears formed in her eyes, and she sniffled. "I hate how much I've been crying recently, and you being sweet isn't helping." She laughed, looking down at her hands in her lap. "I love you too, Colt. Of course I do. How could anybody not love you? You make me smile when nobody else can—even when I should be in a bad mood. You make me happy beyond anything I've ever felt. I feel like I can do anything, be anything I want when you're with me. You make me feel like I'm more than an analyst, and I appreciate that so much because, for the longest time, the only way I knew how to describe myself was as a numbers girl. And now I can be anything."

Colton's heart thumped hard in his chest, hope filling every vein and artery in his body. Her confession was better than a hundred Super Bowl wins.

He grabbed her chin gently, pulling her head up and meeting her eyes as he opened his mouth to speak. She smiled wickedly. "Let me finish, Superstar."

He smiled back.

"I can't promise that I'll magically get over this fear of mine, but I promise I'll try. I'll tell you if I'm ever feeling like running or if something happens and I get the urge to push you away. I'll make sure you know so we can talk it out. Because I trust you more than anybody in this world, and I want to prove myself wrong. I want to show my younger self, and even me from a few months ago, that love can be for me. That I'm deserving of it, no matter what I've experienced. That not all relationships have to end in heartbreak."

That's all he'd wanted. He hadn't expected her to leave all her fears behind just because they loved each other. But he did want her to try, because he was sure he could prove to her that she deserved love. If it took their entire lives together, he would prove that to her.

"That's all I want, Luc. That's all I will ever ask for. Just give me the privilege of proving to you that you deserve love. Because you do. You are the most deserving person in this world, and I want to be the one who gets to show you that every day."

Lucia leaned forward, her forehead resting on his for only a moment before she kissed him passionately. When they pulled away, she said, "You better start by eating the breakfast I made you before it gets cold."

And then they grinned at each other like a couple of idiots in love.

Chapter Thirty-Two

Lucia

Lucia stared at the three emails in her inbox. She hadn't told Colton about them yet because the moment he'd asked her to spend the night after the Vipers game, she'd decided she was staying in Charleston. She needed to talk to Coach Turner before she turned the other offers down, though.

Lucia hadn't stopped smiling since the morning after the Vipers game. She hadn't realized how easy it could be to be loved. Colton made her feel chosen every day, and that's all she could have asked for.

The man in question stepped into her office, a winning smile on his face. He'd donned a pair of black, tailored pants and a button-down for their dinner like he'd known exactly what fire to stoke inside of her, and she realized by the setting sun that it was already five. With playoffs, they didn't have much free time, but he'd been adamant about taking her to dinner for their first real date.

"You ready?"

She nodded, a matching smile on her face. She slipped her hand into his outstretched palm, grabbed her purse, and followed him out of her office. The elevator opened, revealing Coach Turner.

"Oh, good. You're here. Let's go up to the seventh floor. Colton, you're welcome to come with us, but you'll have to wait outside."

Lucia's brows furrowed, and she looked at Colton to see if he knew what was happening. He shrugged but squeezed her hand tightly.

They followed Coach out of the elevator and onto the floor, then toward the boardroom where they'd first seen each other again. Just like that day, Lucia squared her shoulders and held her head high. She dropped Colton's hand, and he nodded like he understood that she needed to walk in her own way. Clearly, whatever was about to happen had to do with her professional future with the Sabers.

The layout of the meeting was practically the same as when she'd first shown up, all the same key players in the room, though now she had Colton by her side instead of sitting before her, heckling her. She held back a smile at the memory.

She smiled at Colton reassuringly as Coach shut the door in his face.

"Thank you for being here. We heard that you've received some offers from other teams for next season." She was sure Colton could hear through the door, and she cringed, mentally thanking Coach Turner for outing her to Colton about something that she'd planned to discuss with him over dinner.

Coach Turner continued, "We have found your skills to be immensely helpful to the team as a whole, as well as to Colton's game. As such, we're looking to extend your contract for another three years with the ability to renew at a later date. Additionally, we'd like to offer you a raise, effective at the end of the season."

With every word, Lucia internally screamed louder and louder. She couldn't believe any of the things leaving his mouth. Not only did they want her to stay for at least another three years, but they wanted her so badly, they'd decided to give her a raise. She had to hold back her squeal, trying to appear professional as she nodded. She wouldn't have to leave Charleston, or Colton, or Rudy and Jenna, or any of it.

She opened her mouth to respond, but Coach held up a hand, nodding to Tim, who stepped forward. "You will continue working with Colton and running analytics with the rest of the analysts. In addition, we want you included on the draft day team to help us decide who we'll be taking for next season. You will also receive training from a couple of our head analysts with the hope that you'll eventually be promoted to their position and take over your own team of analysts."

She nearly collapsed.

"I…I…" She had to pause, trying not to hyperventilate. Putting on her most professional smile, she said, "Thank you. I'd love to continue working with the Sabers." Her voice shook as she responded, but her acceptance seemed to be all they were looking for.

"Great. HR will get the contract and other paperwork sent up to you by next week."

She started to turn toward the door when Coach Turner spoke. "You and Colton are still operating within the agreement you signed about this relationship, and while you'll continue working together, we'll have to re-evaluate if it begins to impede his game."

"Of course."

Coaches and staff began talking amongst each other, and she took that as a dismissal.

Lucia walked out of the boardroom, and the moment she was out of sight of the men in the room, she turned to Colton excitedly. He was beaming, pride written all over his face. He'd clearly heard it all. She jumped into his arms, giggling as he spun her around.

"Don't think you're getting away with not telling me about the other teams," he whispered into her hair, right beside her ear. She smiled.

"I was gonna tell you at dinner so we could figure out our options, but I knew my answer the moment you asked me to stay the night after the Vipers game."

"I'm so proud of you. Now we have to celebrate." He set her down, slipping his hand into hers again. "Let's get to dinner, and then tonight"—he dropped his voice, low and sensual—"you're the queen of the castle, and I'm gonna be on my knees begging for a taste."

She felt herself warm, her heart galloping at an unhealthy pace.

Every day, Colton proved to her that he wanted to be in her life and that she deserved the love that so many other people enjoyed. She knew her fears wouldn't disappear overnight, and she wasn't sure they would ever fully go away, but at the very least, she and Colton could navigate and attempt to quell them together. For the first time in her life, Lucia felt like she had everything she wanted and more.

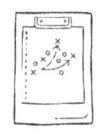

Lucia

One Year Later

Lucia stepped out of the analyst box, swiping across her screen to answer the call from Maya. Halftime had just started, and because it was the conference championship, she could hear the fans screaming even in the hall outside the room.

"Maya? Are you in Colton's player box?"

Maya had suffered an injury that'd taken her out of tennis for a while, so she'd been splitting her time between Charleston and Los Angeles. Both Lucia and Colton had noticed how down she'd seemed, so they'd made sure she stayed with them when she came to visit, despite all the boxes that had littered Colton's massive mansion since Lucia moved in—something that Lucia would only take ownership for in her own head.

"Yeah, I'm here with Dad." Lucia knew that tone meant Maya needed saving.

"I'll meet you at the staff entrance, and you can come hang with me in the analyst box if you want?" Lucia was running a small team of analysts, so nobody would say anything about having Maya in the room. Plus, nobody wanted to piss off the star quarterback who'd given them not one but two Super Bowl wins. In a row.

"Please." Her voice dropped to a whisper. "I can't do this for much longer. I'm surprised Colton even let him have family tickets again."

Lucia stifled a laugh as she walked toward where she'd promised to meet Maya, and when she saw Colton's sister heading toward her, she clicked off the call.

"If I'd known he was coming, I would've had you join me from the start."

Maya blew out a sigh, walking beside Lucia back toward the analyst box. "I'm starting to think Colton's cold indifference toward him is the best way to handle him."

Lucia was inclined to agree, but she tried to stay out of the family dynamic as much as she could. Lucia noted the grimace on Maya's face when she attempted to open the door with her splinted arm. Lucia grabbed the door from Maya, made quick introductions, and cleared a space at the table beside her for Maya to sit.

They talked about Landon, who was just finishing his season since they'd lost their playoff game, and other football-related topics. Lucia tried to keep the conversation away from Maya's tennis, knowing it was still a sore spot. They were all praying she'd find a way through the injury, but Colton had told Lucia a couple of weeks earlier that Maya thought it might be career-ending. Lucia's heart tightened at the thought of her bright friend losing her greatest passion in life. She couldn't imagine how down Colton would be without football.

When the second half started, Lucia had to focus on the numbers and Colton's game. Maya didn't seem to mind, watching quietly, tensing alongside Lucia when Colton got sacked or missed a throw.

As the fourth quarter drew to a close and it became obvious that the Sabers wouldn't be making it to the Super Bowl for a third year in a row, Lucia began packing up her equipment.

She turned to Maya. "Wanna come with me to my office to drop these things off before the press conference? If not, I'll meet you in the press room."

"I think I'll meet you in the press room. I should say bye to Cooper before I leave tonight since I may not be back for a few weeks."

Lucia tried to hide the surprised look she knew was on her face. She'd noticed Maya and Cooper sharing looks here and there and recalled the night she'd gone out to drinks with Maya, Isa, Jenna, and Leigh. Jenna had talked about how Cooper looked at Maya, and Lucia wondered if there'd been more to that than simple teasing. She needed to talk to Colton about it.

Maya seemed to have picked up on her thoughts because she continued talking. "Uh, and Rudy and Jenna and Chris and everyone, of course. I should say goodbye to everyone."

"Of course. I'll meet you in the press room in a few, then."

Lucia and the rest of the team moved the equipment they could from the room to the offices. Once Lucia plugged her computers in, she grabbed her purse and headed back to the stadium, knowing she'd need to put on her bravest face to comfort an upset Colton.

He'd gotten better about dealing with losses, but she hadn't seen him lose a playoff game since they'd started dating, and she was sure it would be far worse than a regular-season loss.

She walked into the room and closed the door silently, questions already being answered. She sidled up to Maya just as Colton was asked a question.

"Tough loss, Colton. What do you think went wrong?"

Lucia sighed, hating their insensitivity. The press had never, and would never, be their friend, and she'd made her peace with that.

She was pleasantly surprised to see a half-smile on Colton's face, his eyes finding hers. "Sometimes, you do the best you can, and you don't win. Sometimes, they're just gonna outplay you. I'm proud of the way the team played. I'm proud of our offense, and I'm proud of our defense. We did our best, and that's all anybody can ask of us. They were just the better team today."

A big grin split Lucia's face at his words. She was immensely proud of Colton. He'd never played better than he had in this past season, and though it wouldn't end in another Super Bowl attempt, her heart swelled with love and pride for all that he'd accomplished since she'd joined the Sabertooths.

Three reporters tried to ask him different questions at the same time, and he put his hands up. "I appreciate all the questions, but I'm gonna let Coach take the rest of them for the night. I have dinner plans with my two favorite people."

A couple of people turned to her and Maya when they noticed where Colton's focus was, and Coach Turner gave Colton an annoyed look but said nothing.

Lucia led Maya out of the room, a smile spreading across her face once again when she heard the other door closing. She turned and found Colton before her, the corner of his mouth ticked up.

She moved toward him, sliding her arms around his torso as he placed his head atop hers.

"I'm really proud of you. You played so well."

He rubbed her back. "Thank you. We'll get 'em next year," he murmured into her hair. They pulled away, and he put one arm around her shoulders and the other around Maya's. "Let's let Maya say her goodbyes, and then it's pizza time."

Acknowledgments

This book is my love letter to many things. My struggles with my culture. The Chiefs. Strong women. My boyfriend, Ethan. But especially football and how it's changed my life.

I grew up in Texas with a dad who played and loved football, which means I have memories of sitting on the couch as a child with my dad standing in front of the television, pointing out different plays to me. It's how we bonded, and even now that we live apart, it's what we text about the most.

After I hit a roadblock with the first book I wrote (currently unpublished, but hopefully out someday soon!), I decided I wanted to pull away from my romantasy writing and focus on something a bit more contemporary. NFL season was in full swing, and as I watched Sunday after Sunday, these characters were born. Four days of outlining and six weeks of drafting later, I had my first sports romance written and ready to go. Kind of.

This final product would not have been what it is without the support of my alpha readers and best friends, Georgia

Wood (coworker turned book club bestie!), Emily Tash (another coworker turned bestie), and Sreeja Ambati (my oldest and most loyal friend, I love you). Thank you to each and every one of you for reading through my first fully plotted book baby.

To my beta readers: Elle F. Sun (who gave me so much Charleston help!), Rachel Bunner, Casey Wood, Lisa Couch (twice!), and Marja Graham (my literal best friend and my biggest champion). Your feedback was invaluable in making GG what it is today and I would have been lost without you. Thank you for taking a chance on my debut.

To Rachel, my editor, my angel, my everything. Please never leave me. Thank you for your late nights of editing, commenting on your favorite parts, hyping me up on social media constantly, being okay waking up to five messages of me freaking out, going above and beyond for me in every facet I could ever imagine and more. I am so much more confident in this book than I was before you, and I cannot ever thank you enough.

To Chelsey Brand, thank you for noticing all the little things. I'm so thankful for all of your help and your excitement for my characters and story.

To Laura Hartley, one of my best friends in this world, thank you for listening to me talk about my characters ad-nauseum, and for being excited even when you had no idea what I was talking about. Seeing your comments on my manuscript made me giggle every time, and I'm so glad to have met and loved you.

To my mom, for teaching me what it means to be hardworking and to my dad for teaching me about this sport that I love so much. To my brother for going out of his way to help me, whether it be in finding an editor, figuring out social media, or just lending an ear. And to my sister, for being excited for me from the start without knowing a thing about this book.

To Marja, who took a chance on friendship when I slid into her DMs, and who has become so much more to me since. Thank you for being with me through every single step of this process. From beta reading GG (twice!) to our Sunday sprints to helping me with social media to formatting my book for me, you are my soulmate and I love you so. Thanks for being one half of Frog and Toad with me, for being the otter anchoring me in the raging river that is indie publishing, and for being the big sister I always wanted. I can honestly say that I would not be where I am without you.

And finally, to Ethan, my alpha reader, my beta reader, my biggest fan and the man who inspired me to write this series in the first place. This is my love letter to you. Thanks for always answering me every time I took out an AirPod to verify that something I was writing about football was correct (even though we both know I know more about football than you do). I hope I made you proud.

About the Author

Vai Denton is an American author, romance enthusiast—especially if sports are involved—and book lover. She has spent much of her life struggling to find her identity between her two cultures, using books as an escape. Though she experimented with writing from a young age, once she began writing seriously, Vai started weaving those cultures and struggles into her characters' journeys. Her hope is that her stories provide readers with the escape she once sought. In each of her books, you can expect swoony, healthy relationships that will have you kicking your feet.

When inspiration strikes, you can find her flipping between texting herself and the notes app on her phone. If she's not reading or writing about love, you'll find her watching football, tennis, or any number of her favorite romcoms.

If you'd like to contact Vai, find her on instagram @vaidentonauthor or via email at vaidentonauthor@gmail.com

Printed in Great Britain
by Amazon